Apologies
to My
Censor

The High and Low Adventures of a
Foreigner in China

MITCH MOXLEY

HARPER PERENNIAL

NEW YORK • LONDON • TORONTO • SYDNEY • NEW DELHI • AUCKLAND

HARPER ● PERENNIAL

HarperCollins books may be purchased for educational, business, or sales promotional use. For information please e-mail the Special Markets Department at SPsales@harpercollins.com.

FIRST EDITION

Designed by Michael P. Correy

Library of Congress Cataloging-in-Publication Data is available upon request.

ISBN 978-0-06-212443-2

13 14 15 16 17   OV/RRD   10 9 8 7 6 5 4 3 2

For Mom & Dad

Prologue

My greatest fear was about to become reality: sober dancing.

I stood atop a set of stairs at a faux-Italian outdoor mall in Beijing, my face in full makeup and my hair styled in the weird, poofy way of urban Chinese, wearing skinny jeans and a short-sleeve black shirt unbuttoned halfway down my chest. Beside me was a small-time pop star from Shandong province named Marry (two *r*'s), rehearsing the upcoming shot in a flowing white wedding dress. Next to her was a Chinese male model with pursed lips and a perfectly trimmed goatee. At the foot of the stairs awaited the nervous director, a cameraman, and forty-odd pairs of curious eyes: crew members and passersby, all eagerly anticipating, I was sure, the disaster that was about to unfold.

The camera started rolling. Beads of sweat trickled through the stubble on my cheeks like pachinko balls as I descended into a true-life nightmare.

I started to dance.

A few days earlier, I had been approached on the street by a stranger and asked to appear in a music video as the star's European love interest. As random as it might sound to be asked to be in a music video, ridiculous incidents of this nature are not totally uncommon in China. I once posed as one of

China's 100 "Hottest Bachelors" for a special Valentine's Day issue of *Cosmopolitan* magazine. The vetting process was not very thorough, and by "not very thorough" I mean totally non-existent: the project's editors had never laid eyes on me before I showed up for the shoot.

I should mention, however, that I'm not your typical music video star. I'm a journalist. I'm tall and a bit lanky, and although I've had my share of movie star fantasies, I can be terribly awkward in front of a camera. I have certain features—say, a long neck—that can appear unusual in pictures and on video. From certain angles my face can seem cartoonish, and it's often when I'm trying to look cool that I look most uncool. In the *Cosmopolitan* Valentine's special, I ended up looking like a vampire in a checkered suit two sizes too small.

Thinking that appearing in a music video might be a worthwhile story, I agreed under one condition: no dancing. Sober dancing is my kryptonite. On the rare occasions when I do dance, I break out in a nervous sweat, swing my arms awkwardly, and buckle at the knees. I'm convinced everyone's watching me. *Look at the tall loser freak!* I imagine them all saying.

Now there we were, filming the video's key scene, my body writhing in awkward, robotic movements. We tried several takes, each worse than the last. During a break, I pleaded with the director to cut me from the video entirely and spare everybody the hassle of having to figure out how to salvage the footage.

They begged for a few more takes. I reluctantly agreed.

Atop the stairs once again, I looked out at the eyes staring back to me. I became lightheaded and began to have an out-of-body experience, where I was able to see an image of myself in my skinny jeans and unbuttoned black shirt, my hair made up like a bird's nest. "Action!" the director yelled, and before I could stop, my body contorted itself into a strange little jig. I forced a stupid grin and pretended to be in love with Marry as she lip-synched her awful, pitchy song. I could imagine what the video might look like once edited, and where it might be played, and what my friends would think if they ever saw it.

As these images of impending doom played in my mind, I thought: Oh fuck, YouTube.

I was thirty years old and this was my life: a series of random China adventures that seemed to stretch on forever. Toward what, I still wasn't sure.

How did it all happen? I asked myself that question every day. In fact, I shouldn't even have been there at all—in Beijing, in China, on the stairs of that outdoor mall.

I came to Beijing in the spring of 2007 to take a job as a writer and editor for *China Daily*, the country's only English-language national newspaper at the time. My journey to China was by accident. One freezing afternoon in Toronto a few months earlier—depressed, bored, failing as a writer, and unsure of where my life was headed—I opened an online journalism job board and noticed a posting for a position at a government-owned newspaper in Beijing I'd never heard of. I had never imagined going to China, but anything was better than the state I was in. So I applied, and a few months later, after a writing test and a brief phone interview, I was offered a one-year contract.

In China, everything was happening. The economy was booming, the Olympics were on the horizon, and Beijing was being transformed into a world-class city overnight. *China Daily* was changing, too. Somewhere in the bowels of the *China Daily* headquarters in Beijing, someone had decided the paper needed some sprucing up before the Games. Money flowed in, the paper was redesigned and expanded, and, in an effort to improve the quality of the writing, the management recruited a growing team of "foreign experts" (the official wording on our visas) from all corners of the English-speaking world. When I arrived in mid-April, there were three dozen of us, mostly new arrivals. We were going to play a big part in the "new" *China Daily*, they told us. We were important.

Before I left Canada for Beijing an e-mail landed in my inbox from a friend's father, who was working in Chinese state media at the time. "It's important to know that journalism here ain't quite the same as over there," he wrote. "Not by a long shot. It's journalism with 'Chinese characteristics.'" Shortly after, I received another message from an American editor at *China Daily*. "Just so you don't have any illusions about this, *China Daily* is a State-owned newspaper, as is all media in China. That means you would be dealing with two ultimate bosses: (1) The Information Office of the State Council and (2) the Propaganda Department of the Communist Party of China."

In other words, despite my official position as writer and editor for *China Daily*'s business section, I was essentially accepting a job as a propagandist for the government of the People's Republic of China.

My original plan was to stay for just over a year, work out my contract, have some fun, stick around for the Olympics, and return to normal life. China was meant to be a break. A chance to reboot.

Almost four years later, I was dancing like a robotic idiot in a Chinese music video, and self-admittedly addicted to the random, chaotic nature of expatriate life in China. Normal life had most definitely *not* resumed. Among other adventures, I had crisscrossed the country doing journalism, sat front row to the Olympics, posed as a fake businessman, indulged in many a booze-fueled night, and paid to feed a goat to a hungry lion.

Along the way I learned that there is no such thing as normal life for a foreigner in this crazy, exhilarating, intoxicating nation. You might settle into a routine, and the things around you start to seem ordinary and mundane, but then you blink and find yourself in the middle of a surreal situation, such as running hand in hand through an imitation Italian mall with a wannabe pop star. You remember that you're in China, that you're at the new center of the universe.

Friends of mine in China often compared our foreigner experience to Peter Pan's Neverland: a fantasyland where you never really have to grow up, and if you're not careful, you might never leave. I was, like many others, one of the Lost Boys of Chinese Neverland. By the fall of 2010, when in the course of a few weeks I filmed a music video, traveled the length of China by train, almost died hiking on a mountain, and fielded calls from Hollywood producers over an article I wrote, I wondered if I would ever go home, or if I was lost in China forever.

The country had changed me. I was, in ways both figuratively and literally, a different person from the one who arrived in China. I'm shy in front of a camera. I don't smile in pictures. I certainly don't dance. The person in the video wasn't the man who stepped off the plane in Beijing in the spring of 2007. That man, when asked to star in a music video, would have said something along the lines of . . . "*Hell* no."

I was the person China had helped create.

I was Mi Gao. Tall Rice.

1

Unite. Diligent. Progress.

During those first jet-lagged days in Beijing, three and a half years before, I would wake early, make a cup of instant coffee, and watch the spectacle unfolding outside my kitchen window. On the basketball courts across from my apartment, several hundred middle school students stood in rows wearing matching blue and white tracksuits and lazily swung their limbs in unison as horrible Chinese pop music blasted from the loudspeakers. If there was ever a more half-assed display of mass calisthenics, I'd never seen it.

A coach hollered commands through a megaphone while teachers in baggy trousers and sports jackets did laps on the track. On the brick wall beside the basketball courts, words painted in English read, UNITE. DILIGENT. PROGRESS. The whole display was astonishing. I took pictures on my cell phone camera for future reference, sipped coffee, and soaked in the strangeness of it all.

————

China wasn't my first foray into life abroad. In the fall of 2005, I finished a contract with a newspaper in Toronto and set off to work as a freelance writer in Asia. Earlier that year, I'd taken a three-week vacation to visit my childhood friend Will in Nagoya, Japan, where he was working as an English teacher. During that trip I managed to sell a number of stories to newspapers and magazines at home. Freelancing seemed promising, and I left Toronto that September confident that I could easily survive overseas.

That fall, I traveled to Vietnam, Thailand, and the Philippines, freelancing a few articles for foreign publications. Between each trip, I would return to Japan and stay at Will's place. We would party all weekend, recover from our hangovers by watching movies, relaxing in *onsen* bathhouses, or going to the beach, and then do it all over again. During one of our more epic nights, an all-night affair in Nagoya, we set off a fire extinguisher in an elevator, covering ourselves in salty-tasting pinkish powder as the door closed on us. Life was great.

But things started to sour shortly after Christmas. I realized there was no way I could sustain myself on the pathetic earnings of a freelance writer, especially when I was blowing wads of cash partying until 7 a.m. in one of the world's most expensive countries, and jet-setting across Asia to write stories I wouldn't be paid for until months afterward. I decided to settle in Nagoya and find work as an English teacher. I soon learned, however, that they didn't hand these jobs out at the airport as I had originally thought. Most of the turnover at English schools occurred during semester breaks, and I was looking during the middle of the semester. Job opportunities were scarce, and several weeks went by with not so much as an interview. My parents were putting cash into my account to keep me afloat. (This, sadly, would become a recurring theme in my life over the next few years.)

Other parts of my life were disintegrating as well. I had a girlfriend back in Canada, and our relationship was slowly drawing to a close. So it was with mixed emotions that I left for Japan that September. "I need to do this," I told her a few days before I left. And I did—I needed to travel while I was still young, to see if I could make it as a writer. Although we were officially broken up, we talked and e-mailed regularly while I was away, and we ended up in a relationship purgatory where neither of us really knew what was going on but we were too afraid to talk about it. The uncertainty weighed on me every day I was abroad. Over time, my calls home grew more infrequent, my e-mails shorter and more distant until it became clear I was losing her, at which point I began to panic.

Meanwhile, I developed a mysterious infection during my trip to the Philippines over Christmas that caused a rather horrible case of acne, something I'd never had in my life. Acne combined with a looming quarter-life crisis is an unfortunate and miserable combination. By mid-January, back in Japan, I was sleeping until noon, drinking too much, and putting very little effort into finding work. I showed up to one interview hungover and half an hour late, and I wasn't able to answer a question about the grammatical difference between "I ate a hamburger" and "I have eaten a hamburger." When I got turned down for a job teaching kindergartners at a school inexplicably called the Potato Academy—despite a master's degree and a once-promising career in journalism—I decided it was time to cash in my chips and head home.

When I returned to Toronto, things didn't get much better. I spent the summer subletting a room in a house full of crazies fit for a sitcom. I was working as a freelance reporter, and after a few months of writing business articles I didn't care about and wandering around alone, counting the cracks in the pavement, I figured this must be the loneliest profession on earth.

Most days I sat alone in coffee shops with my laptop open on the table in front of me, back hunched, struggling to find the motivation to perform even basic work-related tasks, such as opening a Word document. Sometimes the thought of walking from my apartment to the coffee shop was too draining, and I would work in my tiny third-floor room, which had a slanted roof and no air-conditioning. Many mornings, I didn't bother to get dressed. I checked my e-mail obsessively, because the Internet seemed to be my only companion. The solitude, the apartment, the heat, the roommates—I was slowly suffocating.

My girlfriend and I made a valiant effort to make it work when I got back to Canada, but we were running on fumes. We tried out all of our little inside jokes and old quirks, but they felt forced now. I was twenty-six and terrified of domestic life: dinner parties with other couples, weekly softball games, a neighborhood pub filled with grumpy boozehounds, kids—*kids!* I wasn't ready for any of that, and neither was she. We loved each other, but by mid-July we were officially done.

My social life, meanwhile, had diminished greatly from the last time I lived in Toronto. As a freelancer, working alone, I had fallen off my friends' radar—not that I was trying very hard to engage with anybody—and most nights after spending the day in my own head, I would watch episodes of *Entourage*, lying in bed in the throbbing heat of my claustrophobic room, noting the many discrepancies between Vincent Chase's life and my own, wondering where it all went wrong.

I began to exercise obsessively to sweat out my anxiety. I went to the doctor even if it was only a minor ailment (thank you, Canadian health care), just to fill my day. I started to see a therapist and do yoga, trying in vain to clear my head. I sometimes replied to personal ads on Craigslist to kill time. I did drugs on weekends whenever they were around, as a temporary balm for my hurting brain. I was twelve thousand dollars in debt and earning not much more than the summer in college when I worked as a dishwasher, which now ranked as only the second-most demoralizing period of my life.

One morning in the winter of 2007, I was sitting in a Starbucks in Toronto working on a story when my cell phone rang. It was a long-distance number I didn't recognize. On the other end was an American who said he worked as an editor at *China Daily* in Beijing. It had been months since I'd submitted my résumé and weeks since I wrote the editing test. I assumed they'd forgotten about me.

"The bosses were impressed with your editing test," the man said. "I can't say for sure, but it looks good."

I could feel my heart hammering inside my chest but tried to sound composed on the phone. "That's, that's . . . great news," I said. He asked me a few questions about my experience, told me a little about the job, and said to expect an e-mail shortly.

Over the next few days, I checked my e-mail constantly, and when the offer finally came, three weeks later, I was ecstatic. One-year contract, accommodation, plane ticket each way. I was in a coffee shop and it was blizzarding outside. I wanted to laugh at the swirling snow and its attempt to keep me rooted and miserable in Toronto. I bit my fist, barely able to wrap my head around the idea of moving to Beijing. I was going to do it right this time, I told myself. Not like Japan. I was going to make this trip count.

After the initial euphoria faded, doubts crept in. Despite the terrible year I'd had, I couldn't help but wonder if *China Daily* was a step in the wrong direction. Based on the warnings that soon began landing in my inbox from foreign editors, it didn't seem like what they were doing over there was *journalism* exactly, and being a journalist was the only thing I had ever wanted to be.

As a kid, I would sit in my basement penning tales of sporting glory and intergalactic adventure, a long-haired and ear-pierced version of my young self in the role of protagonist. In high school, I interned at a local weekly paper, writing for the sports section, and during my undergraduate studies I worked at my university's student newspaper. I loved it. Journalism, and writing in general, gave me an identity. I went on to do a master's degree in journalism, and during my course I interned at a newspaper in Toronto called the *National Post*, where I continued to work after graduation.

My dream was to live abroad and write long-form magazine articles and books, but I was realistic enough to know that those things wouldn't come right away. At the *National Post*, I was placed in the business section, and although I gave it my best (at least at first), it became clear that a career as a business reporter was not my calling. I wrote stories about investing although I had no investments and no interest in investing. I reported on dividends and bonds and EBITDA and interest rates, without truly understanding what any of those terms meant. I was perhaps the world's most inadequate business reporter, and toward the end of my contract it began to show. I made small mistakes, rarely pitched stories to my editors, and whined incessantly about my job to anyone who would listen.

I grew anxious to get out into the world and do the writing I wanted to do. When I eventually left the paper and traveled to Asia in the fall of 2005, I wrote a few magazine articles that stirred my passions, including a dozen-page magazine feature about the legacy of Agent Orange in Vietnam. This, I thought, is what I want to do. I wanted *big* stories, stories I could live and feel, stories that would make a difference, stories that would take me out of an office and into places I never knew existed.

But despite a few successes, I never figured out how to make freelance writing sustainable on that first trip to Asia, and by the time I was back in Toronto I was writing business articles again, only now I was doing it for half of what I earned at the *Post*. I had envisioned that at this stage of my career I would be writing for *GQ* or *Esquire* from jungle war zones and sinful foreign metropolises. Instead, I was writing weekend features about how to get a better deal on your cell phone plan.

China was a chance at redemption. In the days after I was offered the job, I pictured myself cracking A-list publications, maybe even writing a book about my experiences at *China Daily*.

At the same time, I had serious doubts. I didn't know the language. Didn't know much about the city or country, and I had no friends waiting for me. What if I hated Beijing? What would the job be like? Would I even be able to freelance while working at *China Daily*? Would I be able to make it work? Or would I be back in Toronto within a year, my tail between my legs, feeling like a catastrophic loser again?

I couldn't sleep the weeks before I left for Beijing, lying awake, obsessing over nothing. I had trouble focusing, my mood oscillating between near exhilaration at moving across the world and a crushing fear that I was making a terrible decision. Friends and family said it was a once-in-a-lifetime opportunity, that it would all work out, etc. I wanted to believe them, but moving to *China*? To work for a government newspaper? It seemed so ridiculous.

One day, struggling to finish a story, I walked up the street to a bookstore to buy a Beijing guidebook. I was in a fog during the walk, oblivious to the frozen city around me. I sat down in the store with a couple of different guidebooks, and flipping through Lonely Planet's *Best of Beijing* I stumbled across a section called "Newspapers & Magazines."

"The Chinese government's favorite English-language mouthpiece," it read, "is the *China Daily*."

I opened the *Rough Guide to China* and searched for mention of my new employer. *China Daily* was good for local listings, the *Rough Guide* said, but "the rest of the paper is propaganda written in torrid prose."

My heart, already weighed down, sank to the pavement.

I had second thoughts up until I stepped onto the crowded Air Canada flight bound for Beijing, at which point it was too late to change my mind.

The next morning, I sipped a cup of instant coffee, exhausted but relieved that I was finally there, in Beijing, China, watching kids outside my apartment window perform lazy morning exercises as I tried to make sense of the words, painted on a brick wall, Unite. Diligent. Progress.

2

The Chinese Propagandist

Life in Beijing got off to a fittingly inauspicious start. On my first morning, Jenny, the Chinese staff member assigned to handle foreign editors at *China Daily*, took me to my state-required physical examination at a nearby hospital. On the way, we passed a commotion at a busy intersection. A crowd had gathered around a police car, and as we drove by, several men were yelling at one another.

In the middle of the crowd, I noticed a man lying twisted, motionless, and bloody. Nobody was helping him.

"Holy shit," I said, my face pressed against the taxi window. "I think he's dead."

Jenny giggled. She was a jittery woman in her mid-twenties with a ponytail and thick glasses. I told her that a story about a subway tunnel collapse that killed six workers in Beijing had recently made news in Canada.

She looked at me and said, "How many dead people do you think makes the news in China?"

"I don't know. One?"

She laughed again. "At least ten."

I offered an uncomfortable chuckle before realizing she wasn't joking but pointing out my naïveté. In a country of 1.3 billion people, one dead pedestrian wasn't news at all.

The examination, required for all foreign workers in China, included a blood test for HIV/AIDS and heart monitoring. I caused some confusion when I stated my height and weight in inches and pounds, and a question about narcotics prompted a flashback to a long and regrettable cocaine-fueled night a few months earlier at a friend's wedding in Cancún. I worried for a moment that my time in China might be over before it began.

After the examination, I had a lunch of pork and fish with my new boss, Mr. Wang, a nervous little fellow with glasses, a bowl cut, and an oversize University of Tennessee sweater-vest. Mr. Wang, who was in charge of all foreign staff, hunched over his plate and studied the fish we were eating. He determined that it was a lake fish—"some kind of carp," he said. He went on to talk at length about Norman Bethune, the Canadian doctor who joined Mao Zedong's communists during the Revolution and who is a legend in China but barely known outside of it. I asked him about his vest and he told me that he had once been a visiting scholar at the school, studying mass media. "It is very polite," he said of Tennessee, "but conservative."

Mr. Wang told me I'd be working the night shift, at least to start, editing the business pages. My heart immediately sank. Editing the *China Daily* business section's "torrid prose," as the *Rough Guide* put it, was one thing, but doing so at night, while I wanted to be out diving headlong into Beijing's boom, was a whole different ball game. I made a mental note: this will need to be remedied.

After lunch, Jenny whisked me away for a tour of the office. *China Daily*'s headquarters were in a four-story, faded yellow building near the fourth ring road in north Beijing, far from the Forbidden City and Tiananmen Square, located in the center of the city. Guards who looked no more than twenty, wearing poorly fitting green uniforms and armed with walkie-talkies, stood at lazy attention at the front door. Everything about the place looked drab and dated, from the water stains on the outside tiles to the bizarre cubic architecture throughout. The interior was as bleak as outside, with humming fluorescent lights, gray cubicle walls, and the constant waft of onion drifting in from the canteen down the hall. Jenny sat me down at my cubicle. The chair squeaked and there were enough crumbs in my ancient keyboard to feed one of the young guards working out front.

I wandered the streets around the *China Daily* compound that night. I could hardly believe I was there. The setting sun had turned the sky purple, and the streets were busy with locals walking in and out of brightly lit restaurants. The air smelled of garlic and burning meat. Potbellied middle-aged men with their pants pulled high smoked cigarettes on the sidewalk while mothers fussed over small children. I was energized. I felt more optimistic about life than I had in a year.

The next day, my second in China, I started work. I was told to shadow a balding, nervous Scotsman, a *China Daily* veteran who introduced me to some of the foreigners around the office. There seemed to be a clear divide in the expat staff. Some were young and international, here for an adventure and to experience the Olympic buildup. A few were wandering professionals who had spent a career bouncing from one developing world English-language paper to another. Others were lifted directly from a Hemingway novel—heavy drinkers, bar fighters, frequenters of prostitutes. Many were career expatriates, some having been in Asia for a decade or two.

My cubicle neighbor at *China Daily* was a well-dressed young Chinese reporter who went by the English name Harry. He had a firm handshake and a flattop brush cut, and he spoke in robotic English. On one of my first days of work, Harry showed me a Flash presentation he'd made for his former employer, a political magazine.

"This is for propagating at the beginning of a campaign," he told me.

I had no idea what he meant. The video was slick, with pictures of Chinese leaders throughout history mixed with images of battles and slogans. Chinese characters and English words—totally out of context—flashed on the screen. VICTORY. HISTORY. I would have thought it was a joke if Harry's facial expression didn't betray such pride. He was beaming.

"I love this Flash," he told me. "It is one way in China we have of propagating. Here at *China Daily*, we use careful chosen words for propagating. It's a different way." Harry nodded. "It's good."

A few days later, over lunch at a local noodle shop, Harry told me with a straight face, "There are too many foreigners in China." Again, I would have thought he was joking had he not looked so serious. Harry had been by far the most accommodating Beijinger I'd met since arriving; he had even paid for the noodles I was eating. He shook his head. "Far too many."

It turned out, foreigners weren't the only group of people Harry frowned upon. His countrymen from Shanghai were "the most disgusting people in the country, other than Taiwanese. Taiwanese want their own country," he scoffed, moving his hand in a sweeping motion, "so forget about them. Shanghainese, they think the rest of Chinese are all *peasants*! They think they are the only ones who are sophisticated, that they are *soooo* well educated. They are disgusting."

The next time Harry asked me for lunch, I politely said no.

My first friend at *China Daily* was a thirty-year-old Englishman named Rob. He had been at the paper for three months when I arrived and introduced himself on one of my first days on the job.

"I heard there was another young guy here. That's good," he said, nodding. He told me he liked Beijing well enough but was eager to find a wingman for the weekends. "We should party sometime."

"Definitely," I said.

Rob reminded me of a balding James Bond, only in boot cut jeans instead of a tux. He had broad shoulders, blue eyes, and a wide smile of fake-looking front teeth. Rob had lived in Asia for seven years—in Japan and the Philippines before coming to China—and had slept with more women than anybody I'd ever met. His nickname at the paper, I soon discovered, was Yi Bai Wu, the Chinese word for one hundred and fifty. That was supposedly the number of women he'd bedded, although after hearing him talk I figured it was a conservative estimate.

On my first weekend in Beijing, Rob and another coworker, an Australian in his mid-thirties named Max, took me out to a few bars in Sanlitun, Beijing's rowdy nightlife area near the Workers Stadium. We visited a half-dozen bars, packed with foreigners and Chinese. There were dive bars, expensive bars, music bars, hooker bars, and massive, booming nightclubs that stayed open until the last customer left. We drank until four in the morning and finished the night off eating Big Macs at a McDonald's down the road from *China Daily*.

The next morning, hungover, Rob regaled me with stories of his many conquests in Asia as we strolled around town. We bought lattes in the Starbucks in the Forbidden City, and as we walked through the old imperial palace talking about women and drinking American coffee, I felt like we were pissing on two thousand years of Chinese history.

I was a stranger in a strange place, and even though I was hardly alone, I felt unique simply for being there. The city's global prominence was growing. The Olympics were on everybody's mind, and I was there to see it.

When I came home that night, after spending the evening walking around the city with Rob, I sat at my computer and wrote for hours, recording the details of the beginning of my new life.

Although I was hired as a writer, my initial duties were editing, or "polishing," as it was known around the office. I started work at two-thirty in the afternoon and ended around eleven or eleven-thirty. During the empty hours before work I would take long walks around the *China Daily* building (almost all of the foreign editors lived in an apartment complex next door), or go to a nearby gym, which, like everything else in Beijing, smelled of onions. My apartment, the office, people's breath. It all smelled like onions.

Everything was new and strange and exciting. The streets, the sounds, the unique Beijing energy—it was invigorating. One morning, I stopped at a narrow, polluted river near my office. Old people walked up and down the banks, slapping their backs and doing strange exercises. One elderly woman massaged another with her fists. A city worker raked the ground around a small tree while debris floated in the toxic-looking green river behind him.

Each day was a small adventure. I had arrived in Beijing armed with an arsenal of Chinese words that topped out at one: *ni hao*—hello. To communicate, I relied on colleagues, maps, and body language, which I discovered did not work very well in China. Ordering food was a crapshoot, especially if restaurant menus lacked pictures. During my first week in the city, I stopped for lunch at a restaurant across the street from *China Daily*, where the waitress presented me with a menu featuring columns of Chinese characters. I was hungry and too proud to walk out without ordering, so I simply pointed at random to an item I felt fell in an appropriate price range for a lunchtime meal for one. What arrived was a massive metal bowl filled with spicy red broth, bony chicken, and vegetables. It was delicious, and it could have served five.

Despite the language barrier, I did my best to explore. Rob and I bought cheap bicycles, and on a Saturday morning we rode south to Chang'An Dajie (Avenue of Eternal Peace), Beijing's main artery, a wide boulevard lined with government buildings. We cycled west past Wangfujing, a popular pedestrian street, down to Tiananmen Square and the Forbidden City, where tourists in from the countryside took photos of a portrait of Chairman Mao. We headed south through the winding *hutong* alleyways, many of which faced demolition as the Olympics approached. In late afternoon we arrived in Dashilan'r, a former slum that was being renovated into a tourist attraction. We had a late lunch of pork with green pepper, ground beef and green beans, spicy tofu, and dumplings dipped in vinegar, and we drank throat-numbing rice wine and Yanjing beer with a gregarious restaurant owner.

One morning, I cycled along the north fourth ring road, not far from the *China Daily* compound, to the Olympic Green. Finishing touches were being put on the National Stadium, better known as the Bird's Nest, and the National Aquatics Center, aka the Water Cube—self-congratulatory national backslaps that stood honor to China's rise. The Olympic Green was surrounded by a blue metal wall. Workers in yellow construction hats squatted on the surrounding pavement, slurping noodles from metal bowls. Around them were the temporary barracks in which they slept, and the trucks and diggers and bulldozers they worked in by day. Visitors peered through cracks in the blue wall and hoisted digital cameras over the top, snapping pictures of the nearby future.

At night, during those early days, I would stand on my balcony smoking cigarettes and looking out at the glowing city, and my heart would thump. Beijing—home to emperors and tyrants and thousands of years of history—was my new home. It was an incredible feeling.

Walking back to my apartment one afternoon, I ran into an Australian editor named Martin, who was in his forties with a friendly smile of smoke-stained teeth and wiry gray hair. Martin had been in Beijing for more than a year. "Things are changing here," he told me, pointing to the influx of foreign staff. "Sure, it's a drab government paper. *China Daily* doesn't break news because the government doesn't break itself. But it's changing." He mentioned a few recent stories that had been critical of the government, before noticing the skepticism creeping on my face. "You'll have a ball here," he said.

But I had my doubts. It only took a few weeks for my initial high to wear off and I started to dread going to work. When I arrived in Beijing, I wanted life at *China Daily* to be crazy, movie-premise crazy, communist spies leaning over my shoulder, filtered e-mails, phone taps, and threatening late-night altercations with men in Mao suits. In my imagination, I would be a fly on the wall and expose the massive state propaganda apparatus from within. The book would be huge—maybe I'd be kicked out of China and return to Toronto, triumphantly, just in time for my book launch. China—and *China Daily*—promised so much for me, and more than anything it promised escape from the boring, depressing, and uninspiring life I had been leading in Canada.

So it was a massive disappointment to discover that my job was, above all else, boring, depressing, and uninspiring. The office wasn't crazy at all. A little nutty, maybe, but more in a funny ha-ha sort of way than a Stalinist Russia way.

My shift was quite possibly the worst in global journalism. The office at night was eerily silent—I could hear the buzz of the lights and every tiny squeak of my chair. Not many people worked evenings, and few of them were among the dozen-odd young foreign staff I would see at lunchtime in the canteen and around the *China Daily* campus. While I toiled at my desk during the warm spring evenings, I was sure the rest of my colleagues were out getting drunk and having the time of their lives.

As I settled into my new routine, I soon began to miss things about Canada. I missed my friends back home, and my ex-girlfriend, and my family. After work, I would return to my apartment and watch episodes of *The Wire* on my computer for hours, wondering if I'd made the right decision to take the job at all.

As if the universe was trying to remind me that China would not always be an easy place to live, I soon experienced my first vicious bout of Beijing belly. Every foreigner gets this illness at some early point during his or her stay, and I was no exception. Mine just came at the worst possible time, sparked, I suspect, by a considerable portion of *Gongbao jiding*—Kung Pao chicken— I'd eaten the night before.

The onset happened as my new couch was being delivered. The apartments *China Daily* provided were nice enough, but they were sparsely furnished—a TV, a few uncomfortable pleather chairs, a bed with a thin blanket. Mine was spacious, with a bedroom, dining room and kitchen, and a living room. But it also felt empty. So a few weeks into my tenure at the paper I followed the lead of the other foreign staff and made a trip to IKEA.

I strolled through the massive store—the second-largest IKEA in the world at the time—with patrons who didn't so much shop as they did lounge on the couches, nap in the beds, snap photos, and order absurd amounts of food at the cafeteria. Fighting my way through the masses, I bought a small couch, a few towels, some lamps, and other odds and ends to make my place feel a little more like home.

A few days later, I was set to have my first class with a Chinese teacher, named Ms. Song, who taught the expat staff at *China Daily*. She was coming to my apartment at 10 a.m., around the same time I had arranged for IKEA to deliver the couch. At about 9:50 a.m., I got a call from some workers at the base of my building ready to bring up the couch. In the elevator on the way down, I felt a rumble in my gut. I have never experienced anything as sudden and lethal as the pain that developed in my stomach that morning. When I met the workers at the foot of my building, I was ready to explode.

I rushed them into the elevator, and they struggled to get the couch to fit. Everything seemed to be happening in slow motion. The door shut. I watched the lights above the elevator door. Two . . . three . . . four . . .

I burst out of the elevator on the eighth floor, flung open the door to my apartment, and pointed the deliverymen toward the living room. The explosion that occurred once I got in the bathroom was inhuman. It was rapid-fire, machine-gun diarrhea. It sprayed all over the toilet, the floor, the walls. Not to mention all my clothes.

Once all was said and done, I took one of my new IKEA towels and wiped up what I could. I sprayed down the bathroom with the shower head, threw my underwear and socks in the garbage, and put my jeans back over my still-filthy legs. There was a knock on the bathroom door, and some chattering in Chinese. I opened it a crack to find a small Chinese woman I'd never seen before looking back at me with curious eyes, standing in front of the crew of IKEA deliverymen.

"Ms. Song?" I asked, my forehead damp with sweat.

She nodded.

"Nice to meet you," I said. "I'll just be a minute, okay?"

"They want to know if they can go," she said, nodding toward the workers.

"Uh, yeah, tell them they can go."

I shut the door and washed myself off as quickly as I could. I wiped up whatever was left on the floor with a second brand-new IKEA towel, dried the sweat from my face, and reluctantly made my way out of the bathroom, praying that Ms. Song didn't have to use it.

"Okay," I said nervously. "Maybe we should go to a café for the lesson? It's not very good light in here. I just need to change into shorts first. It's very warm today."

We walked to a nearby coffee shop, and for the duration of our two-hour class, my first Chinese lesson ever, I couldn't stop wondering if Ms. Song was noticing the pungent smell of shit wafting off my legs.

One of my frustrations at work was that many of the stories I was assigned to edit at *China Daily* didn't make sense. Talking to the Chinese reporters often left me even more confused, so I would often clean up the copy or rewrite it entirely without actually understanding the point of the story, and then send it along to the Chinese sub-editor. If I didn't understand what was going on in the story, they certainly didn't.

China Daily features, a colleague told me, were to be positive and "happy." News involving the Three T's—Taiwan, Tibet, and the 1989 Tiananmen Square massacre, all highly combustible issues—was tightly controlled, and anything remotely sensitive was so biased it became laughable. On one occasion, at a meeting with the business editors, I was told *China Daily* would not write stories about Germany for the time being because Chancellor Angela Merkel had recently met with the Dalai Lama. Thus the world's fourth-largest economy, according to *China Daily*, had simply vanished.

This type of "journalism" went on in spite of the *China Daily* Code of Journalism Ethics, which had been included in a booklet I had received upon arrival: "Factual, Honest, Fair, Complete."

Before I came to China, I wondered if working at a state-owned newspaper was a step in the wrong direction. Now I wondered if it wasn't a giant leap. Among foreigners in Beijing, *China Daily* was a laughingstock. And although I'd had hopes of serving in a mentor role to the Chinese reporters, imbuing them with all the vast wisdom I'd gained in journalism school and in my brief career as a reporter, nobody at *China Daily* seemed especially interested in what I had to say. Foreign experts' editorial suggestions were routinely ignored; we had next to no input about what went into the paper. That applied especially to me, one of the youngest foreigners on staff.

Meanwhile, my freelance ambitions were dead upon arrival. The city and country were so enormous and confusing, I had no idea what to write about. Every time I came up with an idea I thought would sell, I discovered within the span of a five-minute Internet search that the story had been done—about five years earlier. After two months in Beijing, I hadn't sold a single freelance article. When I told some of my foreign colleagues about my book idea, they laughed. "You and everybody else," one scoffed.

At work, I went through the motions, but it was difficult to take the job seriously. A regular feature in the paper called China Scene gathered unusual stories from around the country. Many of them were obviously exaggerated, and some days I was asked to edit these on top of the business pieces. China Scene could be highly entertaining, but editing these puzzling little blurbs was certainly not what I had in mind when I embarked on a career in journalism.

Speaking, Dancing Parrot Wins Bird Skills Competition

A thirty-six-year-old parrot that can speak and dance won the all-round title at the first China Bird Skill Competition in Yuelushan, a scenic spot in Changsha, capital of Hunan Province, on Tuesday.

The parrot can also push a cart, do sums, distinguish the denomination of renminbi and play on a swing.

Participants included babblers, quails, mynahs and doves.

Something had to change.

3

Foreign Friends

Tall Rice was born on a business card.

A month after I started at *China Daily*, I went to the business editor—a tiny, middle-aged woman with graying hair named Ms. Feng—and asked to be moved to the day shift as a writer. "I'm a writer," I told her. "I was hired as a writer. I want to be a writer."

Before granting my request, Ms. Feng wanted to test my reporting chops. She assigned me to accompany a Chinese reporter to an interview with a foreign executive of a major American company. (It would be a fateful interview, though I didn't know it at the time.) For the meeting I needed business cards, which are essential for formal interactions in China, handed over proudly with two hands at every introduction. But before I could get business cards, I needed a Chinese name.

I enlisted one of my cubicle neighbors, a Chinese reporter

who went by the English name Lois, to help me. Lois was a lovely twenty-seven-year-old who accepted my request with vigor and spent the better part of an hour scribbling different characters on a piece of paper, trying to create my perfect Chinese name.

As I edited a story, she slipped the paper on my keyboard. There were two characters written on it.

"That means rice. That means tall, or high. It's Mi Gao," she said.

"Rice Tall?"

"Tall Rice is better."

Harry peaked his head over the cubicle wall. "Ha! That's a stupid name."

"No it's not!" Lois insisted. "*Mi*, because your name's Mitch. And *Gao* because you're tall. And the characters are beautiful."

They were beautiful characters. "Mi Gao. Tall Rice." I thought for a second. "It's great. I love it."

Although when said aloud it could be confused for the Chinese word for "rice cake," my new name was fitting, since as far as I could tell I was the tallest employee at *China Daily*. Introductions to members of the Chinese staff I had not yet met usually included compliments about my height, and word traveled quickly that there was a tall guy working at the paper. Basketball is massive in China—millions play and it's the NBA's second-biggest market. Since Yao Ming's emergence as an international star, China had fallen in love with basketball, and the folks at *China Daily* were no exception. The paper hosted a game on Saturday at nearby courts and put a team together to play against other media companies and government departments around the city.

Not long after I started working at the paper, a member of the Chinese staff came by my desk to recruit me. I told him I've played my whole life, and I would be happy to play with the team. That Saturday, I went to the outdoor courts at the university across from *China Daily* with a dozen or so members of the staff, mostly Chinese and a few foreigners who hadn't played much basketball. I am six foot three, and other than Rob, who was about my height, I was several inches taller than anyone else on the court. My shooting and driving abilities played well in the Chinese game, in which absolutely *zero* defense is played. The hoops were about nine and a half feet high, which meant I could dunk. This caused quite the stir.

Within a few weeks I was the basketball sensation of the three-square-block area around *China Daily*. I wish it was because I'm a naturally gifted athlete, but basketball in China is simply different from the Western game. For one, in North America players don't often wear jeans. On the indoor courts where we sometimes played, a layer of dust covered everything, so you didn't so much run down the court as you did skate or ski. Players often refreshed themselves between games with a cigarette, which they smoked inside the building at the edge of the court.

Soon after my debut, *China Daily* organized a game with a team from the Ministry of Health. Our captains had recruited another basketball talent, an Australian in the features section named Ben. He would be our point guard. The excitement around the office was palpable, and the paper's Chinese-language monthly newsletter ran a Q&A with me—or rather my new alter ego, Mi Gao.

China Daily: Please give some comments on our basketball club.

Mi Gao: I think more games need to be arranged against teams outside China Daily. A couple of times I was told we had a game only to show up at the gym to find it was a scrimmage against other players from China Daily. *Real games will help us play better as a team.*

CD: *What did you learn or benefit from our basketball club?*

MG: *I learned I am the tallest person at* China Daily.

A few days before our game against the Ministry of Health, the foreign editor came to my desk and told me with great disappointment that the game had been postponed.

"What happened?" I asked.

"They found out you could dunk," he said solemnly.

"But I can't *actually* dunk on a regulation net."

He shrugged. "They want a month to prepare."

The extra preparation proved futile: we played the game a month later and pummeled them. I didn't dunk.

The interview with the foreign businessman that Ms. Feng had assigned was scheduled to last three hours on a Friday morning, the one day of the week I worked the day shift, editing the opinion pages. I mentioned this to the reporter, a husky man with a bowl cut who was surnamed Lu, the week before the interview, and he said it was no problem; we'd cover my questions first and then I could step out and return to the office to work my shift.

The interview came and went, and I awaited word from editors about my hoped-for switch to the day shift as a writer. The night shift did not suit me; it made me feel comatose and envious of anybody who worked normal hours. I was still struggling with freelance story ideas, and I hoped that moving to a reporting position would propel me into action. There was an exciting world to explore beyond the *China Daily* gates, and I felt like I was being robbed of the opportunity to get out into it. I focused all my resentment on *China Daily*.

"Anybody who believes *China Daily* is a real newspaper is fooling themselves," I told Rob on one of my bad days. "It's a fucking joke."

A few weeks after my interview with the foreign business executive, the time came for my two-month evaluation. Mr. Wang, of the Tennessee sweater vest, sent the evaluation in an e-mail and asked me into his office for a meeting. "This is an overall reevaluation of your work, which was done among copy editors and editors who have been working with you in the past months," the e-mail read. "On the basis of the assessment sheets collected, we got the following results. Your average score is 10.25 out of 20 points, which is 51.25 out of 100 points."

Fifty percent? What had I done wrong? It would be a lie to say I was enjoying the work, but I arrived on time, did what was required of me, and hadn't heard any complaints up until now.

I pulled up a chair in Mr. Wang's office as he leaned over his keyboard and browsed the document he'd sent me. "Everything is okay . . . editing skills are fine . . . headlines . . . attitude . . . We are happy." He said the editors had decided to make me a writer in the features section.

"But why is my score so low?" I asked.

Mr. Wang dodged the question. "I can tell you're a bright young man and I look forward to seeing more of your stories." He played with his glasses. He looked nervous and I decided to press him.

"But fifty percent. I'm just curious to know why the editors ranked me so low. What are they unhappy with?"

Mr. Wang hesitated for a moment. "There is some concern," he said, "that you walked out of an interview."

I shook my head. "Excuse me? *Walked* out of an interview?"

"Yes, with a foreign business executive."

"What? No. I mean, I left the interview early, yeah, but I had cleared that with the reporter in advance."

"The reports I have been given indicate that you walked out of the interview. I will look into it, but for now we look forward to seeing more of your good stories in the paper."

The next day I approached Lu, the reporter I had accompanied to the interview, and told him about my evaluation. "They're upset because I left the interview early," I said.

"Yes." He smiled sheepishly. "Some people thought that was"—lowering his voice to a whisper—"quite *rude*."

"Rude? I cleared it with you before we went! What did you tell them?"

He waved me off. "I will talk to them," he said, continuing to type on his computer.

A few days later, I attended a meeting with the features editor and writers. The features editor took me into his office. "You're being moved back to the business section," he said.

"But they just moved me here."

"Yes, there's some concern you walked out of an interview. But the editor in chief said you have to stay in business."

For the next week, I was moved between the business and features sections a total of thirteen times. One editor would tell me I was in the business section; fifteen minutes later another editor would say otherwise, and so on.

Nobody bothered to tell me what was really going on, so I sat at my desk and did nothing. By now word had spread around *China Daily* that I had "walked out" of an interview, and both the Chinese reporters and foreign staff were asking me what was going on. I had no clue.

"I heard you walked out of an interview," Jenny, who took me to my medical exam on my first day, wrote to me one day on instant messenger.

I explained the situation and insisted I wasn't at fault.

"Hee-hee. You'll never understand China," she said.

It wasn't until a few weeks later, once I had been resettled into the business section, that I found out what really happened. Over drinks at a bar one night, Ram, an Indian editor who had the most influence of any foreigner at *China Daily*, pulled me aside. Ram had been at the paper for years and had built up significant *guanxi*—"relations" or "connections," hugely important in Chinese culture and business—with the bosses. He told me that most of the editors and reporters at *China Daily* were angry that there were so many foreigners at the paper and that we were being paid starting salaries triple that of Chinese reporters. They were especially livid that there were now foreign writers at *China Daily*, something entirely new at the paper. The business editors, who viewed their section as superior to the others, were especially displeased. When the opportunity arose, Ram said, certain editors deliberately tried to make me look lazy and unprofessional, in an attempt to demonstrate to the higher-ups that there shouldn't be foreign writers in the business section and at the paper in general.

"So," I said, smoking one of Ram's cigarettes, "I was . . . set up?"

"Yes. But don't worry. The editor in chief knows about it and he's very upset. He's let them know there are going to be foreign writers here and there's nothing they can do about it."

By the following week, things had changed. Ms. Feng, the business editor, asked if I wanted to write an opinion column and told me, "We need to do a better job of communicating with our foreign experts." She cleared her throat. "I mean foreign *friends*."

With so much time on my hands during the tumultuous few weeks, I tried to tackle Chinese. Because I was planning to stay only until the Olympics, I didn't see the need to fully immerse myself in the language. "Just the basics," I told Ms. Song during our first infamous lesson. "Enough to get around, order food, you know."

I started by taking one two-hour lesson a week but soon realized that would get me nowhere. Chinese, a tonal language with some ten thousand characters, is a massive mountain to climb. I knew it wouldn't be easy, but it didn't take long before it simply felt futile. For a few weeks I arranged to meet Ms. Song for $7.50-per-hour lessons every day, but laziness soon overpowered what little determination I had. Ms. Song loved to gossip, and I latched on to her as an excuse to avoid studying. Ten minutes into our lessons, she would be gossiping about my colleagues at *China Daily*, in English, and I never tried to set her back on course. Before long, I was regularly canceling lessons, using myriad excuses, and I eventually scaled back to three times a week, then two, then one—right back where I started.

Our lessons would begin with a review of the previous class. Ms. Song would allow me to look over a chapter in our textbook, and then she would take it away from me, hiding it against her chest so I couldn't see.

"What's *huanjing*?"

"Hmm. No idea."

"But you just looked at the book."

"But I don't remember."

"But we study this word every week for last three weeks."

"Sorry."

"Sometimes I think you only speak Chinese with me."

"Maybe."

And then on to the next word I didn't remember. Soon I would bring up the latest *China Daily* gossip, knowing Ms. Song would take the bait, or I might complain about whatever recent injustice I perceived I had suffered at the hands of *China Daily*. Two hours later, I was one hundred yuan (fifteen dollars) poorer and no closer to knowing any Chinese.

China Daily began offering group classes twice a week with Ms. Song. About eight foreign experts initially attended the classes. Seven of us were beginners, while one colleague, an American in his mid-twenties named Jon, who worked in the Web division, was upper-intermediate. Classes were a mix of Jon and Ms. Song speaking in Chinese, and the rest of us chatting in English.

I decided that regular testing was the only way I would scratch the surface of Chinese, so I paid Ms. Song extra to prepare weekly tests based on what we had studied in our private classes. A few days after the first test I was waiting for the *China Daily* group class to begin when Ms. Song arrived carrying a stack of papers.

"We are having a test today," she said.

She handed out a sheet of paper to everybody in the class, and when she got to me, I noticed it was the same test I had paid her to make for my private classes. I should have let it slide, since I was paying her a total of eight dollars a week to make the tests.

Let it slide I did not.

"Ms. Song, I have a bone to pick with you," I said as my classmates scribbled on the sheets of paper.

"A bone to chew?"

"A bone to *pick*."

"What's a bone to pick?"

"It's an expression . . . never mind. Anyway, the thing is, I paid for you to make these tests for *me*, not to make them for everybody in the class. If I knew you were going to hand out tests in the class, I wouldn't be paying you to make them for me."

Ms. Song's eyes widened. For a second I thought she was going to cry. She said nothing.

"Uh . . . I'm sorry," I said, instantly regretting being a baby. "It's really not a big deal. I just thought I'd, you know, I thought I'd let you know how I felt."

After class, Jon approached me at the elevator.

"Hey Mitch, I think Ms. Song was really embarrassed."

"I wasn't really angry. I just thought she shouldn't use tests for the class that I'm paying her to write for me."

"Yeah, I know, but in China there's a certain way of dealing with things like that. It's a face thing."

A face thing. Face is an enigma central to Chinese culture. It would take me years to figure out how to navigate the labyrinth of face, but I figure it essentially works like a currency. Face can be given and taken away, in small, medium, or large increments. The giving and taking of face can be deliberate or accidental. By confronting Ms. Song in class, I had taken away her face. Or at least that's what I understood.

Later that day an e-mail arrived in my inbox with the subject "paper case."

hi mitch:

i am ms. song. i want to explain the paper giving to you. i think i should say sorry to you, because i havent tell you i gave the paper to other class. But i don't think i am wrong.

i am very happy you love to study chinese very much, so i want to help you. i hope all of my student can speak chinese very well, actually, i dont care about you money, i just want you can get improve and feel more fun with studing chinese, yesterday i spent 2 hours to make you paper, comperad you *payment i think i spent more time maybe i shouldnt tell you this but i just want you to understand me, i hope you kown you are my student also friend. . . .*

i think you shoud not talk to this thing in my class, you made me so embarrassing, except you and me nobody know this, and i can not explain in the class using everbodys time. so mayby because of you words somebody will misunderstand me, thinking about me is a cheater. anyway, that's why i give the paper to basic class, i hope you, friend of mine, can understand me.

I might have been lost in Chinese class, but being an asshole, it turned out, translated into any language.

Unmotivated to work or learn the language, I needed a break—from the city, the heat, from *China Daily*. A friend from Canada was coming to town, and we decided to make a weekend trip to a former German colonial town on the coast called Qingdao, where an annual beer festival was about to begin.

On the flight from Beijing, I was reading a book and sitting beside my friend George, a former colleague from Canada, when the plane shook violently. It felt as if we had collided with another plane. A few seconds later we hit turbulence so bad it made the cabin lights flicker. The flight crew hit the deck and the toddler behind me started to wail. Beside him, an old man laughed hysterically, as if to say, *I knew man couldn't fly!*

The trip went all downhill from there.

I was excited about Qingdao. The *Rough Guide* described the city as some kind of Bavarian wonderland. Chinese colleagues had sung its praises, too: beach city, boomtown, beer festival.

"The port city of Qingdao in the east of Shandong province makes a remarkable first impression," the *Rough Guide* said. "Emerging from the train station and walking north with your eyes fixed on the skyline, you could almost believe you had got off at a nineteenth-century Bavarian village, nestling on the Yellow Sea."

As far as I could tell, the only thing Bavarian left in Qingdao was the rain and the German guy who stole our cab during a torrential downpour our second night in town. Every number listed in the *Rough Guide* was incorrect (seven digits instead of eight) and the hotel it recommended, and where we stayed, smelled of bad seafood, as did much of Qingdao itself. Our room, at one hundred dollars a night, overlooked the city's busiest intersection, which meant that as of 7 a.m. we were greeted with the whistles, honks, and hollering of a thousand umbrella-wielding Chinese tourists marching up and down the boardwalk.

Our first night in Qingdao, after a day spent walking around town in the rain, we went to Tsingtao Beer Street. (Qingdao is known for its beer and is famous for the popular brand Tsingtao.) The beer festival was kicking off the next day, so visiting a street of beer seemed appropriate. Beer Street was packed, lined with indistinguishable seafood restaurants. There were some suspicious smells, but the food was good: tiny clams, garlic shrimp, grilled fish, all washed down with fresh beer brewed across the street.

The atmosphere, however, was not as appetizing. When I went to the washroom, the floor was covered with urine, and though it was a one-man bathroom, two drunken men invited themselves in and peed in the drain while I used the Western-style toilet. One of them gave me a thumbs-up. Later, as we ate dinner, a man beside us placed his index finger on his left nostril and blew a wad of snot on the ground, his nose inches from our bowl of shellfish. Meanwhile, an old lady in an apron emerged from the kitchen, sat in a chair, and picked her nose as we ate our shrimp.

At this point, we were still giving Qingdao the benefit of the doubt, assuming there was more to the city than met the eye. After a good night's rest, George and I figured, we would discover the city's true charm. But Qingdao had other ideas. As soon as we decided to leave Beer Street, the rains came. It poured from 10 p.m. until past 2 a.m., flooding the streets. It was clear we were in for a long weekend.

The next day the rains continued and we were slow moving. After lunch we took a bus to the Beer Festival, where we sat at a table drinking bottles of German beer as a waitress tried to sell us chicken feet and duck liver. Around us were several hundred drunk Chinese huddled at picnic tables under a large circus tent. Onstage, a performer in a black tank top and ripped jeans, with a beer gut and Elvis hair, swung his hips and punched the air to the tune of horrendous pop music played at what was surely a dangerous decibel.

At around 7 p.m. we decided the Beer Festival was beyond salvaging and headed back downtown. After the aforementioned German stole our cab, we eventually made it to our destination and decided to unwind with a pizza and a massage. We headed to a four-star hotel near ours and ate a pizza with toppings that included sausage, lettuce, and corn.

Then we went downstairs to the "spa." I should have known something was amiss when two young women took George and me to separate rooms, at which point my masseuse, whose thong was exposed at the back of her jeans, began to massage nothing but my lower abdomen and inner thigh, moving slowly inward.

"You want?" she said, eyebrows raised.

I shook my head. "Bu yao, xie xie." No, thanks.

I covered my eyes with my hands and tried to will away what was happening in my pants.

She typed the number 1,200—about $150—on her phone and showed it to me. "Okay?"

"No, thanks."

She pouted and typed 600. "Okay?"

"No, thank you. Just massage."

George was having a similar problem. "Mitch, what's happening over there?!" he cried from the other room.

"She's trying to jerk me off!" I hollered.

"Me, too!"

George successfully fought off the happy ending, but my masseuse was loath to give up. She keyed 300 into her phone. "Okay?"

"No, I don't want that!" I said.

She threw up her hands in exasperation. The rest of the massage was terrible. She spent most of the time unenthusiastically kneading my back with one hand, and text messaging with the other.

After waking the next morning to more rain, George and I went across town to drink coffee at a Starbucks. We basically just wanted to kill the day before boarding the flight back to Beijing. By midafternoon the clouds broke for the first time, revealing a lovely blue sky. Of course, we were wearing jeans and shoes, and too far from our hotel to change into shorts and enjoy the weather.

A few hours later, we were sitting on the plane, having never set foot on the beach during our weekend beach getaway, and looking paler than ever.

During the weeks that followed I did very little work at *China Daily*. The editors would assign me a story, I would take two weeks to write it, and then the story had a 50 percent shot at going to print. Throughout the summer and into the fall, I wrote maybe three or four stories. The rest of the time I did whatever I wanted.

It became clear to me during that time that the influx of "foreign friends" to *China Daily* was little more than window dressing, not much different from the coats of paint they were throwing up on apartment buildings around the ring roads to beautify the city before the Games. We were a small part of the biggest public relations campaign in history—Beijing's Olympic makeover.

To that end, *China Daily* brought in people with *real* journalism experience. In the past, the foreigners at the paper were travelers, university students on summer break, or outright nut jobs. One foreign expert, whose career at *China Daily* lasted two weeks, frequently and firmly made known his belief in aliens and claimed to have fourteen doctoral degrees, one of which was being suppressed by the Vatican. Now the foreign experts appeared legally sane, or at bare minimum did not talk openly about their belief in aliens. We were told we would have real influence at the paper and that we could help decide its direction. But in the end, what *China Daily* really wanted was for us to sit down, shut up, and edit. There were changes, but they were glacial and superficial. It was a sugarcoating, and we were the sugar.

Periodically the foreign staff would discuss the ethics of working at *China Daily*. Some felt we had a responsibility to make the paper better. Others disagreed. "There's nothing wrong with what we do," my friend Max, the Australian, said one night as we strolled around the *China Daily* compound. "You have to realize what this is. We're not a newspaper, mate. We're PR. You have to give the bosses what they want."

He was right, and once I accepted that fact I could tolerate working at *China Daily*. I was no longer a journalist, but I could be one in my off-hours. By midsummer I had sold a few freelance articles, and I became determined to do better. I would be like a media Batman: propagandist by day, journalist by night.

Although I would always have my issues with *China Daily*, I eventually began to appreciate the unique experience for what it was and to enjoy myself. And I still hoped that I could, in some small way, change the paper for the better, to make it somehow more palatable, to blur the line between propaganda and journalism until a reader might barely know the difference.

"How does it feel to be a government propagandist?" a woman asked me once at a bar in Beijing, barely masking her contempt. It was a question I received often, and I answered her honestly: "Great!" It had become a reason to be in China during an incredible time, a chance to be a part of history.

Since my editors asked very little of me, that's what I gave them, and in the slow, sweltering weeks of summer I settled into a lovely routine in my new career as a wallflower. Sometimes, out of sheer boredom, I would offer to edit a story, but mostly my days looked like this:

9:30—Wake up. Press snooze button.

10:15—Walk to nearby café.

10:30—Arrive at office.

10:30–11:00—Check e-mail.

11:00–noon—Surf Internet.

Noon–1:30—Lunch with colleagues. Having grown
weary of the canteen's food, several of us often split a cab
to a deli fifteen minutes away from the offices, where we
relaxed over coffee long after we were expected back at
work.

1:30–4:15—Sporadic checking of e-mail, chatting on
MSN, surfing Internet. Flirt with Lois.

4:15–4:45—Coffee with other members of the foreign
staff.

4:45–6:00—Work. Mostly researching potential freelance stories that had nothing to do with *China Daily*.

6:00—Home.

China Daily and I had come to a happy truce. In September,
after a lazy four months on the job, I walked into Mr. Wang's
office and asked for a raise.

I got it.

4

Young Turks, Old Hacks

It was my colleague Potter's birthday. We got drunk.

I didn't know how old Potter was. He was probably in his late fifties or early sixties, though it was hard to tell since he was a heavy smoker and drinker, a lifetime of which was taking its toll. His cheeks were sunken and the bags under his eyes were large and black, as if he never slept, which was entirely possible. Potter was half Indian, half Welsh, Hong Kong–born and raised, a tiny man with a thin goatee and bald head except for a horseshoe of jet-black hair that wrapped around the back of his skull. He was cigarette slim; in the year I knew him I don't think I ever saw him eat. He dressed immaculately in white or black collarless shirts, with black pressed trousers and polished black shoes.

His birthday party was on a hot weeknight in midsummer. Everybody met after the late shift at the Goose & Duck, a sports bar with a Filipino cover band next to a park on Beijing's east side. When Rob and I arrived around 11:30 p.m., the party was already in full swing.

Potter sat in the middle of a long table beside Filipino David, a Beijing-based photographer and Potter's good friend from back in the day in Bangkok. David had a bushy black mustache and wore a faded denim jacket even in the heat. His laugh was contagious and he came across as the friendliest guy you'd ever met. Some of the other expat staff were there along with others I didn't know, mostly Filipinos, including a man known as the Ambassador, short for "Maggie's Ambassador," a name he earned due to the frequency with which he visited Beijing's most notorious nightlife establishment, Maggie's, a club known as a pickup joint specializing in Mongolian prostitutes.

Rob and I pulled up chairs at the table, where everybody was eating Filipino food. Potter was drinking a bottle of Carlsberg and sipping from a bottle of Johnnie Walker Red Label that David had brought. When Potter's glass was empty, David filled it, his arm resting over his old buddy's shoulders.

"Any birthday resolutions, Potter?" Rob asked. "Anything you're going to do different in the next three hundred and sixty-five days?"

Potter smiled. He looked like he was thinking of something witty to say, but nothing came.

"Be a better propagandist?" Rob suggested.

Potter laughed, a throaty chuckle that seemed to rattle his rib cage. "Yes, yes. That's it."

This was my crew: a gang of misfits from around the globe—nomads, drinkers, aging journalists with young girlfriends. Wanderers with no place else to go. Runners from reality.

In *The Rum Diary*, Hunter S. Thompson describes the staff of the fictional San Juan *Daily News* as either "wild young Turks" or "beer-bellied old hacks" barely able to write a postcard. This, more or less, was *China Daily*. Asia attracts the latter kind of man. Many are in or beyond middle age, reliving their youth through copious amounts of alcohol and regular (sometimes paid) intercourse with women young enough to be their daughters. I had seen them before, in cities like Bangkok and Manila and other stops in Southeast Asia. These were men who refused to grow up: the Lost Boys of Neverland. And *China Daily* offered what they craved most—escape.

At *China Daily*, we lived cushioned existences outside the realities and pressures of our lives back at home. Everything was provided for us. We could spend weeks at a time without ever having to leave the *China Daily* compound, a life revolving around a piece-of-cake job, heavy drinking, bootleg DVDs, and not much else. We could eat breakfast, lunch, and dinner for almost nothing at *China Daily*'s canteen, a two-minute walk from our apartments (although it's debatable whether to describe what the canteen offered as "food"). We each hired cleaning ladies to come in on weekends to tidy up our apartments and do our laundry. Reality and responsibility were things that existed outside the gates.

Potter had spent years working copy desks in Hong Kong and Bangkok. He was now late in his career doing the same thing, at the same pay, as people thirty years his junior. His life, or what I knew of it, consisted of work, betting on Hong Kong horse races over the Internet, and drinking with his buddies until dawn.

There were others, too. There was Wooden Tooth Dan, a boozer from Alaska I met my first day in China. His hair was disheveled, dandruff-ridden, and cut at different lengths, in some places down to the scalp, as if it had been cut with a Flowbee. His teeth were large and brown and looked like they had been carved out of driftwood. I would often see him after work walking back from the convenience store on the corner with a plastic bag filled with a dozen or more cans of beer. In the evenings, I could hear him and his young local wife screaming at each other in their apartment. The next day he would show up at work reeking of liquor so badly you could smell it from down the hallway.

There was the white-haired man who worked upstairs at one of *China Daily*'s sister publications and whose name I never learned, who told stories of 'Nam even though it seemed to me he was at least a decade too young to have served there. There was one editor, a recovering gambling addict, who once won a dubious award as his country's *worst* journalist after he was found fabricating stories.

There was Rob, Yi Bai Wu—One Hundred and Fifty. Rob, my first friend in China, was half Potter's age but on the same path to reality and morality warping and eventually dissipating like a fog. Rob was on his way there; Potter had long passed.

Rob was at once one of the most fascinating and frightening people I had ever met. He was one of those people who would require a team of scientists monitoring him 24/7 to figure out what was going on in his brain, and even then I don't think they'd get it right. There were times when Rob was genuinely insightful and thoughtful. You could give him a book and he would tear through it in a weekend and come in on Monday with a full report. One day he bought me a book of short stories from an English-language bookstore just because he thought I would enjoy it. Rob was a good writer and often talked about chronicling his seven years of debauchery (a book I would read). He could be philosophical, and he tried harder to learn Chinese than any other foreigner I knew at *China Daily*, myself included.

At other times, his moods turned dark, often vicious. He could be combative and withdrawn, stumble home drunk at 7 a.m. with a strange girl on his arm, and otherwise tear through life like a tornado, leaving a trail of destruction in his wake. After a few months of knowing him, I became convinced he was bipolar.

Rob had a remarkable way with women, and God help them all. He slept with dozens in the time I knew him, without remorse, including one in a hotel room in Shanghai he was sharing with me and a friend of mine, both of us trying unsuccessfully to sleep.

When I first met Rob, he was dating a naïve Chinese girl in her early twenties. One day he decided it was over and stopped replying to her text messages. She sent him dozens that day, a rapid and teary downward spiral. I came home in the early evening to find a young woman sleeping outside Rob's apartment door, waiting for him.

"How long have you been here?" I asked.

"Since this morning," the girl replied, her eyes red with tears.

I called Rob and told him about the girl waiting outside his door.

"Just text me when she's gone," he said.

And then there was me. When I arrived at *China Daily*, I was both appalled and thrilled by many of the men I met. Appalled for all the reasons above; thrilled because observing and drinking with them could be so entertaining, and because I figured no matter what I did I could always point to one of them and say *at least I'm not like that.*

But, really, was I so different? I was also running from something, looking for escape in my own small corner of Asia. And I would be lying to say Rob's life didn't intrigue me. It was a guilty pleasure listening to his stories of drunken adventures and sexual hedonism. When I was heartbroken and miserable after breaking up with my previous girlfriend the year before, it was Rob's life I fantasized about. The previous fall, single and unmotivated to date or meet anybody new, it was somebody like Rob that I needed most, to pry me out of my self-loathing by thrusting a shot of tequila in my face.

Rob was nobody's role model, but in some ways, during those early days in China, he was exactly what I needed. He provided an avenue to escape.

On the night of Potter's birthday party, after the Goose & Duck we ventured to the Den, Potter's favorite haunt. The Den was a classic Asia expat bar, filled with single, middle-aged men drinking Carlsberg and eating burgers and pizzas while watching English Premier League soccer, the kind of place where waitresses flirted with you no matter how drunk or ugly you were. The other half of the crowd were Mongolian prostitutes, and Potter claimed to have been with all of them.

We sat at a long table and ordered rounds of beer and shots of tequila and whiskey. A replay of Ali and Fraser's Thrilla in Manila played on one of the televisions as cigarette smoke floated through the crowded bar. The Den had the vibe of the Mos Eisley Cantina in the first *Star Wars*—where we first meet Han Solo. I got the impression that the people in this bar had all done some things, had been places. People at the Den had secrets.

We talked about our jobs and Potter spoke nostalgically about his time in Bangkok and Hong Kong. "Beijing is a backwater," he said. I asked him what he thought about working at *China Daily*. He shrugged. "It's a job."

Around 2 a.m. we went to Maggie's. I had never been to Maggie's but had heard its legend. The club was a Beijing institution, the embassy of Beijing's down and depraved. It was the Den on steroids, the bar of choice for foreign businessmen looking for action, for older expats in need of a nightcap at four in the morning, and for Mongolian hookers looking for after-hours freelance business. If the Den was the Mos Eisley Cantina, Maggie's was the garbage pit in the Death Star.

As we strolled through the dark, smoky club, fat foreigners in boxy suits wrapped their meaty hands around the waists of young Mongolians. The bottom of a beer bottle was downed, and a new couple would walk hand in hand out of the club and back to whichever hotel was home for the night.

We made our way to a pool table at the back of the bar. Rounds of drinks were ordered, and we chain-smoked cigarettes. There were more women in the bar than there were clients, and each potential customer had two or three women competing for them. The Ambassador seemed to know every girl in there, and he introduced every one that came by to Potter.

"It's his birthday," he told them, patting their lower backs. "Give him a kiss."

The seediness left me feeling hollow, and after a few drinks, I had seen enough. I took a cab back to *China Daily* to sleep while the others stayed until dawn. I ran into one of the foreign editors the next morning outside the building, and he sheepishly told me he had solicited the services of a Maggie's working girl. "It's all part of the rich tapestry of life," he said.

Rob and I hung out most evenings. Sometimes we joined Potter and the others at the Den and other bars around town. Other nights we stayed in Rob's apartment, drinking beers and watching American movies on pirated DVDs.

Often we found ourselves at the main *China Daily* hangout, the Noodle Shop, across the street from our compound. The Noodle Shop had a name, but nobody ever bothered to learn it. So it was simply the Noodle Shop. The rumor was that the Noodle Shop was owned, operated, and frequented by Chinese gangsters. I doubt that gossip was true, but it made a good story to everyone I brought there.

In the evenings it was packed with noisy and drunken locals, who sometimes stayed until dawn. Peanut shells and green pea pods littered the floor, and bottles of beer collected on the tables by the dozens. The noodles were oily and the meat skewers—the ubiquitous Beijing street snack called *chuan'r*—were of questionable quality. Once I bit down on a chunk of soggy denim in a bowl of beef noodles. After that, I stopped ordering food from the Noodle Shop.

Fights were common. I strolled by the Noodle Shop one evening after work to find two ambulances, each containing a Chinese man with bloodied gauze wrapped around his head. On the cement outside were thick pools of blood and shards of glass from smashed beer bottles. Two *China Daily* foreign experts once fought outside the Noodle Shop. Both men were drunk; one called the other's girlfriend a "whore," for no apparent reason, and blows ensued. One participant had a hip injury and weighed 140 pounds soaking wet; the other was Wooden Tooth Dan, who was already a dozen drinks deep, possibly more. I didn't see the fight, but the next day a colleague described it as "the most pathetic display I've ever seen."

Mostly we drank beers and vented about work. We debated about the quality and direction of the paper, about whether there was anything we could do to improve it, about whether we were just wasting our time, wasting away at *China Daily*. And then we'd order another round.

On weekends, Rob and I were wingmen. Most of the other *China Daily* guys were not very adventurous when it came to nightlife, sticking mostly to pubs popular with expats, like the Den. The crowds at these places tended to be older and depressing, and Rob and I were eager to explore some of the more youthful nightlife destinations.

To say that we went out "a lot" would be a drastic understatement. For me, living in China was a chance to say "yes" to everything. Yes to drinking, to smoking, to partying until dawn. Yes to it all. Beijing was cheap and we were well paid and free to do anything. It was liberating and terrifying.

Longtime expats liked to wax nostalgic about the old days of the city's nightlife, before the clubs took over. In the years before I landed in Beijing, a good night out largely meant huddling on plastic chairs in dingy bars, where people sipped bottles of lukewarm Tsingtao and "just got drunk," as a friend who had lived in Beijing for five years told me.

Those days were fading. There were still dingy bars along Sanlitun Bar Street and surrounding Houhai Lake, but many of the more popular bar districts had been demolished to make way for apartment blocks and shopping malls, and bottles of Tsingtao were being swapped for bottles of Chivas mixed with ice tea, a Chinese club staple. The holes-in-the-wall were being replaced by lounges, *hutong* bars, pubs, and massive nightclubs. These clubs, with names like Angel, Babyface, Coco Banana, Vics, and Mix, were often packed seven nights a week with hundreds of people, mostly Chinese, drinking in private booths and dancing until dawn listening to some of the world's top DJs. New bars and clubs seemed to open every other week, and it was impossible to keep track of which ones were cool at a given moment. The Olympics were still a year down the road, but the party was well under way.

There were plenty of drugs in Beijing—cocaine, ecstasy, hash. It was all available, and it was easy to find, a fact I immediately found alarming. I had been smoking pot periodically since my early teens and had experimented with mushrooms and ecstasy by the time I was twenty. A few years before moving to China, I started taking coke from time to time. But for me, coke come-downs were brutal, life-questioning nightmares that took me two or three days to get over. In Toronto, before I left for China, I was doing coke every few months and it was something I was looking forward to escaping in China, where, it being an authoritarian state, I assumed drugs would be scarce.

Not so. The first night I went out in the city, Rob, Max, and I were approached on the street by a half-dozen African men in the darker sections of Sanlitun. Trade between China and Africa was booming, and thousands of Africans were coming to China to buy cheap goods to sell back home. Some who didn't make it as merchants ended up on the streets of Sanlitun selling drugs, and they did so in the open. Nobody seemed to be trying to stop it.

"Pssst. Yo, what's up," they would say. "You good? Need anything?"

About once a month we supplemented our nighttime activities with "extracurriculars." Although I had been hoping to avoid drugs, I struggled to do so once I arrived in Beijing, and they seemed to be everywhere. Since what I was looking for in Beijing most of all was escape, narcotics fit nicely into the equation.

The quality varied. One hot July night, we bought ecstasy from a Nigerian drug dealer on Lady Street, a bar area near the American embassy. We met him after dinner and he led us around the corner, where he pulled out a small plastic bag filled with baby blue pills. We bought two each. (On the way to get a cab, Rob pulled into a sex shop to buy some generic version of Viagra. "For later," he said.)

We went to a bar in Sanlitun and I popped my first pill. An hour later, nothing had happened. Frustrated, I told Max I was going to take the other. "I would wait a little," he said. "See if the first one kicks in. I'm feeling it." I ignored Max's advice and swallowed the second pill with a swig of beer.

Soon the walls were melting. I sat down at the bar and could barely lift my arms. People tried to talk to me, but I couldn't respond. "Are you all right?" Max asked, patting me on the back. I was not. I stumbled to the bathroom to wash my face and saw devils in the bathroom tiles.

I emerged from the bathroom, and Rob and Max laughed at me when I told them I needed to go home. I caught a cab, and when I made it back to my apartment, I took two allergy tablets in a desperate attempt to sleep it off. It didn't work. My heart raced and I hated myself. I stared at the ceiling, eyes wide open, until the sun came up, when the panic finally subsided and I managed to get a few hours of shaky sleep.

I eventually drifted away from the Potters of *China Daily*. One Sunday, when I was filling in for a colleague editing the Monday paper, still hungover from a late night of boozing the night before, I grew annoyed with myself. I surely felt a hundred times better than I did in Toronto, but was this why I'd come to China? To hang out in seedy bars and coast through life either drunk or hungover? Partly, yes. But still, I thought, there must be more to Beijing life than this. The summer had been fun, but I hadn't fulfilled my promise to make more strides with my freelance career, even though I spent large chunks of my day surfing the Internet for story ideas. My Chinese was virtually nonexistent. I could barely motivate myself to pick up the phone for the articles I was supposed to be writing for *China Daily*. I was partying too hard and needed things to calm down in the fall.

I eventually found more friends my age and grew less intrigued with the darker side of Beijing, avoiding the Den or Maggie's whenever possible. But the more I got to know Potter and his friends, the more I felt I understood them and I realized they could also be decent people. A friendship like David and

Potter's struck me as truly rare. They would die for each other; they just lived by a different set of rules, lived in a different reality. They lived in Chinese Neverland—they had permanent residency, in fact.

Later, Rob and I grew apart, too, and as time went on he became increasingly isolated, spiraling into a deep depression. He stopped hanging out with many of the *China Daily* staff, myself included. The only people he seemed to trust were Potter, David, and a few of their friends, and he refused to attend any event that included the majority of *China Daily*'s expat staff.

Rob seemed to know what he was becoming and he mostly embraced it. But he had doubts. A friend relayed to me a story about one afternoon when Rob and Potter sat in the *China Daily* lobby, smoking cigarettes and talking. Rob needed advice. He was single, lonely, drinking too much. He was lost.

"But this is the life, right? Freedom. Doing whatever I want," Rob said. "I mean, look at you; you're happy, right?"

"What do you think, mate?" Potter replied. "I'm fucking miserable."

Two years later, Potter died of a heart attack. After being laid off from *China Daily*, he moved to another state-owned paper that had launched an English version. He was found alone in his apartment after several days, when colleagues wondered why he hadn't shown up for work.

After Potter's death, his friends created something of a shrine to him in one of his favorite Beijing bars. On the wall at the back of the bar were photos of Potter and his buddies drinking Carlsberg and Johnnie Walker, smoking cigarettes, laughing it up. Living a life I would later worry might suck me in, too.

5

On Assignment

Ms. Feng's instructions for most of the stories I wrote for *China Daily* were straightforward: "Find out what Westerners think."

It was clear early on that Pulitzer Prize–winning journalism would not be expected of me as a writer for *China Daily*, and before long, I owned the "What Westerners Think About Stuff" beat. Property prices, Chinese products, websites about China—I was tasked to find out what foreigners thought about it all. It seemed the editors simply wanted me out of sight, out of mind, and that was fine with me.

The stories I was assigned were mostly puff pieces that would be tucked into the business section's back pages or in a weekend supplement called *Business Weekly*. One of the first stories I wrote for *China Daily*, with a Chinese cowriter, was about an Israeli products fair downtown. We sampled olives and hummus and wine. It was a lovely afternoon, but it wasn't a story. It shouldn't even have garnered a brief, but we wrote a feature about it anyway, reporting—despite a total lack of substantiating evidence—that Israeli goods were taking the Chinese market by storm.

For another story, the editors sent me to Beijing's famous Silk Street market. Silk Street, or Xiushui, had long been a symbolic thorn in the side of Western governments and companies that wanted China to crack down on counterfeit products and intellectual property rights violations. In a rare victory for legitimate brands, Chinese authorities had recently "reorganized" Xiushui to concentrate on high-quality silk while eliminating fake goods. *China Daily*, in fact, wrote a story declaring the market to be 100 percent free of counterfeit products.

"Find out what Westerners think about that," Ms. Feng said.

I arrived at the Silk Market to find the place full, from floor to ceiling, with fake products—jeans, jackets, shoes, underwear, everything. Whatever one wanted, it was all there, and it was almost all counterfeit. The silk was real, so I was told, but there were no foreigners buying it. In fact, fake stuff was exactly what foreigners wanted. "I just want cheap crap to bring back as presents," one young American told me. (I did a little shopping myself, buying a pair of knockoff Calvin Klein underwear.)

The next morning at *China Daily*, I relayed my conclusion that the reason foreigners went to Xiushui was for cheap knockoffs, not expensive silk. I was wearing the evidence.

"You can't mention counterfeit," the *Business Weekly* editor said. "We could get sued."

"But the stuff *is* counterfeit. The whole market is counterfeit."

"But the government has really cracked down on the intellectual property rights issue, *sooooo* . . . ," he trailed off.

After some debate with my editor, I was allowed to report

that foreigners liked the market for its "low-cost goods." All mentions of knockoffs were stripped from the story.

While writing government-friendly puff pieces took up most of my workweek, Friday was the one day I still worked an editing shift, polishing the *China Daily* opinion pages. Many of the articles weren't so much arguments supported by fact but rants supported by nothing. Many violated everything I had ever learned about journalistic ethics, including *China Daily*'s own code: "Factual, Honest, Fair, Complete." It was sometimes hard to stomach editing the opinion pages, but I didn't have much choice. I knew any complaints would fall on deaf ears.

The articles themselves proved tricky to edit. When articles I edited for the business section were poorly written, I would return them to the reporter for rewrites before I took to editing the story. I couldn't do this with the opinion pages, however; the authors were often senior editors or important Chinese academics from leading universities.

One day I edited an op-ed praising China's state-required college entrance exam—the bane of every senior high school student in the country. Universities selected students based almost entirely on their exam scores. The story was repetitive and nonsensical. It was the fifth of seven stories of a thousand-plus words I was supposed to edit that day, and I was getting fed up. I completely rewrote the story, which we were discouraged from doing. I removed all redundancies, awkward sentences, and unnecessary jargon. The resulting story was about half the length of the original. Although it still lacked a point, at least it was written in clear, proper English.

Late in the afternoon, one of the opinion page's editors, a friendly middle-aged Chinese man with a gap-toothed smile, approached my desk. He removed his glasses and sighed.

"Moxley," he said, confusing the order of my names. "We have a problem. You have polished too much. We cannot fit the stories onto the page. It's too short."

"A lot of it was repetitive," I said. "In some paragraphs the author was trying to make one point but saying it in four different ways. So I changed it to one way."

"Yes, the polishing is okay, but we cannot fit it on the page."

After a few moments of stalemate, I agreed to redo the edits. As the editor walked away I opened the original story. Without making any changes, I sent it back to him, the word-for-word original—the same way it ran in the next day's paper.

Nobody said a thing.

The next week I showed up at work, and Harry, my anti-foreigner, anti-Shanghainese, anti-Taiwanese deskmate, was gone. My new neighbor introduced himself as Wang—"just Wang is okay," he said. (For newcomers to China, keeping track of people surnamed Wang can be daunting.) Wang was the same age as me, thin and bespectacled, with immaculate hair parted to the side. He was a Communist Party member, he told me, not because he was necessarily interested in politics or the Party but because it was key for career success. Membership mostly entailed spending the odd weekend away at Party conferences, where officials would drone on about policy and ideology for hours. Wang covered natural resources for the paper, and he was good at his job. He worked the phones all day and filed clean copy.

One Friday, a few weeks later, I noticed Wang was proofreading the opinion pages I had edited. Initially I took this as a slight to my work, and then I became nervous that my bosses had figured out that I didn't actually *read* the proofs.

"Why do they need you to work as a proofreader anyway?" I asked. "You're already working all day as a reporter."

"They need me to look for political mistakes."

"Political mistakes? Like what?"

"Like Taiwan and Hong Kong, for example. Or another example: the other day there was a reference to South Korea as 'Korea.' That is not acceptable. Because there are two Koreas, South Korea and North Korea, and one Korea cannot represent both Koreas. If we have that, North Korea will call *China Daily* and be very upset with us."

"I see."

I pulled out a proofreading sheet and found a story that mentioned Taiwan as a Chinese province.

"Hey, I found a political mistake here. Shouldn't this say 'China *and* Taiwan,' which are two *separate countries*? Like North and South Korea?"

Silence. Wang grabbed the paper and held the sheet of paper inches from his glasses.

"I'm joking," I said.

Wang just laughed nervously.

I was much better suited to the day shift, and my mood perked up accordingly. Working from ten to six improved my social life, but I still wasn't finding much in the way of freelance success. I wrote a piece about China's stock market for a Canadian business magazine, and I was commissioned a few stories for local English magazines. I pitched North American newspapers and magazines regularly but without much luck. Many e-mails were ignored completely—so frequently, in fact, that I sometimes e-mailed myself just to confirm my messages were actually going through.

I often met foreign journalists who worked for well-known publications—the *New York Times*, the *Wall Street Journal*, *Time*, *Newsweek*, and others. Beijing was stocked with foreign correspondents, and I felt grossly inadequate whenever I socialized with them, imagining them laughing at my career misfortune whenever I went to the bar to order a drink.

At night, lying in bed on hot summer nights—one year away from the Olympics—I would ruminate about my station in life. I wanted to be writing for marquee magazines, to some day walk into a bookstore and see a book I'd written. But I had no idea how to get there. And when I looked around the office at some of my colleagues—beat-down, dreary-eyed, wearing the same outfit they'd worn all week—it was clear that *China Daily* was not a path to great success.

One day in late August, Ms. Feng approached my desk and told me I would be sent with a team of Chinese reporters to cover the first World Economic Forum held in China, called "Summer Davos," in the booming coastal city of Dalian. I would be the token *laowai* on our reporting squad. (*Laowai* is the colloquial term for "foreigner" in Chinese, literally meaning "old outsider.")

I was at once flattered at being sent and slightly concerned that it would lead to actual responsibility at the paper, something I wanted to avoid so I could use office hours to covertly concentrate on finding freelance stories.

"You'll be staying at a four-star hotel," Ms. Feng said, with a nod that suggested, *How about that?*

Until the day of our departure a great deal of enthusiasm was generated among the business reporters about the "four-star" hotel in which we were booked. From the Beijing airport all the way to Dalian the talk was all about the four-star hotel. I got swept up in it as well, imagining the trip as more vacation than business trip: watching HBO in my four-star room and lounging in a sauna at the four-star spa downstairs.

After arriving in Dalian we drove in a cab through the city, passed the Shangri-La, the Kempinsky, the Sheraton, and a luxury Japanese hotel, before pulling into the Dalian Delight Hotel. It wasn't horrible, but four stars it was not. (At least not by international standards; behind the receptionist desk was a plaque from the China Tourism Bureau with four stars prominently displayed.) My room was small, with dim yellow lights, faded carpets, and cigarette burns in the sheets, despite a no-smoking sign on the wall.

The Chinese staff was two or more to a room. I was given my own room, which made me feel uneasy. The Chinese reporters worked hard and carried the burden of actually putting out a paper, while I knew that very little would be expected from me on this trip.

After check-in, Xiao Zhang, a handsome young editor who worked on the international desk, gave me my first assignment.

"Please write a story about your impressions of Dalian," he said.

"My impressions of Dalian?"

"Yes. What do you think of Dalian?"

"I don't know. We just got here."

"Maybe you should go and walk around, and then write about your impressions of Dalian."

"Like, related to business? Or travel, or what?"

"Just impressions."

"Okay . . ."

So I set out to discover Dalian. The city was by far the prettiest I had seen in China—clean, with wide, tree-lined streets and green spaces, and a decent beach close to downtown. Big squares defined the city center, paid for by growing software, tourism, and shipping industries. The city looked more like it belonged in Japan or Korea than China.

I strolled down by the shore, which was dominated by massive apartment buildings that looked like castles from Disneyland. A friendly young Chinese couple approached me. They were curious to know what I was doing in the city.

"China is changing very fast," the husband said via his wife, who translated.

"This was all once seaside," the wife told me. "Twenty years ago there was nothing here." She spoke not with regret—the apartments were colossal eyesores—but with tremendous pride. "We hope you enjoy our beautiful Dalian."

The city was emblematic of China's economic miracle and a fitting home for the Economic Forum, which was held at a new conference center across town from our hotel. The meeting, dubbed "the Inaugural Annual Meeting of the New Champions," was to celebrate the emergence of multinational companies from developing countries. Business and government leaders from around the world were in attendance. Chinese premier Wen Jiabao gave a speech on the opening night. Three-time Pulitzer Prize–winner and *New York Times* columnist Thomas Friedman was there, as were many prominent CEOs from global companies.

Journalists from *Time*, the *Wall Street Journal*, the *Economist*, and every other major news organization that had a presence in China were covering the forum. This brought back my feelings of inadequacy. During the days of the forum, *China Daily* gave me free rein to attend whichever talks I wanted to. Whereas other *China Daily* reporters were tied down to the media center, I was free to wander around all day with no obligation to even check in with the team. I should have been out making contacts, developing sources, and setting up the exclusive interviews with bigwig business types that *China Daily* so lusted after. Instead, I wandered around aimlessly, my ID badge shamelessly flipped around so no one would know where I worked.

The forum was very much a China lovefest, and if anything of significance was accomplished there, I didn't see it. The majority of sessions were behind closed doors, and the discussions open to the media were mostly contrived and bland. Each panel invariably had one Chinese member who would rattle off facts and figures and boast about China's economic might, its commitment to the environment, and the development of a "harmonious society"—Chinese president Hu Jintao's catchphrase. The foreigners on the panel would smile and nod, never questioning anything that was said.

After two days and after only contributing a few blurbs alongside my "Dalian impressions" story, I was feeling guilty about my insignificant contribution. I flipped through the forum's schedule and noticed a session called "Soft Power: Influencing the World with a Chinese Touch." The discussion would be moderated by *Fortune* magazine Asia editor Clay Chandler, featuring panelists such as Thomas Friedman; Sha Zukang, the United Nations undersecretary-general for the Department of Economic and Social Affairs; and prominent businesspeople from China and abroad. It sounded interesting and I decided to attend.

At the session, Chandler started things off by criticizing Premier Wen's speech from the night before. Wen had given a boilerplate speech, listing off GDP figures, economic and environmental promises, etc.

"It was an opportunity for him to say something new," Chandler told the audience. "But he didn't."

What ensued was a lively and candid debate that, for the first time I'd seen, contained both praise for and criticisms of China.

After the discussion wrapped up, I went to the media center and told Xiao Zhang about the session. He suggested I write a story about it. I told him I would but only if I could write it honestly, including the criticisms made about China.

"That's okay. Write about the different opinions," he said.

So I did. The story I filed focused on the debate about China's use of "soft power" and included a back-and-forth between Friedman and Sha about China's role in the world. Friedman said China should take a hard-line stance against Iran and Sudan; Sha argued that China should lead by example, not by shows of dominance.

Back in Beijing, the hatchets came out. During dinner that night in Dalian, a colleague told me the editors were removing any mention of Iran or Sudan from the story.

"But that defeats the purpose of the story," I protested.

I text messaged Max in Beijing, who I knew was editing the Dalian stories. I asked him what changes were being made. He called back a few minutes later and said someone had cut the story from 750 words to about 250 words. All mentions of Iran and Sudan had been axed, as had Thomas Friedman and all of his quotes.

"So what's left?" I asked.

"The China stuff."

"Please take my name off it."

The next day's story, which didn't include a byline, was titled, "China, Leading by Example." "A panel of experts and officials was in hot debate about how soft power could work better, particularly about how China could use its soft power to attract and persuade others," the opening paragraph, not written by me, went.

I wasn't angry about the changes. I would have been surprised if the story was published as I wrote it. *China Daily* was changing, but change happens slowly.

Still, my colleagues could tell I was a bit annoyed. In the news center the next day, Xiao Zhang apologized for the changes and offered a rationale for the edits: "It didn't go along with China's views."

That was the last battle I fought with *China Daily*. I realized that any skirmish was going to be a lopsided affair. It was China's century now. The rest of us were just living in it. I had come to *China Daily* determined to change the paper for the better, to instill in it my Western journalistic sensibilities. Now, I figured, I'd best learn how to enjoy the ride.

"I wonder what it's like . . . ," I said, a few weeks later, running my finger over a map of China hanging on an office wall, looking for the most remote place I could find. "Here. *U-RUM-QI.*"

We were sitting around Rob's office at *China Daily* one afternoon, marveling at the scale of the country we were living in. I had never really taken the time to appreciate the vastness of China. I'd been in China four months and only visited Shanghai, Qingdao, Dalian, and an unimpressive beach resort near Beijing called Beidaihe, popular with Siberian tourists. I glanced over the map and wondered what, exactly, was going on in all these strange places—Gansu, Qinghai, Shanxi, Shaanxi. I had never even heard of most of China.

I stood up and analyzed the country laid out before me. With my finger placed on the map, I sounded out the name of the capital of Xinjiang province, a sprawling, desert-covered region in China's far west.

"Urumqi," I said, looking at the map even more closely. "*Xinjiang Uighur Autonomous Region.* I can't believe people even live out there." Xinjiang was bordered by a bunch of "Stan" countries. I read them off. "Kazakhstan. Kyrgyzstan. Tajikistan . . ."

Summer had turned to fall, and the National Day holiday, a weeklong celebration of the founding of the People's Republic of China in 1949, was approaching. It would be my first week off since I started at *China Daily* six months earlier, and I wanted to get out of town. I tossed around different ideas with friends and was leaning toward Southeast Asia for a week on a beach, when a friend of mine, Gemma, a British woman who worked in the carbon trading industry, whom I'd met through mutual friends that summer, asked if I was interested in something more adventurous: Xinjiang.

"I don't know," I wrote her in an e-mail, my mind focused on beaches and palm trees. "Couldn't we go somewhere more . . . exotic? Like Cambodia?"

"Xinjiang's as exotic as it gets," Gemma replied.

She e-mailed me pictures she had found on the Internet—photos of sand dunes, snowy mountain ranges, camels, and locals with colorful outfits. My arm was twisted.

A few weeks later, Gemma and I were driving the Karakoram Highway, the highest paved international road in the world, connecting China and Pakistan, in a rickety Volkswagen Santana with a small and bespectacled Chinese man named Xiao Xu at the helm. Xiao Xu, who ran a café in the nearby city of Kashgar and also organized excursions, was testy that morning. He'd expected two people, but the night before, Gemma and I had met an Australian couple in the hotel bar and invited them to join us.

I asked him how long the trip would take.

"Three hours with two people," he huffed, nodding toward the couple, Tom and Kelly. "But four hours with four people. Because it's uphill."

Gemma and I had been in Xinjiang for a week, and the trip had been eye-opening. Xinjiang was different from what I'd seen in China so far in almost every way. It was hard to believe it was even the same country. The region spanned 640,000 square miles and had been home to Uighurs, a Turkic ethnic group, for centuries. It had massive oil and gas reserves, which China was eager to develop, but also suffered from a drug epidemic, fueled by opium smuggled from Afghanistan.

The drive to Karakul Lake was harrowing, not so much because of the terrain, which was rugged, but because of Xiao Xu's driving. He rode the Santana from one side of the highway to the other, as if practicing downhill ski turns. Whenever his eyes caught a mountain or lake, or whatever else was on the side of the road, the car would drift to whichever side he was looking toward until he eventually noticed and heaved the car back toward the middle of the road. Our anxiety was compounded by the fact that the Santana's backseats had no seat belts.

It was a remarkable drive, the terrain like nothing I'd seen before. The mountains were massive and snow covered. Glacial lakes gave way to sand dunes, and the landscape was stripped of vegetation. We drove past men bundled in winter clothing, herding sheep on rocky cliffs. We stopped for photos, and locals would try to sell us trinkets and watches and whatever else they had. The women wore bright colors and the men dark. Their faces were uniformly reddened, with deep creases around their eyes and dry, chapped lips.

Sometime after noon we arrived at Karakul Lake, 11,000 feet above sea level in the Pamir Mountains. Muztagh Ata Mountain, at 24,000 feet high, stood in the background, not far from the Tajikistan border. Xiao Xu had arranged for us to stay in a yurt belonging to a local family of Kyrgyz farmers.

Along the way Gemma became sick; food poisoning, she thought, or maybe altitude sickness. The mother of the Kyrgyz family quickly adopted her into their brick home next door, covering Gemma with blankets and brewing up a thermos of hot tea.

While Gemma slept, Tom, Kelly, and I set out for a hike around the lake. The terrain was rocky, with small tufts of grass. I dipped my fingers in the cold lake. We walked by camels with thick brown coats, grazing on the sparse grass. Camel shit was everywhere and I kicked clumps of it as I walked, noting that they were as hard as hockey pucks. Not long after setting off, I began feeling the altitude and had shortness of breath. I wondered if we would be able to make it all the way around the lake.

An hour into the hike, Tom convinced me to try to climb a hill on the far side of the lake. Dressed in jeans, Nike Air Max, and a fake Arc'teryx jacket I had picked up in a Beijing market, I started to climb. The first section almost finished me off. I was hungry, thirsty, and faint. On a steep and rocky section I looked out toward the lake and felt completely disoriented. For a second, I forgot where I was. Tom kept going and I stopped to get my bearings. I thought about turning back, but watching Tom climb I became more determined to reach the top, and about an hour after we started, I did.

The view was incredible. The mountains seemed endless and the lake below was turquoise. I wondered if I was looking out at Pakistan or Tajikistan. I sat down, sucked in what little oxygen the air offered, and did my best to appreciate where I was. It was by far the most beautiful place I'd seen in China.

Near sunset we made it back to our Kyrgyz family. They spoke no English so Xiao Xu translated. They fed us a dinner of yak meat with rice, cabbage, onion, and tomato, with bottomless cups of black tea. The yak was tough with a strong, overpowering taste, a taste that contaminates your mouth for hours. I forced it down because I knew I needed the nutrition, and I washed it down with tea. We ate and chatted, and I thought about how different the family's life was from my own.

We talked about Chinese politics with Xiao Xu. He had been born in Kashgar and spent his life there, married a Uighur woman, and seemed more sympathetic to his Muslim neighbors than to his fellow Han.

"In China, rich government, poor people," he said.

"Do you think China will ever change?" Tom asked.

"It would take thousand years," Xiao Xu replied.

An hour later we went to our yurt, a tentlike dwelling common on the Central Asian steppes. It was freezing and none of us could sleep. I'd forgotten my sleeping bag and struggled to keep warm despite several layers of woolen blankets. Drinking so much tea also proved to have been a terrible idea. In the middle of the night I had to get up to go to the bathroom. Struggling to navigate my way out of the pitch-black yurt, I slammed into the fireplace.

Outside, the sky was full of stars, from horizon to horizon, big ones, brighter even than those I grew up with in northern Canada. Looking up at the sky, I could barely believe that this was China. In Beijing, I'd seen maybe . . . three, four stars in six months. This place, these people, were was all so foreign, and it occurred to me that I knew *nothing* about China, that there remained this massive, curious country to explore, and I knew that a year would not be nearly enough time.

I stayed outside in the cold for a few minutes and promised myself that I would do a better job of appreciating the opportunity I was being afforded. I had yet to fall in love with China— that would come later. But there were incredible places outside the walls of *China Daily*, and it was slowly dawning on me as I stood outside of our yurt looking up at a sky full of Xinjiang stars.

I took a deep breath and went back into the yurt. As I struggled to find my bed, I accidentally stepped on Xiao Xu, who woke in a panic. I crawled under the blankets and lay awake, staring into the dark.

"How did you all sleep?" I asked.

"Poorly," Tom said. "Somebody kept banging into things."

"Hmm."

We were exhausted. We ate cold bread and drank more black tea, even though the only thing I wanted was a coffee. We said goodbye to the family, paid them about ten dollars each for accommodating us for the night, and boarded the shaky Santana, which barely started in the cold. We were quiet on the ride home. It was cloudy outside and cold in the car. At one point, our car began to slow and I noticed that the engine wasn't running. Xiao Xu drifted to the side of the road, stopped the car, and sighed. There were no cars in sight and no help for miles. He waited a moment and turned the key. The engine started on the first go.

We flew from Kashgar to Urumqi, Xinjiang's capital, two days later. With eight hours to kill before our flight to Beijing, Gemma and I headed downtown. It was cold and gray in Urumqi, and I was feeling depressed that the trip was over.

We walked in silence to a public park in the middle of the city, where we rode the most terrifying Ferris wheel on earth—old, rusted, and lethal—and as we did, I imagined it collapsing and crushing us, two foreigners in this frozen, forgotten city. I wondered if *China Daily*, where I'd be back at work again the following morning, would even report the story.

6

Bad China Days

As fall turned to winter, the cold came suddenly and with force. The city government wouldn't turn on public heating until mid-November, and as the temperature dropped, there seemed to be no escaping the cold. I wore sweaters and a hat while watching movies at home, and I used an extra blanket at night. At work, the cold was numbing. My fingers felt arthritic as I typed.

And then the heat came on. Immediately, on November 15, my apartment became a sauna. I opened my windows to let in the cool fall air and used sheets to cover the radiators. I complained to Jenny and other officials at *China Daily* and was always met with the same response: "There's only one setting." The heaters also sapped out what little moisture was in the air, and soon after the heating went on, I developed a chronic, hacking cough that lasted for two months.

Meanwhile, the high-pollution days added up. There were days when the sky was a gray-brown postapocalyptic haze. Pollution so thick a building a hundred feet away would be a blur; so dense you could taste it on your tongue. There are days in Beijing when you would wake up feeling hungover even though you didn't drink the night before.

The weather influenced Beijing's usually vibrant social scene. Whereas summer was a nonstop stream of dinners, parties, and other events, the fall-winter schedule revolved almost solely around bootleg DVDs. Chinese television was all low-budget historical epics, variety shows, and dating shows. The only English channel on regular cable was the news station CCTV 9—essentially *China Daily* put to camera. The televisions in our apartments had CNN, but the satellite was frequently down. Going to the movies wasn't much of an option, either. Cinemas in China played just twenty foreign movies a year, most of which were big Hollywood blockbusters. There was no such thing as independent cinema. There were no legal movie rental shops, and the Internet was too slow for downloading.

But bootleg DVDs were everywhere. Vendors varied from the haggard-looking migrant woman—selling filmed-in-the-theater copies of *The Bourne Ultimatum*, *Pirates of the Caribbean: At World's End*, *Transformers*, and more from a shoe box outside the Noodle Shop—to fully stocked, seemingly legitimate stores, selling illegitimate copies of movies from around the world.

I bought most of my DVDs from a shop called Tom's in the expat neighborhood of Lido, which was on the way from *China Daily* to the airport. Tom's was located in a basement under an antiques shop, and it was remarkable, stocked with thousands of DVDs, old and new, Hollywood and foreign. New releases often made it to Tom's before they premiered on movie screens in the States. On Sunday afternoons, especially during the cooler months, Tom's was shoulder-to-shoulder packed with expats filling carts with DVD boxes, stocking up for the week ahead.

A good friend of mine at *China Daily*, Ben, a thirty-year-old Australian who worked in the features section, reviewed movies for an Australian website to supplement his income. He watched five films a week from Sunday through Thursday, and with his fiancée, Helena, often hosted dinner and a movie at their place, two floors above mine in the *China Daily* apartments. I often attended along with our friend Jeremy, a tattooed copy editor and Columbia journalism grad from Michigan in his early thirties. The movies ran the gamut from black-and-white classics, like *The Maltese Falcon*, to modern Academy Award winners, to 1990s sexual thrillers and action movies. The latter categories were my favorite. Sometimes we would drink whiskey and end up laughing on the floor while watching movies like *China Moon*, an incredibly awful yet unintentionally hilarious film noir starring Ed Harris.

I loved movie nights, but life in Beijing was becoming routine. The gray weather often mixed with isolation to create boredom—a potent combo for me—and it was during this time that I became familiar with Bad China Days. These days are known to all foreigners who make China their home. They are the days when the country makes you want to explode, when you feel at the brink of a murderous rage, when even the simplest task becomes an Olympian feat. Life in a foreign country can be difficult; in China it can sometimes seem impossible.

It's the little things that get to you. The big things—the traffic, the smog, the masses of people—you expect. But the little things, the simple problems of day-to-day life—trying to buy batteries, for example, or the Odyssean quest to find decent deodorant—those are the things that drive you crazy. When I first arrived, a simple chore might be a half-day gauntlet of frustration.

I had reached the point in my China life where not everything seemed exciting anymore, where every day didn't feel like a small adventure, as it had when I first arrived. Xinjiang had opened my eyes to China's possibilities, and I felt trapped at *China Daily*. I was unfulfilled at work, and even though I had sold a few free-lance pieces, I was frustrated that I hadn't done more writing for Western publications, despite my increased efforts.

I also grew increasingly irritated with myself that my Chinese was so dismal. Despite several hours of class a week, it felt like I was making no progress at all. Chinese words were learned and forgotten as if I was reading names from a phone book. My Chinese colleagues all spoke English, and I had Chinese friends outside the paper as well, but our relationships depended entirely on their English ability. It was obvious that without better Chinese I would never really connect with the city.

The up-and-down waves of life in China, which initially arrived in hourly and daily increments, were becoming much more profound. The swings expanded into weeks, and the pivot could happen suddenly. I would love Beijing one minute and pat myself on the back for being smart enough to come, and then the next moment I might find myself in a state of near panic that would last for weeks. As I sat at my desk, staring at my computer screen, homesickness would set in and I would forget all the reasons I left and focus on the good things back home: reading the news-paper at my favorite café, having drinks with friends in a nice cocktail bar, watching indie movies at the cinema near my apart-ment, cycling by the lakeshore during Toronto summers.

It was at night when the loneliness of living abroad hit the hardest. Sometimes I would wake up in the middle of the night and stumble to the bathroom. I would remember that I was in Beijing and be suddenly disoriented. I'd look at myself in the bathroom mirror as I peed and be gnawed by fear. Fear that I would never make it as a writer. That I was wasting my life. I thought about all the decisions that had led me to China and wondered if every major choice I had made in my life was the wrong one.

But then I would think about walking around Toronto the year before with my shoulder bag giving me back pain, the grueling existence of a failing freelance journalist, and all the things that drove me to China, and the panic would subside.

What I needed, I decided, was a girlfriend. A companion. A fling would do. I found one, by accident, on Halloween.

A group from *China Daily* had tickets to a Halloween party in a club in a mall downtown called the Place. That afternoon, Rob and I went to the Silk Market to pick out costumes. Options were limited so we decided to dress as gangsters. I bought a black tie, suspenders, a gray fedora, and a toy gun to go with a truly tragic pinstriped charcoal suit that I'd had made for my trip to Dalian. When I put my outfit on later that night, I looked more like a gay Swiss yodeler than a 1930s Chicago gangster. The pants were too baggy, the shirt too tight. The hat made my head look like a shrunken miniature.

Jon, my American colleague from the Web division, had picked up tickets for Rob and me, and we were all supposed to meet at 8 p.m. at his apartment. Rob, however, had gone to the gym after dinner and was more than two hours late. I grew more furious with each passing minute.

We arrived at the party around eleven. I quickly got over my costume when I realized that all the girls at the party had used the event as an excuse to wear pretty much nothing. We got drinks and made the rounds, introducing ourselves to whatever group of liberally clothed young women we could find.

Not long after our arrival, Max said he and his girlfriend were leaving. "Take my drink tickets," he said, handing me a reel of a dozen tickets.

As soon as the tickets were in my hand, Rob swooped in and ripped off about eight of them. "I'll take those," he said, darting off.

A few minutes later, Rob handed me four drink tickets and asked me to get him an orange juice. This was during one of Rob's euphoric upswings when he was working out religiously and cutting down on drinking and smoking. ("My body is a temple," he told me once, without a hint of irony.)

"Why can't you go yourself?" I said, still angry with him for making me wait two hours.

"I'm dancing."

I went to the bar with a friend, an Australian photographer named Chris who was already drunk. I ordered a beer and an orange juice.

"Get me a beer," Chris said.

"Two beers and an orange juice," I told the bartender.

When our drinks arrived, I asked Chris for his tickets.

"What tickets?"

"Shit," I said, counting out eight tickets—four of mine, four of Rob's. Enough for two drinks.

I sent the orange juice back, figuring Rob could wait a minute for his vitamin C dose while I went and bought new tickets. I went back to the dance floor.

"I didn't have enough tickets," I told Rob. "I'll go buy more and get your juice in a minute."

Rob looked at me with crazy eyes. He snapped. I heard some mutterings through his clenched teeth—"fuck" this and "fuck" that—and the next thing I knew Rob had knocked the beer out of my hand and two-hand-shoved me over a table. I tried to get up, but he shoved me back down, standing over me, screaming something I couldn't make out. I thought he was going to stomp on my face, when suddenly Chris hauled me to my feet.

"Let's get out of here," he said.

In the hallway outside the club, Chris and I smoked cigarettes while I fumed about Rob. My hands were shaking.

And then, through a throng of partyers standing outside the club, I saw a girl. She was wearing a black bra under a see-through mesh top, her tanned brown stomach exposed, and skin-tight blue jeans. Around her neck was a collar that led to the hand of a young foreign man dressed in Goth. She wore heavy makeup, but underneath she was gorgeous. She posed for photos with a group of guys.

Chris noticed me staring at her.

"You want to talk to her?" He nodded toward the girl. "Give me your phone."

I handed him my phone and he led me by my suspenders across the hall. He tapped the girl on the shoulder. She turned around with a big smile.

"Yes?" she said.

"Hey, there. Can we take your picture?" Chris said.

"Sure."

"Okay, you two together," he said, motioning for the two of us to squeeze together.

I wrapped my arm around her cool, bare shoulder and Chris snapped a photo on my phone. Then he handed her the phone.

"Great. Now can we have your number?"

"Ha-ha. Nice try, guys," she said.

I couldn't place her ethnicity. I thought she was Chinese, but she was speaking with a Russian accent.

"Are you Chinese?"

"No, I'm Russian."

"You don't look Russian."

"Well, I'm Korean. But born in Russia."

I was mesmerized. She was beautiful. She was sexy. She was perfect. She was . . .

"A slut!"

"Excuse me?"

"My costume. I'm dressed as a slut, ha-ha. I didn't have anything else to wear."

"Interesting. You probably shouldn't tell people that."

"Yeah, I know. Actually I don't know what I am. I just wore whatever clothes I had like this."

Her name was Julia. I asked her a few questions about what she was doing in China (studying) and for how long (two years), and then I ran out of things to say. I wanted to ask for her number, but I froze.

As we left the club, I turned back, waved goodbye, and walked out.

That week at *China Daily*, Rob and I played the silent game. We passed each other a few times in the corridor without speaking. We each told colleagues our versions of the story, and we each thought the other was in the wrong.

Midweek, at lunchtime, Rob and I passed each other on the sidewalk outside *China Daily*. We stopped and Rob smiled.

"I just wanted to say . . . sorry," he said.

I was shocked. I didn't think he was capable of apologizing. "Thanks," I said. "I'm sorry, too."

"Give me a hug, mate."

We hugged it out right there on the sidewalk. Rob said he would make it up to me on the weekend . . . by buying a gram of coke.

On Saturday night, we went out to Suzy Wong's, dipping in and out of the bathroom to snort Rob's peace offering. As Rob hit on a Chinese model at our table, I looked around the bar and spotted Julia, the Korean-Russian. I stood up immediately. I approached her at the bar and reminded her that we'd met the weekend before. Her smile was wide and beautiful. It lit up the room, and I was intimidated. I took a deep breath, hoped that Rob's makeup present was masking my nerves, and asked her if she wanted to go for a drink sometime.

"Sure," she said.

"Sure?"

"Yeah, let's go for a drink. Let me give you my number."

We exchanged phone numbers, my coke-strained heart beating furiously. I thanked her and returned to the table with Rob and his model.

"Who was that?" Rob asked as I sat down.

"This girl I met last weekend."

"Where's she from?"

"She's Korean but from Russia."

"Hmm," he said. "Krussian."

I went out for dinner with Julia, who would forever be known among my friends at *China Daily* as the Krussian, the following week at an Indian restaurant near her apartment in Wudaokou, a university neighborhood in northwest Beijing. It was awkward at first; she looked lovely, and I was nervous. At first we had little to talk about and I thought she wasn't interested in me. She ordered Sprite—a bad sign. Good first dates should always include alcohol, I reasoned. The dinner was slow, and as I paid for the bill, I thought that perhaps this was a dead end.

On the walk home, I asked her what she usually did on weekends.

"Go dancing," she said.

"You like dancing?"

"I love dancing."

"That's too bad. I hate dancing."

"Why?"

"Because I'm usually the tallest guy in the bar. When I dance, I feel like everybody's staring at me. Plus, I'm a terrible dancer. I move like this."

I started doing an awkward robotic dance, pumping my fists up and down. She laughed.

"You are a bad dancer," she said. Her cheeks were dimpled and rosy when she laughed, and I thought she was adorable.

We had dinner the next week, and the following Friday I went out with her and her friends. She wore a slim black and white dress, and I barely let her out of my sight. We went to a Latin club, and she even got me dancing a little. Before long, we were kissing in the corner of the club.

She came to my house that night, and my winter doldrums began to lift.

All of a sudden life at *China Daily* didn't seem so bad. I tackled new feature assignments, pitched a few more freelance stories, and began to focus as best I could on learning Chinese. I met Ms. Song twice a week at my apartment and attended the two free classes she taught at *China Daily*. I even started learning Chinese characters. It was slow and painful, but at least I was making an effort.

But for every China high, there's a China low. After a few weeks, I was back to the Bad China Days. Beijing was cold in late December, and after seeing each other at least once a week for close to two months, Julia went away for vacation. I would have to work throughout the holidays.

On Christmas morning I sat at my desk, staring blankly at my computer screen and thinking about all the things I was missing in Canada. It was the first time in my twenty-seven years I hadn't been with my family on Christmas.

It was a white Christmas in Beijing, but not in the Bing Crosby sense. Outside the office windows, the sky was a toxic white haze of suffocating pollution. The hours passed by glacially. My colleagues and I took a long lunch and exchanged gifts. We tried to put on happy faces, but it didn't work.

For the first time, I was truly homesick.

Every year during the Chinese Lunar New Year, otherwise known as Spring Festival, occurs the largest human migration on earth. In the span of forty days, almost three billion passenger trips are made around the country. Train stations become desperate seas of humanity, where anxious travelers camp for days and weeks to purchase tickets that sell out in minutes. For many of China's 200 million–plus migrant workers, the Lunar New Year is the one chance they have each year to return home, the one chance to see family and friends.

For me, escape from Beijing was imperative as well. During Spring Festival, the entire city goes on a massive fireworks binge at all hours of the day and night. For three consecutive days that February, I had been going about my routine amid constant explosions, waking up at dawn to deafening *pop-pop-pop*s, car alarms, and children squealing. For a day, the fireworks are pretty cool, an entire city of eighteen million alight with dangerous explosives that can be purchased on any street corner. After two days, it's annoying. By day three or four, thoughts creep to murder.

I was anxious to begin exploring the country again. My life felt lazy and routine: work, DVDs, dinner/drinks, rinse, repeat. I wanted some excitement, and Harbin, a city in northeast China, seemed to offer it. A colleague had visited Harbin a few weeks earlier and stumbled upon a rare attraction: bears wrestling while wearing capes. The strange event occurred at the site of Harbin's annual ice festival, which featured ice replicas of the Acropolis, the Egyptian pyramids, the Eiffel Tower, and other famous landmarks. My colleague spoke highly of the city's vodka-fueled nightlife, and taken together it seemed crazy enough to warrant a look.

I had a few days off and many of my friends, including Julia, were out of town. Through *China Daily*'s travel agency, Jeremy, Ben, and I managed to buy tickets to Harbin, capital of Heilongjiang province, nine hours to the north, near Siberia.

We took a morning train and arrived in late afternoon. The temperature was minus twenty degrees Celsius. We promptly took a taxi to an ice bar on the main street and downed shots of vodka under a pair of reindeer horns harnessed to the ice wall.

Fortified for the cold, we walked toward the yellowish glow of Harbin's ice city, not far from downtown. Hundreds of families, bundled up in layers of winter clothing, snapped photos in front of ice sculptures and buildings lit up in red, yellow, green, and blue. I followed my colleague's instructions to the back of the ice city, where she had spotted the wrestling bears a few weeks earlier. We climbed to the top of the Acropolis and spotted the venue we sought: a rest area with Nescafé and Harbin beer signs surrounding a circuslike ring.

We pulled up to a table next to a foggy window and ordered a round of beers. Families with young children sat at tables around us, anxiously awaiting what was to follow.

The show began with a Chinese trainer leading a dozen or so mangy wolves around a ring, their gray hair a patchy mix of thick tufts and bald spots. The wolves jumped through hoops and did an assortment of other unimpressive tricks. One particularly haggard wolf was whipped by his master and took a frightened dump in the middle of the ring.

The wolves were followed by house cats that performed equally lame hoop jumps, followed by a boar that could identify

Chinese characters in exchange for a snack, followed by well-groomed poodles that did nothing but sniff each other.

Exit poodles, enter two lions and a tiger. One male tiger tried, unsuccessfully, to mate with the lion, which was also male. The lion was swapped for a second tiger, and the two were led around the ring by the trainer, jumping through flaming hoops. Toward the end one tiger swiped at another and a skirmish ensued.

While there was no wrestling in the finale, there was a bear. And it wasn't wearing a cape. Instead, this poor creature in this freezing northern Chinese city was wearing women's lingerie. Extra-extra-large women's underwear and a bra.

It's true—I have witnesses.

The lingerie-wearing bear was led out by the trainer and presented with a two-wheel bicycle, which it proceeded to pedal with its short legs, doing circles around the ring. The bear followed that by skipping a rope swung by the trainer and his assistant and dunking a basketball on a miniature hoop.

Inside the Nescafé/Harbin beer tent, the crowd went wild. Kids hopped up and down on plastic chairs, clambering for more. Satisfied dads lit up cigarettes and clapped.

Our jaws were on the floor. "Well, that was fucked-up," Jeremy said, summing up the entire episode nicely.

One member of our group, a friend of a friend from North Carolina, looked stunned. He sat hunched over his beer, shaking his head slowly from side to side. "That was just . . . wrong."

None of us knew what to make of what we'd seen. I was somewhat ashamed to have even witnessed it. We sat in the smoky Nescafé tent drinking beer and shared a few minutes of contemplative silence.

Alcohol, we figured, would wash away what had just taken place, and so we went out in search of Harbin's nightlife. Friends from

Beijing had recommended a popular expat hangout called Blues Bar. When we arrived, there were only a few tables of young Chinese, drinking beer and playing a dice game. We ordered drinks and soon more people started arriving.

We met a group of teachers from Australia and Canada. They ordered bottles of a Chinese-made vodka that tasted like acid. I flipped over a bottle and noticed on the label that the vodka was made by Anhui Ante Biological Chemistry Co. Ltd.

"Yo, you know this is made by a chemical company," I said, presenting the bottle to a spiky-haired Australian.

He shrugged. "I like to party," he said, downing a glass of vodka and Coke.

The teachers took us to a club called the Box, which was packed with both Chinese and foreigners. The foreigners came from all over—the United States, Mexico, Russia, parts of Africa. Some were teaching in Harbin, some studying at the university. Whenever I traveled to places like Harbin, I always marveled that anyone would actually choose to live somewhere like that. For some reason, imagining their lives in this lonely, frozen outpost made me a little sad. I didn't even want to imagine how the search for deodorant would go down in a city as remote as Harbin.

The next afternoon we headed for our second animal-related adventure, at the Harbin Siberian Tiger Park, where visitors could feed live animals—including chickens, goats, and cows—to tigers and lions. The park was lively when we arrived in midafternoon, the parking lot abuzz with tour groups and families. A sign at the ticket booth said, in English, "No. 1 Adventure Bus: You're welcome to take No.1 Adventure Bus to experience the tense feeling of looking at the tigers in close distance, viewing the thrilling scene of tigers' preying on other animals." We pooled our money together and bought a goat for about five hundred yuan—seventy dollars.

On our bus were children as young as five, their curious eyes pressed against the window. We toured the park, where tigers dozed in the cold surrounded by chicken feathers, until we reached a feeding ground. We watched as a park worker in the Jeep in front of us threw a live chicken out of the passenger-side door. (Passengers couldn't actually feed the animals themselves.) A tiger snatched the chicken in its teeth and ran off into the bushes.

Our bus continued into the African lion's den for the goat feed. As soon as we entered the gate, hungry female lions swarmed our minibus, jumping up and pawing at window. Kids wailed. Parents laughed nervously. At the front of the bus a park worker prepared our goat, which looked concerned.

It all happened so fast. Goat tossed out the door . . . lions pounce . . . chaos . . . goat reappears . . . a lion's jaws clamp down on the goat by the neck, another lion snatches it by the back . . . goat bleats, its stomach exposed . . . another lion, sensing opportunity, bites the goat's bare belly . . . guts explode.

A moment later, one lion ran off with the goat's front section, another with its hind legs, and several others fought for various body parts littered on the ground.

The passengers in our van applauded. I felt like I'd witnessed a crime, or worse, that I'd actually paid to commit one. My stomach churned as I watched through fingers splayed over my face as tigers ate the goat's insides.

I looked over to Ben, who was shaking his head.

"I'm glad we didn't buy the cow," I said.

We took the train back to Beijing first thing the next morning. Even after such a short trip, I was ready to get back to the city, back to my cozy apartment, to DVDs, to Julia. But my curiosity about China grew exponentially during the trip to Harbin. Bears in lingerie, tiger feeds, industrial vodka. That's the stuff dreams are made of. I thought that if all that and more happens in Harbin—a city of four million people, an industrial and administrative hub of northern China—what went on in China's even more remote regions?

On the train I jotted notes from the trip in my journal. I stopped for a moment and looked out the window at the freezing landscape.

So many stories, I thought. So many stories to tell.

7

The Failed Propagandist

I was entering the third mile on a treadmill at a gym not far from the *China Daily* compound, exhausted and dripping sweat, trying to shed a few pounds put on during a winter spent watching movies and eating extravagant meals. I'd recently returned from a two-week trip with friends to Southeast Asia. We relaxed on beaches, gorged ourselves, and drank liver-pulverizing quantities of beer and whiskey buckets, the effects of which hadn't helped my already hurting physique. When I arrived in China almost a year earlier, I was in the best shape of my life. I was working out daily and eating well. My abs were visible.

Now I was back near the two-hundred-pounds mark with no semblance of muscular definition. Showering one morning at home, I looked at myself in the mirror, pinched my love handles, and admitted to myself what several Chinese colleagues had cheerfully pointed out more than once: I was getting fat. The

good news (and perhaps the main reason for my bloated waist-
line) was that I was, for the first time in two years, mostly . . .
happy.

Above the treadmill a television was playing CNN. Larry
King was on, and his guests were former escorts and brothel
owners discussing what might have been going through the mind
of New York governor Eliot Spitzer when he solicited the services of a young employee of Emperor Club VIP in Washing-
ton, D.C., the month before. During a discussion about whether
paying for sex is ethically wrong, and whether or not Spitzer
should serve jail time, CNN cut away to breaking news. A blond
anchor appeared and text flashed on the screen. "Breaking News:
Riots in Tibet."

The anchor spoke. "Riots broke out in the traditional Tibetan
capital of Lhasa today—"

And then, suddenly, the screen went black.

It was March 2008 and life in Beijing was good. I had a big
group of friends and we spent our spare time having long dinners and plenty of drinks. Eating out is the norm in China, and
the food is affordable and delicious: spicy fare from Sichuan and
Yunnan, dumplings from northeast China, Shanghai noodles,
Xinjiang lamb—Beijing was an amazing place to eat.

Dinner is also a social event in China, a tradition we embraced
vigorously. We would eat in gritty, smoky alleyway restaurants,
or big, noisy places that served Peking duck or hot pot—thinly
sliced meat, leafy vegetables, mushrooms, tofu, noodles, all
tossed into a boiling, often spicy, broth. Sometimes we ate at
French or Italian restaurants, Thai restaurants, or Japanese restaurants. Social life revolved around eating, and going for dinner
was among the highlights of living in the city. Our groups at
dinner came from all over the world, and we talked about China,

politics, our jobs, our futures. Later we would go to music clubs, or little bars tucked in the *hutong* alleyways, or, when we were up for it, out to the lounges and clubs that continued to pop up all over the city.

Notably absent from most social occasions was Rob. We had drifted apart in the weeks and months after the Orange Juice Incident. I'd forgiven him, but I didn't really trust him anymore, if I actually ever did. If something as minor as that could set him off, what would happen if we *really* got into an argument? We still spoke and hung out sometimes, but I didn't often reach out to him, and I got the impression he blamed me for his isolation from my group of friends at *China Daily*. But it wasn't intentional. I'd just grown comfortable in my new life. I still partied a lot, but I'd cut out the drugs and had generally calmed down.

Mine was a comfortable life. I played in a weekly basketball game, went to a pub quiz once in a while, and finally had a firm grasp of the city. I was making slow progress with my Chinese; I continued to meet Ms. Song a few times a week and did at least some homework most days. Beijing, which had once seemed so foreign, was starting to feel like a second home. I had a little over a month and a half left at *China Daily*, and once my contract ended, I planned to focus on learning Chinese and freelancing, and then stay for the event that had drawn most of us to Beijing in the first place: the 2008 Olympics.

At work, I had long ago abandoned any notion of trying to change or improve the paper, and in the New Year I had decided to by and large retire as a reporter and offer my services, once again, as an editor—on the condition that I didn't have to work the night shift.

My bosses assigned me to edit a weekly business supplement, a job I split with another foreign editor. The assignment involved editing about six or seven features a week, almost all of which I saved for Wednesday, the day before the section went to print. My role at the paper was so slight that I no longer appeared on the work schedule e-mailed to foreign experts every week. To make the most of my free time, I picked up the pace of my freelance work, contributing travel stories and other features to Canadian publications and local magazines. Editors back home were realizing I was in China, and assignments were slowly starting to come to me. I still hadn't reached the level where I wanted to be, still hadn't cracked big American publications, but I felt for the first time since I came to China that I was on the right track.

The rest of the time I read U.S. presidential campaign news, chatted with friends and colleagues online, surfed various blogs about China, and took extraordinarily long lunches with Ben and Jeremy. As far as I knew, my editors didn't know about my freelance work, and they seemed content to let me coast through to the end of my tenure at the paper.

From the beginning, I knew I wouldn't renew my contract with *China Daily*, even if they offered—by late winter it was clear they would not. Who could blame them? If I was my editors, I would have fired me. But with the Olympics just around the corner, many expat editors were jumping ship for better jobs or no job at all, so they could enjoy the Games without other obligations. My neighbor in the business section, an Australian woman, had recently told Mr. Wang she wouldn't be coming back when her contract ended in April. Mr. Wang, shocked upon hearing the news, leaned forward and rubbed his forehead. "Another problem," he said.

But even with an exodus of foreigners, there was no way Mr. Wang could justify keeping me around afterward, even if I wanted to stay. I had grumbled my way into a role of doing basically nothing, and as the end of my contract approached, I knew one of two things was going to happen. One: My last day would arrive without any mention of renewing my contract; there would be a little going-away party; and off I would go. Or two: Mr. Wang would call me into his office and tell me they were getting rid of the business writer position entirely.

My editors must have wondered what I did with all those hours sitting in my cubicle, but nobody said a thing. Finally, in my third week back from my trip to Southeast Asia, one of the business editors, an avian-looking woman who had shown utter disdain for my existence as a *China Daily* business writer since my first day on the job, approached my desk.

"Your contract ends next month," Bird Lady said. "You're going back to your country?"

I smiled. "I haven't decided yet."

She frowned and walked away.

A few days later, Lois said she heard I was going home.

"Why does everybody think that?" I said.

She shrugged. "I don't know. They just do."

I hadn't actually told any of my Chinese colleagues my plans, and my guess was that Bird Lady and Lois had been tasked to figure out my intentions. Chinese are generally averse to confrontation—as I had learned when I called out Ms. Song for handing out my test to class eight months earlier—and if my editors could find out through the grapevine that I was going back to Canada, they could avoid the awkwardness of officially letting me go. I liked this approach. So I started to spread the word that I was going freelance.

Julia and I, meanwhile, had managed to maintain a weekly dinner/movie/sex, no-strings-attached relationship. It was perfect. I liked her and it was the first time since my last girlfriend that I had even remote feelings for anybody. I was buoyed when she texted, and I looked forward to seeing her. We held hands when we walked down the street and e-mailed each other when one of us was out of town. I was happy with the rhythms of my life in China, and she was part of that. But I still wasn't ready to call her my girlfriend.

That started to change one night that spring. As we sat in my living room talking, she let slip that a few months ago she had been seeing somebody else. She was allowed to, of course, and so was I. But hearing her say it was unsettling. She noticed and pulled away.

"I'm sorry, but . . . I'm not your girlfriend," she said. "We're just having fun. Right?"

I told her I agreed. "It's okay, you didn't do anything wrong. I guess I just never thought about it."

The next day at work she was *all* I could think about. I opened her Facebook page and browsed her photos. I saw pictures she had posted after a trip to Thailand. There was one image in particular: a black-and-white of her on a beach. She was lying on her side, wearing a striped summer dress, her face in profile looking out to the sea. She looked impossibly beautiful and it stirred all kinds of emotions. I thought to myself, You're lucky. You shouldn't take this for granted.

She meant more to me than I realized, and I wondered if I was ready for a relationship again. The problem was, in a few months she would be gone, back to Russia to finish university. And I didn't know where I'd be at all.

On March 14, 2008, riots broke out in Tibet. It began as an annual observance of Tibetan Uprising Day, which commemorates the 1959 rebellion against the Chinese government. Street protests led by monks descended into rioting, burning, and looting, and spiraled into violence, perpetrated mostly by Tibetans on Han Chinese. Police cracked down to halt the violence, and there were fatalities on both sides.

Finger-pointing began immediately, with the Chinese government claiming the riots had been orchestrated by the Dalai Lama, and Tibetans in exile blaming what they perceived as illegitimate rule from Beijing. The riots might have been happening fifteen hundred miles from Beijing, where life went on as normal, but it was the biggest news story coming out of China and the main topic of conversation around the office.

Anger in China was vented on instant messenger. Almost all my Chinese colleagues' messenger statuses read "[Heart] China." My former cubicle neighbor, Harry, who had long since left *China Daily* for another government employer, wrote as his status message, "CNN go to hell!" The network had become synonymous with what many Chinese perceived as an anti-China bias in the Western media. Some Westerners in Beijing feared an anti-foreigner backlash not seen since 1999, when NATO planes accidentally bombed the Chinese embassy in Belgrade, killing three Chinese reporters and sparking outrage across China.

Some of the hostility toward the West became directed at us, *China Daily*'s foreign friends. One day a reporter lectured Jeremy that the West was interested in separating Tibet from China because of the geographic advantages of having an American puppet state close to China, Pakistan, and India.

That same week, I met Lois and two other *China Daily* reporters for drinks in a bar near the Drum and Bell Towers, in the center of the city. Over casual conversation, I told them I was having trouble figuring out a visa for the summer, and one of the reporters said the Chinese government shouldn't have allowed so many foreigners into the country in the first place.

Lois, whose opinions I valued, said that foreigners', and especially the Western media's, opinion of Tibet was informed by "ignorance" and that they shouldn't be allowed to have an opinion at all because "they haven't been there."

"Have you?" I asked.

"No," she huffed. "That's why I don't have an opinion."

She did, of course. Everybody did, and those opinions were being expressed with more hostility every day. In the States, a Chinese student at Duke University had become a public enemy in China simply for encouraging dialogue between pro-Tibetan and pro-Chinese protesters at her university. Chinese nationalists on the Internet threatened to dismember her and posted her parents' home address in Qingdao, which led someone to put a bag of feces on her parents' front steps. A *New York Times* article said the events had forced the girl into hiding.

I forwarded the *Times* article to Lois, and she said it was simply another attempt by the Western media to smear China.

"What's the point of this article?" she said. "To make all Chinese protesters look like idiots?"

Getting news about Tibet from within China was getting more difficult each day. I was still able to get information from the sites of many mainstream English-language news organizations, but the Chinese government was blocking some Internet and television reports about Tibet. Google searches would produce "Not Found" messages. The *Economist*, which had one of the only Western reporters in Tibet during the riots, was sporadically blocked. YouTube was down, and so were the proxy servers that we usually used to access blocked websites.

The state media's take on the Tibet riots was the polar opposite of international media reports. "The state media has tightly controlled its coverage to focus on Tibetans burning Chinese businesses or attacking and killing Chinese merchants," the *Times* wrote. "No mention is made of Tibetan grievances or reports that 80 or more Tibetans have died."

China Daily, meanwhile, ran a front-page story under the headline TIBET RELIGIOUS LEADERS CONDEMN LHASA RIOTS, provided by Xinhua, the state newswire service. It quoted the Panchen Lama condemning the riots as "sabotage acts." Of course, the Panchen Lama is handpicked by China. The Dalai Lama, the Tibetan holy leader in exile, was characterized in state media reports as being little more than the leader of a gang of petty thugs.

On page three of the same day's paper, *China Daily* published another Xinhua story with the headline FEARS AND TEARS IN HOLY PLATEAU CITY. The story referred to a school damaged by "saboteurs" and "vandals carrying backpacks filled with stones and bottles of inflammable liquids" who "smashed windows, set fire to vehicles, shops and restaurants along their destructive path." According to an official quoted, the chaos was "masterminded by the Dalai clique."

One afternoon, I sat at my desk watching a news conference given by Chinese premier Wen Jiabao at the National People's Congress, as it played on a television mounted to the wall beside me. A crowd of Chinese reporters and editors had gathered. Someone turned up the volume. Everyone around me was quiet.

During the press conference, questions focused on Tibet. Wen's answers were stock and predictable.

"The events in Tibet caused by a few people were meant to undermine the Olympic Games," the premier said. But he promised the Games would go off smoothly—a showcase of the new China. "During the Olympics," Wen said, "the smiles of 1.3 billion Chinese will be reflected by the smiles of people around the world."

As he spoke, I found myself growing irritated with my colleagues, who nodded along in agreement. I was also ashamed that I worked at a newspaper that was presenting such a lopsided account of what were truly horrible events—for both sides. And as I watched the press conference, the Chinese premier glossing over the chaos that was happening on the other side of the country, I knew that at *China Daily*, his message was front-page material.

The riots exposed fault lines between China and the West, fault lines that were worsened by Olympic torch relay protests. The relay, called the "Journey of Harmony," was to last 129 days and span 85,000 miles—the longest relay since the tradition began in 1936. The torch would be lit in Athens, pass through six continents, stopping at Mount Everest on the border of Nepal and Tibet, and ending in Beijing on March 31, 2008.

The name "Journey of Harmony" was becoming more ironic by the day. The torch relay resulted in "violence and farce" in London (according to the *Daily Mail*) and "waves of chaos" in Paris (*New York Times*). In San Francisco, protesters scaled the Golden Gate Bridge and unfurled pro-Tibet banners before the torch even touched down in the city.

One wouldn't have known any of this by reading *China Daily*. Whereas the Western media focused on protests in London that resulted in thirty-two arrests, *China Daily* ran a front-page story titled WARM RECEPTION IN COOL LONDON.

"Olympic fever yesterday gripped snowy London—host of the 2012 Olympic Games—on the latest leg of the torch relay's global odyssey. . . . Despite the bad weather, the flame received a particularly warm welcome from crowds in the city." The story dismissed the protests as a "small number of criminal attempts to disrupt the safety, security and safe passage of the torch."

The next day, in Paris, protesters swarmed torchbearers, and police made about twenty arrests. Along the Seine, protesters forced officials in charge of the flame onto a bus, and the flame was briefly extinguished. Ultimately, the "eternal flame" was forced out four times that day.

China Daily painted a slightly different picture of the Paris leg. FRENCH PASSION GREETS TORCH IN PARIS, the headline read. "Tens of thousands of Parisians swarmed the streets while many waved and cheered, like their ancestors did in 1884," the story said. The next day, however, the Chinese reaction to the torch protests turned from denial to outrage. *China Daily*'s story, titled SEPARATISTS' ATTACK ON TORCH DENOUNCED, characterized the protests as "despicable" acts that "defiled the Olympic spirit and defied people who love the Games."

With each passing day my temples grew increasingly raw from rubbing. I was thankful that I didn't work in the news section, so that I didn't have to edit the stories *China Daily* was publishing. Some days I was furious at what the paper printed, other days bewildered, and once in a while I couldn't help but be amused at the differences between our version of events and the rest of the world's.

As a foreigner at *China Daily*, it felt like I was straddling an ever-widening gulf between two different universes. But the events didn't make me want to leave China, as it did some other foreigners. For me it was the opposite. China was dominating global news coverage, and I was in the middle of it. I was, in some ways, living a journalist's dream: I was a part of history.

A story idea came to mind: an insider's account of working within the state media during this time of turmoil. I contacted an editor at the *Globe and Mail* and pitched the piece. He expressed interest but wrote back, "Are you sure you should write this?"

I asked my foreign colleagues for their opinions. Their advice ranged from "Yes, definitely write it" to a sort of *I'm not so sure* wince. In the end I decided that I should write it; that my position at *China Daily* could help explain the differences between China and the West on Tibet. Besides, I had only a month left on my contract.

I wrote the story in a day, from my desk at *China Daily*, and sent it to my editor that night. In the piece, I talked about my own experiences working at the paper and discussed the government's censorship efforts. I noted that state media had focused almost exclusively on how Tibetan rioters had looted and damaged property owned by Han Chinese and had attacked or killed Chinese civilians, in an attempt to undermine ethnic unity in the lead-up to the Olympics. Meanwhile, the state media made virtually no reference to Tibetan grievances or to reports from rights groups that nearly one hundred Tibetans had been killed in the violence.

I referred to a story published in *Vanity Fair* titled "Beijing's Olympic Makeover." In the piece, its author, William Langewiesche, visited *China Daily* and spoke with several local reporters. "It surprised me that [Chinese reporters] showed no sign of regret about their roles, or of envy about the possibilities offered by freedom of the press," he wrote. "They seemed to believe genuinely in the need for censorship, and executed most of it themselves before even beginning to write."

I wrote about how the *Vanity Fair* piece reminded me of a number of conversations I'd had with Chinese reporters over the year, which went a long way in illuminating the paper's coverage of issues such as the Tibet riots: the greatest form of censorship at *China Daily* was self-imposed. There were no shadowy Party agents leaning over reporters' shoulders telling them what to write, and as far as I knew, day-to-day stories didn't go to some high-up government official for approval or rejection. As the *Vanity Fair* article pointed out, and as I reinforced in my *Globe* article, there was no "thought police" at *China Daily*. Instead, reporters and writers simply knew what they could and could not report, and nobody ever challenged those limitations. In this way, change wasn't coming from the bottom, and it certainly wasn't coming from the top.

Whenever I asked Chinese reporters about their thoughts on censorship, their answers tended to meander, but they always emphasized that change happens slowly and almost always concluded by saying, "What can I do?" Of course, in a country with no tradition of press freedom, there was no telling what might happen if reporters did challenge their roles. As Lois once told me, with eyebrows raised, during a conversation about media freedom: "This isn't Canada."

I was nervous about how my colleagues would react to the piece, but I knew it was a good story. I finally felt like a journalist again.

But the day before the article went to print in the *Globe and Mail*, I panicked. I was at a cocktail bar in Sanlitun drinking a martini with Jeremy when I was hit with worry about what my editors would do once they found out. I had no doubt they would discover it, since *China Daily* monitored all mentions of the paper in foreign media. I tossed back martini after martini, and with each glass I grew more paranoid. They were going to fire me. Strip me of my visa. I would never be allowed back in China.

It hadn't been that long ago that I'd fantasized about being tossed out of China. But now China was where I wanted to be— where I *needed* to be—and getting exiled would be devastating so close to the Olympics.

On Monday, I came into work early and hid at my desk. All day I looked over my shoulder, waiting for a furious Mr. Wang to call me into his office and tell me I had twenty-four hours to clean out my apartment and leave the country.

Instead, nothing.

Maybe it was because the article was hidden behind a pay wall. Or maybe they couldn't afford to lose another foreign editor when we were so short-staffed. Or perhaps they just didn't find out. Or didn't care.

But instead of relief, I felt an overwhelming sense of guilt. I had betrayed the people who provided me with the opportunity to live in China, who bought my plane tickets to and from Beijing, gave me a free apartment, paid my salary, and put up with my terrible attitude for a year. Mostly, I worried about what Lois would think if she saw the article. I liked her, I respected her, and I didn't want to hurt her feelings.

The next three weeks went by without incident, without any mention of the article. My contract ended not with a bang but a whimper. With each day that passed, I became excited for the summer ahead and nostalgic for the year I'd had. It had been an enlightening year, and I had especially enjoyed the last few months. I had met interesting people and had a life experience I would never forget, one that taught me about China and journalism and myself.

On my last day at *China Daily*, I finished the first story I'd written for the paper in months. I edited a few small pieces for the business supplement. I deleted all the files on my computer (mostly freelance stories), cleared out my desk (mostly articles and notes related to freelance stories), said goodbye to my colleagues, and thanked Mr. Wang and the business editors for the opportunity to work with them at *China Daily*. They all smiled, thanked me, shook my hand, and wished me luck.

At 6 p.m., I slung my bag over my shoulder, took a final look around the dimly lit, pale gray office, and with a touch of sadness, I walked out for good.

I spent another week in Beijing before going home for the first time in a year. *China Daily* threw a going-away party for a colleague and me. We toasted one another and drank until late. Rob didn't even bother to show up.

I found a small apartment with a roommate from New Zealand in an old neighborhood close to the center of the city, on the east second ring road, not far from Sanlitun. The second stage of my China odyssey was beginning.

But as I packed up my place at the *China Daily* compound, I felt empty. Many of the friends I'd made that year—Jeremy, Ben, Helena, and others—would be gone from Beijing when I returned from Canada, some back home, some to Hong Kong, and the rest to other cities in Asia. The comfort of living and working together with friends would be gone with them. I was happy to be leaving *China Daily* but also distraught at letting its comforts go.

The months ahead of me, though exciting, were largely blank, and I was uncertain about what to do after the Olympics. Would I stay in Beijing? Move elsewhere in Asia? Back to Canada? No clear path had presented itself. My life was about to change again, and I wasn't sure it was going to be for the better. I would miss the long lunches, movie nights, and boozy dinners. I would miss Lois and my Chinese coworkers. I would miss the comedy, the incompetence, the characters.

I never would have guessed it, but I would miss *China Daily*.

A few days before I left for Canada, I met Lois for coffee at the university across the street from *China Daily*. We took our coffees to go and sat down on a bench near the school's basketball courts. It was a comfortable, warm spring day, with a light breeze and clear sky. I encouraged Lois to apply for journalism school abroad, but she said she was happy to stay at *China Daily*, which surprised me. She was a talented reporter, and I had assumed she would want to someday move on to bigger and better things, to become a *real* journalist.

After a lull in the conversation, Lois looked at me with hurt eyes and said, "I read your article." She paused. "So that's what you think of us?"

I felt guilty and struggled to offer an explanation.

She shrugged. "I understand. It's just different here."

We sat in silence, sipping our coffees and watching the basketball game on the asphalt court in front of us. All I wanted to do was look her in the eye and tell her that I was sorry.

But I didn't. I couldn't. Because even though I felt awful, I knew I wasn't wrong.

Was I?

In the weeks after leaving *China Daily*, I wrestled over whether I didn't fit in at the paper because, well, it was *China Daily*, or if my failed tenure at the paper was because I am, by nature, exactly how I felt after the *Globe and Mail* article was published: an asshole.

As much I would have liked to write off *China Daily* as a ridiculous charade, I concluded that I, in fact, bore the brunt of the blame for being a Failed Propagandist. I never gave it 100 percent—not for one day, not for one minute. I didn't even give it close to 50 percent. I gave it about 7 percent.

Day after day, I did no work, made no effort to make *China Daily* a better newspaper. Lois was right: it's *different* in China. I didn't play by their rules, I complained endlessly about working nights and editing. I bitched my way into a writer's role and then barely wrote anything. I moaned about every assignment I got. I didn't aggressively report anything. I blogged about the absurdities of working in Chinese state media. I freelanced, violating my contract.

But now that it was over I was embarrassed about my attitude over the previous year. I had treated *China Daily* as a joke from day one, and that wasn't fair to anyone—not to my employers, not to my editors, not to my colleagues. And it wasn't fair to my friends, to people like Lois. If I could have lived the year over again, I would have done things differently. I would have tried to maintain a more open mind and I would have worked harder.

But it was too late for that now. All I could do, I decided, was come back to Beijing with a fresh start and fresh eyes. I wanted to be a better *laowai*.

That April, a few days after my twenty-eighth birthday, I returned to Canada for three weeks. As part of my contract, *China Daily* provided a car to take me to the airport: comfortable, air-conditioned, chauffeured.

Julia texted me while I was on the way. "Have a great time at home," she wrote. "I'll miss you."

"I'll miss you, too," I replied, and I meant it. She still wasn't my girlfriend, but we were getting there.

I flew to Toronto, on *China Daily*'s dime, and landed in a blizzard. The air was clean and cold when I stepped off the shuttle bus downtown. Wind and blowing snow whipped my face as I dragged my suitcase to a friend's apartment.

I fought through jet lag and went with a few friends to a pub downtown, where I ordered the first decent burger I'd had in a year and drank a few pints of good Canadian beer, not the watery beverage served in China. It felt surreal to be back in Canada. The bar smelled of cleaning products and spilled alcohol, not of cigarette smoke like Chinese bars. I caught up on my friends' lives, but when it came time for me to explain my life in China, and *China Daily*, I struggled to convey what I experienced. I pointed out the obvious differences, told them about some of the adventures I'd had, and did my best to paint a full picture.

The next morning I visited my old neighborhood—a bohemian district east of downtown called Cabbagetown—and read a newspaper at the café where I used to write many of my freelance articles. The streets felt small and deserted compared to Beijing. I walked around reliving the summer of 2006, the worst summer of my life. So much had changed. I thought about the person I was before I left for China, and the person I was only twelve months later. It had all turned out all right. I was happier, more confident, more excited about life—and I had China to thank.

I took a streetcar to the Chinese consulate, where Falun Gong protesters were gathered outside, as they were a year earlier when I first applied for a visa. It was mayhem inside, a single waiting room that felt similar to the *China Daily* offices, dated and mute of color, with white sunlight shining in from the windows. People jostled for a place in the line and hollered loud inquiries in Mandarin to the employees behind the glass.

As I waited in line to apply for a tourist visa, I grew excited about going back to China. I was more excited about the prospect of returning to Beijing than I had been about going the first time. It was becoming clear that I was in no way ready to move back to Canada, that my initial plan to stay until the end of the Olympics would soon have to be augmented.

It had been only a few days, but I was disillusioned again with Toronto, where most conversations seemed to revolve around organic food, careers, and complaints about public transit. After a week, I traveled to my home province, Saskatchewan, and on to Vancouver. I enjoyed being back in Canada, but it seemed strangely foreign now. Exchanges at restaurants and coffee shops felt awkward and people came across as both absurdly polite and incredibly cold; I missed the honest bluntness of Chinese people.

There were still things pulling me back, of course. Seeing my parents sparked the guilt I often felt living in China. They had come to visit me in Beijing the previous fall and I was in frequent contact with them, but I knew it was hard on my mom to have her son on the other side of the world, especially in a place that seemed to be in constant turmoil, at least based on news coverage. It was great to see friends, too, and enjoy all the variety Canada had to offer.

But when I imagined going back to my old life in Canada, I quickly dismissed any fleeting notion of moving back.

"So, what's it like in China?" friends would ask.

How could I answer that question? *It's amazing and terrible. Beautiful and ugly, thrilling and boring, inspiring and infuriating.* I couldn't find a short, sound-bite answer, so more often than not I would mumble something like "Oh, it's great. Really interesting. Things are changing so fast." People at home struggled to relate to my China experience, and I couldn't blame them. Before I left, China was this big, mostly blank canvas, except for stock images I'd seen on television or in photos: people on bikes, hazy skies, skyscrapers, and peasant villages. But by then I knew that China is one of those places you need to see and feel, and more than one conversation ended with me saying, "You really just need to be there."

I felt somehow different and I was anxious to get back to Beijing. It was becoming clear to me that I had made the right decision to go to China. For all the ups and downs of my first year in China, it had made me feel alive.

8

The Big Cleanup

A few weeks later, in mid-May 2008, I was back in Beijing, still without a plan that lasted beyond the summer, living in my new apartment, a boxy but adequate three-bedroom owned by Comrade Wu, my old kook of a landlord.

A few days after I arrived back in the capital, Comrade Wu showed up at my apartment unannounced, as was his custom, plopped down on the living room sofa, lit a smoke, and farted. He let out a barking cough, paused, and shifted his weight to one side to scratch his ass cheek. Comrade Wu was retired and in his late sixties, from Henan province, thin as a twig with dark brown skin and massive Pete Postlethwaite cheekbones. He took a shine to me after I moved into his rental apartment, even though we could barely communicate. On this particular morning, Comrade Wu puffed on his cigarette and rattled off a bunch of Chinese I didn't really understand.

After a few minutes he noticed I wasn't keeping up.

"Your Chinese," he said, shaking his head, "is terrible."

He was right. My Chinese was pathetic for having spent a year in the country; it was at a level that could have been achieved after an intensive month-long course. It was something I hoped to remedy that summer, the Olympic summer. I was determined to engage with China differently, to be the better *laowai* I'd promised myself I would be. I wanted to meet more locals, to develop a better understanding of the city and country, and much of that had to do with getting a half-decent understanding of Chinese.

Comrade Wu's apartment was in the Chaoyangmen neighborhood, inside the east second ring road and near the site of the long-ago demolished Chaoyang ("Sun-facing") Gate. My building was part of a large complex of aging six-story walk-ups, made of concrete and built for utility.

The courtyard behind my building was a hub of activity, crowded in spring and summer with locals exercising and gossiping and walking their tiny, yapping dogs. Women wore baggy, dark-colored clothing, and on hot days the men sported T-shirts pulled up over their pale bellies, the legs of their pants rolled to the knee. A geriatric bike repairman with big, filthy hands, wearing a stained muscle shirt and torn jeans, set up shop at the courtyard gate, and business was brisk. Beijing bicycles aren't made to last, and I visited him regularly to fix my sixty-dollar Yongjiu ("Forever") bike.

Just around the corner, across Chaoyangmen South Alley, were rows of old *hutong* alleyways, which I often explored while running or biking in the early evenings. The alleys were the best part of Beijing, full of life and history. Groups of men played cards and mah-jongg; kids walked home from school drowning in their uniforms; old women gathered in the shade of trees to talk and laugh. The alleys smelled of barbecued meat and public toilets. It seemed like the entire community was there, hanging out, living, and often when I went running, the games and chatting stopped and puzzled expressions appeared on the locals' faces as the tall *laowai* darted by, singing along to songs playing on his headphones.

My apartment, which cost $700 a month, split two ways with a journalist from New Zealand named Jon, had three bedrooms, a cramped living room, a kitchen, and a closetlike bathroom. There was no separate shower in the bathroom, so water sprayed directly from the showerhead onto the tiled floor and toilet before going down the often-plugged drain. The bathroom smelled of mold, and the rest of the apartment became onion- or garlic-scented whenever our neighbors cooked. We had two balconies, each attached to a bedroom and closed off with glass windows, rendering them useless as outdoor spaces. The walls were thick; the apartment was dead quiet and scorching hot throughout the summer, whenever the air conditioners were broken, which was often. The walk up the windowless staircase was a struggle in the heat, and I often came through the door panting and dripping with sweat.

It had taken us a month to find the place before I went to Canada. Searching for apartments in Beijing is a nightmare, a lesson Jon and I had learned well. With the Olympics on the horizon, landlords were driving up prices, especially for foreigners, in anticipation of a flood of visitors. We looked at dozens of apartments before finding Comrade Wu's place. I saw shoe box apartments with prison cots, and places that looked like murder scenes going for more than $1,000 a month. They were small, poorly designed, and with furniture that, as Jon put it, "commit various crimes against good taste." Despite its drawbacks, Comrade Wu's was a steal compared to some of the other units we saw: it was clean, minimal, and affordable. The walls were freshly painted white and it had new (fake) wood floor panels.

We weren't far from the main centers of activity: Sanlitun and the Central Business District were ten-minute cab rides away, barring traffic, and I could cycle to my favorite cafés in the alleys near the Drum and Bell Towers in less than fifteen minutes. We had a number of cheap, convenient local restaurants nearby, a 7-Eleven just around the corner, and a Starbucks a ten-minutes walk away, just over the second ring road.

The apartment left something to be desired, but it was central and it helped give me a new lease on Beijing life. I had no office to go to now, no stories to edit, and I was free of *China Daily*. I had accepted a three-week job as a research assistant during the Olympics with the Canadian Broadcasting Corporation, but until then I had nothing but time.

Not long after I came back to Beijing, I enrolled in a Chinese language school across the ring road, signing up for six to ten hours of class each week and making a pledge to myself that I would do homework this time. The day I enrolled at the school, I told the secretary I had studied Chinese for a year, and the school tailored a lesson plan for someone who had not only studied but also *learned* Chinese for a year. But studying and learning are two entirely different things, which I soon found out.

My teacher was a twenty-seven-year-old woman from Heilongjiang province in northeast China, named Guo Li. She was a sweetheart, with a pretty face, dimpled cheeks, and a bowl cut of black hair. She was tiny and looked barely older than a teenager. During our first lesson it became clear that my Chinese was not up to par; nearly everything Guo Li said passed over my head. After a few minutes, she threw her hands up in exasperation and said, in Chinese, "Have you been in China for a year? Or a day?" I immediately liked her.

Meanwhile, with so many of my former colleagues having departed Beijing for home or elsewhere, I was spending more time with Julia. We started spending a couple of nights a week together, and before long it was three or four times a week. In late May, we went with a group of her friends for a weekend trip to Inner Mongolia, where we rode horses and ate roasted lamb and went drinking in the town's karaoke bar. She was planning on returning to Russia to finish university at the end of July, and as we lay in bed in a local family's guesthouse that night, I told her I would miss her when she left.

"I'll miss you too, *sladki.*"

"*Sladki?* What's that mean?"

"It means sweetheart in Russian."

After that, she called me Sladki all the time, and I adored it. (I liked it better than when she said my real name, which in her Russian accent sounded more like a screech—"*Meeeeetch.*") At some point, we started calling each other boyfriend and girlfriend and we spent almost every night together. We took turns staying at one another's place. We went to Xi'an to see the Terracotta Warriors. We had sex in the bushes at the base of the Great Wall during an all-night rave.

She was lovely, and even though we were very different people, we made a great couple. I gave her the confidence she sometimes lacked. She gave me comfort and a sense of calm.

She was my first girlfriend in two years, and our relationship felt good. But always lingering, and always ratcheting up the intensity, was the fact that in less than two months, she would be gone.

I was happy, but I was also adjusting to the burdens of taking care of myself after a year of living like an infant under the super-

vision of a Chinese government newspaper. *China Daily* handled
everything even remotely difficult in our lives—problems with
our apartments, visas, logistics. We had a network of people attending to us. I had gotten used to being supported over the year
and almost forgot that day-to-day life in China can be infuriat-
ingly difficult.

Now I was on my own as a freelancer, and even a menial task
could became a huge hassle. One day, for example, I needed a
D battery. I tried a few little shops near my place. Nothing. The
7-Eleven down the street. No luck. I biked across the ring road
to a market and tried four or five stalls before I found the battery
I needed. A task that would have taken five minutes in North
America took close to forty-five minutes in China, even after a
year.

I was also having constant problems with my apartment.
Only one of the three air conditioners in my place blew cold air,
and the one that did, which was in my bedroom, leaked buckets
of water. I called Comrade Wu four times over a week before
he finally fixed the leak. Less than a week later, it was dripping
water again. After several more phone calls, Comrade Wu finally
came back with a few workers. I tried to explain in my broken
Chinese that I had woken up that morning with a huge puddle
of air conditioner water on my floor. He raised his eyebrows, offered a half smile, shook his head from side to side, and conveyed
what he was thinking with no words at all: "Enough with your
laowai bitching!"

To solve the problem, the workers drilled a hole through the
bedroom wall to the balcony, flakes of paint and bits of cement
falling into a pile on my desk, and then fed the air conditioner
hose through the hole and into a bucket they placed on the other
side. I would need to empty the bucket every second day.

For the most part, I was grateful to be in China during the

Olympic summer, but that didn't stop me from wanting an elevator, a kitchen with an oven, a shower that didn't spray directly onto my toilet, a washing machine that didn't eat my clothes. A landlord that didn't drop in all the time. It felt overwhelming at times, dealing with the little things on top of studying and working. China offered many things but rarely peace of mind.

A major headache of pre-Olympics Beijing was dealing with visas, another problem I hadn't had to bother with while working at *China Daily*. After my "foreign expert" visa expired, I returned to China on a thirty-day tourist visa, which I could renew twice at the Public Security Bureau in Beijing. That would take me up to the start of the Olympics. I asked the Canadian Broadcasting Corporation (CBC), my Olympics employer, if they would sponsor me for the Games themselves, and they said they would look into it, but they never got back to me.

In China, visas could be bought. Many foreigners lived for years on gray-market visas, found through shady visa agents who, thanks to connections or money or both, were able to obtain official visas for foreigners not officially employed in China. I had made inquiries with friends while I was still working at *China Daily* and was directed to look at the online classifieds of local English-language listings magazines. There I found dozens of ads promising tourist or business visas in exchange for a fee. But according to online forums, these gray-market visas were getting harder to come by as the Olympics approached, and those still available were increasingly expensive.

Since I had already accepted a job during the Games and was desperate to see the event after witnessing the buildup, I didn't have much of a choice. One afternoon I met a middle-aged Englishman named Simon, whom I'd found via an ad offering year-long work visas. He was a short man with flushed cheeks and large glasses. He had been working in Beijing for the better part of a decade, running a trading business with a Canadian business partner. He procured visas "on the side," he said, through government contacts he'd made over the years.

I was nervous as I handed him $1,000 and my passport, and he could tell.

"Don't worry," he said. "We've never had a problem getting visas, and if we do, we'll give all your money back—full refund."

He said he would get back within a few days to tell me how it was proceeding. When by the following week I hadn't heard from him, I started getting worried. I called him one afternoon and he assured me there was no problem: my visa would be ready shortly. A few days later he called me back. He said there was a small snag and asked me to meet his business partner, the Canadian, the following day.

The Canadian, a skinny, ratlike man from Calgary, sat across from me in the lobby of his office, not far from *China Daily*. His forehead glistened with sweat.

I had a bad feeling.

"We can get your visa, but we want you to do us a favor," he said.

"What kind of favor?"

"We want you to import a car from Hong Kong under your name. It's for tax reasons. Foreigners don't have to pay taxes on imported cars. Mainlanders do."

I had heard of this before, but usually foreigners who agreed to this scheme got paid several thousand dollars for the risk, on top of a free visa. But I wasn't going to get paid, and my visa was still going to cost me $1,000. Simon and the Rat, I guessed, would make a killing.

I didn't know what the repercussions would be if our plot was uncovered, and I wasn't anxious to find out. I didn't want to miss the Olympics, but my gut told me to run.

"If you're uncomfortable with this," the Rat said, "we'll give you your money back."

I asked for my money back.

As the days passed and the Olympics fast approached, I e-mailed the Olympic press center, which dealt with foreign reporters, and explained my situation. I asked if there was any way I could still apply for a journalist visa. They replied that if I had a press card, which the CBC would be providing for me at the start of the Olympics, then I automatically had a visa for the duration of the event, but it wouldn't kick in until a few days before the Games. Until then, I could stay in China on my current tourist visa, which I still needed to renew every thirty days.

I thought the problem was solved, but my visa woes weren't over. I was able to renew my tourist visa in June, after the first thirty-day period, with no problem. Not so after sixty days.

"There have been some changes," the woman at the Public Security Bureau told me when I visited in mid-July, three weeks before the Olympics.

The building, which served as police headquarters, was located on the north second ring road. On the second floor, where visas were handled, swarms of foreigners lined up at dozens of numbered windows, waiting their turn with visa officers who seemed to put extra effort into their miserable demeanor. It was chaos, and for the first time in my China existence I came face-to-face with the juggernaut of Chinese bureaucracy.

"What kind of changes?" I asked the woman at the counter.

"You must have twenty thousand yuan in your bank account in order to renew your visa. And you must provide a bank statement."

Neither of these requirements had existed even a few weeks before. "Okay. I'll print off a statement from my Canadian bank account."

"No. It must be Chinese bank account."

"What?"

"Must be Chinese account."

I thought about this for a second. "So let me get this straight. Foreign tourists who want to visit China for thirty days must have over three thousand dollars in a *Chinese* bank account in order to obtain a visa?"

"Correct."

I looked at the date on my watch and the date on my visa.

"My visa expires tomorrow," I said. "I've got one day to open a Chinese bank account, deposit twenty thousand yuan, and then bring a statement to you."

"Yes."

"That's impossible."

The woman shrugged. "It's the only way."

I left the PSB and tried to think. I would only be able to withdraw about $1,500 from my own accounts because of daily withdrawal limits, so I'd need to borrow. I called anybody I could think of who might be able to lend me money. Julia lent me $500, and a friend from *China Daily* happened to have $1,000 in cash on hand at his apartment. I rushed to Bank of China and opened an account, depositing $3,000. But in order to get a certified statement of funds, the cashier said I needed to freeze my account for five working days.

In sum: I was (supposedly) a tourist in China, on a thirty-day visa, and I needed to present proof that I had $3,000 in funds in a Chinese bank account that I wouldn't be able to access for a full week of my thirty days in the country.

Bad China Days.

I wasn't the only foreigner having a nightmare with Chinese visas in the lead-up to the Games. Hundreds of people from around the world were denied visas to attend the event, many for no apparent reason at all. Why China would deny visas to ordinary people who only wanted to watch the Olympics, which are supposed to symbolize global camaraderie, is anyone's guess. My hunch was that Chinese officials thought of the Beijing Olympics as their party, no one else's, and they didn't want too much foreign riffraff around causing trouble.

The visa woes were exemplary of something much bigger: Beijing's big Olympic cleanup. It had been happening for years—painting old apartment blocks, ripping up streets and sidewalks, curtailing citizens spitting and line-jumping, closing down factories near the city—but in the months before the Games began, efforts were ratcheted up. It was evident right down at *hutong* level, where old ladies in my neighborhood sat stoically on small stools at all hours of the day, armed with keen eyes and red armbands that said "Public Security Volunteer."

It was on a deeply personal level that I felt the Big Cleanup. One day in June, I traveled to Lido to buy movies at Tom's DVD store. Tom's had become a huge part of my Beijing life, since my free time was divided between 1) drinking, 2) cheap massages, and 3) watching movies.

On this day I was looking for the new *Indiana Jones* movie, but when I arrived, Tom's was closed. I asked two Chinese men loitering outside the antiques store upstairs what was going on, and they said something about inventory. But Tom's had been closed for inventory a few weeks before, and I wondered how much inventory a bootleg DVD store could possibly do. Then a few days later, I read in a city magazine that a DVD vendor in Sanlitun had recently been fined 10,000 yuan and put in jail.

As the Olympics neared, police presence increased around the city. At the traffic rotary on the second ring road near my apartment, cops pulled over drivers all day, checking IDs to make sure out-of-towners had permission to be in Beijing. As a six-foot-three foreigner living in China, I always stood out. But it wasn't until the lead-up to the Olympics that I really felt out of place. From reading the news, it didn't seem that China wanted foreigners there at all. I was never paranoid living in China, even as a journalist, but I did wonder from time to time, as I cycled through the rotary on my way to Chinese class or elsewhere, what would happen if one of the police officers pulled me to the side and asked, what, exactly, I was doing in China. Thankfully, that never happened.

Others weren't so lucky. Several friends were forced to leave the country for the Olympics because they were denied visas. Those deemed undesirable by the Chinese government were forced out. That spring, police rounded up drug suspects in Sanlitun and temporarily shut down several bars and clubs, including the legendary Maggie's. Rumors spread that the city was going to force all bars to shut early during the Olympics, and all patios and outdoor drinking areas would be closed entirely. The government was seemingly sapping all the fun out of the event, and the foreign press responded to these efforts by dubbing the 2008 Olympics the "No Fun Games."

One night after playing basketball, I went with a few friends to Kro's Nest, a popular pizza place owned by a young American expat. The restaurant was at the north gate of Workers Stadium, near two nightclubs that had long been pillars of Beijing's nightlife, Mix and Vics. We passed two security tents set up for the Olympics, which were still two months away. When we arrived at Kro's, it was inexplicably closed. In a few months, Mix and Vics would be forced to shut down as well, for "security reasons."

We walked back through the tents toward the parking lot.

"Stupid Olympics," my friend lamented. "Fucking up Beijing."

The atmosphere around the city was changing, and it oc-curred to me that the Olympics might not be the party everyone was hoping for.

As the summer went on, and my Chinese improved, ever so slightly, I became more comfortable in my classes with Guo Li. Although she had majored in English at a university in Heilongjiang province, Guo Li spoke virtually none, so our one-on-one classes were all in Chinese. During class, she would teach me a few new words from the textbook or go over a new set of Chinese characters, but mostly we chatted.

In class, as my language skills slowly improved, I would slip into character and talk with total confidence even though I had a five-year-old's language ability. I was developing a Chinese iden-tity, becoming the name on my *China Daily* business cards: Mi Gao. Tall Rice.

For me, Tall Rice was a mask behind which I could be whoever I wanted. (This isn't uncommon for foreigners living in China; Peter Hessler also talked about the emergence of his China identity in his first book, *River Town*.) I felt totally at ease around Guo Li, and she did around me as well. She would erupt into hysterics when I mispronounced or mistook a word, as when instead of saying *pi jiu* (second tone on *pi*, meaning "beer"), I said *pi jiu* (fourth tone on *pi*, meaning "fart liquor"). She was immensely curious about my day-to-day life, and during our classes we spoke about anything and everything, often slowly and with difficulty, but the point usually got across. If something was bothering me—visa complications, struggles with work, the frustrations of being a *laowai* in China—I told her. She was like my therapist.

There was no beating around the bush with Guo Li. If I had a complaint about China or Chinese people, I laid it on the table. She told me about her family, her life in Heilongjiang, and about her boyfriend. I marveled at how much she worked—often fourteen hours a day, six days a week—and I gobbled up her insights about Chinese government, society, and people. By the end of the summer, Guo Li was by far the best Chinese friend I had, and our relationship was entirely in Chinese.

It wasn't just around Guo Li that my China identity emerged. Even though it was a struggle to understand him, I enjoyed talking to Comrade Wu, gathering little bits of detail about his family and history. Whenever I used a new word I had learned in class during our conversations, it felt like a minor conquest. I chatted with cabbies and servers at the coffee shops I frequented. These little conversations ("How's your day?" "Do you have kids?") made me feel more comfortable in Beijing by the day.

After class I would go to the gym and then sit in cafés working on my freelance assignments, which were coming at a steady pace as the world turned its eyes on China before the Olympics. I wrote a piece for the *Guardian*, my first story in a major newspaper outside Canada. I wrote a few stories for the *Globe and Mail* and the *South China Morning Post*, a Hong Kong–based English newspaper. I was commissioned to write a story about Beijing's famous Snack Street, near Wangfujing, where I ate scorpions, silkworms, starfish, and lamb penis. I had consistent writing gigs for local publications, and this time around I enjoyed the freedom of the freelance lifestyle.

I spent most nights with Julia, but before long she was getting ready to move back to Moscow. Our breakup was inevitable, and although I had prepared for it all along, it hit me for real one afternoon a few days before she left.

We spent the day together at my apartment and later took a cab to the Silk Market, where she wanted to buy presents for family and friends at home. I dropped her off, and as the cab pulled away, I broke down. It was over and I knew it. She was my best friend in Beijing and would be my girlfriend for only forty-eight more hours.

It felt like everything was ending. Not just her and me, but the summer, one of the best of my life, was coming to an end, too. I had spent the last three months trying not to think beyond August, but now, as the Olympics approached, I was left with a big, empty fall ahead of me.

That night was her going-away party. We went with her friends to an all-you-can-eat Japanese teppanyaki restaurant. We drank warm sake and Asahi beer, and after dinner the group of us walked to Sanlitun. Her friends went into a club while Julia and I sat huddled in a doorway at street level, rethinking our future together even though we both knew better. Should we try to make it work? She could come back next summer. Or maybe I could move to Moscow. But even through the haze of alcohol, we knew the answer. We decided that, after tomorrow, we would be done.

I stayed at her place the last night she spent in Beijing. I slept terribly that night. Once again, Beijing, always reinventing itself, would be a new city in the morning.

On the cab ride to the airport, we barely spoke. The window was down and I stroked her hair until we arrived at Terminal Two. I helped her with her bags and walked her to check-in.

"I'll see you soon," I said, although I had no idea if that was true. We held each other for several minutes, her tears dampening my T-shirt, and then I pulled away, told her to call me when she arrived, and took a cab home.

The week after Julia left was awful. The city felt even lonelier. My friend Will, whom I'd lived with in Japan, came to town with his girlfriend, and it was a welcome distraction. But I still wondered from hour to hour whether Julia and I had made the right decision. As for what would happen to me once the Olympics were over, I was too drained to even consider it.

A week before the opening ceremonies, I went to the Olympic Green to meet my coworkers and pick up my press pass, which would serve as my visa for the duration of the Games. Thousands of volunteers had already been mobilized, and journalists—21,000 of them—were arriving from around the world. My cabdriver dropped me off at the wrong gate, and it took me more than an hour to find the correct entrance, on the opposite side of the sprawling Olympic Green. When I finally arrived, a CBC employee met me at the security check with my pass and escorted me to the main press center.

There I met Dave, the head writer for the two shows I would work on throughout the Olympics. Dave was a quiet, friendly man of about fifty who had worked many Olympic broadcasts. He wore shorts, sneakers, a golf shirt, and baseball cap—an outfit he would wear every day throughout the Games. He seemed kind and decent, a good boss, and I liked him right away. He introduced me to the staff and filled me in on the details of my work, which sounded like an intern's job description: monitoring newswires, looking up information about athletes and events, and doing whatever the head writers and researchers required of me.

Dave walked me over to Ling Long Pagoda, where I would be working. Ling Long was a seven-story tower with studios on each floor overlooking the Olympic Green. The CBC's set had already been built.

"That chair cost two thousand dollars," Dave said, pointing to the anchor's chair.

I sat down and swiveled. It was a fantastic chair—red and made out of some high-tech, super-firm mesh.

"So we'll be working on two prime-time shows that air in Canada at six p.m. every night," Dave told me. "That means an early start here."

"How early?" I said.

"We'll need you here by four in the morning."

I almost puked in his face.

9

Live from Ling Long Pagoda

Ten . . . nine . . . eight . . .

I took a sip of lukewarm Sol beer. Projected images played on a brick wall across from the balcony of the Saddle, a Mexican restaurant and bar in Sanlitun where I was gathered with a half-dozen friends. The Olympics had arrived. Another sip. The city was a sweatbox, about ninety degrees and humid. The crowd was silent as we watched the countdown, which was happening live a few miles to the north. There, in the Bird's Nest, musicians banged drums that illuminated when struck, forming numbers that counted down to the Olympics' auspicious official beginning at 8 p.m. on August 8, 2008.

Seven . . . six . . .

That morning I had watched the sun rise over the Bird's Nest, climbing from behind silhouetted rows of apartment buildings to reveal one of those end-of-times Beijing days that can be understood only when experienced firsthand. Through the haze the sun appeared "lurid red," according to a story that came across the newswire I was monitoring. Far corners of the Olympic Green were barely visible from my station at Ling Long. A good day to open the biggest Olympics in history it was not.

Despite the pollution, the significance of the day couldn't be denied. The seven-year wait was coming to an end. WELCOME, WORLD, read *China Daily*'s front-page headline that morning. China's moment had arrived.

I had been working for a week in preparation for today, living on coffee and adrenaline, worn down but excited that it was finally here. During work, surrounded by my countrymen, I watched montages of previous Olympics and I would get butterflies.

Outside the studio, volunteers in matching teal shirts and gray cargo pants gathered throughout the day. Security was everywhere. I saw girls in pink dresses and shirtless young men rehearsing on the practice track outside the Bird's Nest for the opening ceremonies, which would be attended by dignitaries from around the world. On my way to lunch I saw the entire U.S. men's basketball team leaving the press center: Kobe Bryant out front signing an autograph on a volunteer's shirt; LeBron James trailing behind listening to music on earmuff headphones. It was surreal to know I was a part of the event the world was watching, that I had somehow ended up in the middle of it.

Five . . . four. . .

Starting tomorrow, I would begin my early morning shift at Ling Long Pagoda. The work was not glamorous—digging up data on athletes, keeping the head writers and hosts informed and happy, answering obvious questions about Beijing and China—

but it offered a unique opportunity to contribute to the spectacle in some small way. Sometimes I needed to remind myself how lucky I was, especially when I was furious at having to work so early. Which was often.

I ended my shift on August 8 late in the afternoon, after ten hours of preparing cue cards for the hosts and filing information on athletes that might be needed during one of the next day's shows. As I waited for a cab to take me to Sanlitun, George W. Bush's motorcade drove by.

Three . . . two . . .

I was at the Saddle, drinking Sol and watching the count-down, a tequila shot readied for when the drummers hit *one*. I felt nervous and proud, as if, somehow, these Olympics belonged especially to me. They had been such a huge part of my life for the previous sixteen months. I had seen the city shift and come together for this event. It was the common thread each of us in the city possessed; I felt as if everyone who lived in Beijing, both Chinese and foreigners, could claim these Olympics as their own.

One. . .

Tequila burned my throat and fireworks bloomed throughout the city. We cheered and hugged and high-fived. The ceremony that followed was a spectacle like nothing I'd ever seen before. China had gone all out. We watched in awe.

Later, as the teams entered the Bird's Nest, I looked at my watch and groaned. My friends ordered more rounds of drinks and talked about where they were going to party that night.

I wouldn't be able to join them, however. My alarm was set for three in the morning, when my own sixteen-day Olympic marathon would begin.

I rolled out of bed after four hours of sleep and put on a pair of camouflage shorts and a Nike T-shirt I'd worn the day before. Wardrobe was of little concern to those of us who worked long hours behind the scenes preparing the Olympic broadcast that our friends and families would watch from their living rooms at home.

I guzzled water and forced myself to do fifteen push-ups beside my bed in a futile attempt to wake up. I washed my neck and face, tried to sort out my hair, ate a bowl of oatmeal, and brewed a pot of coffee to put in a go-cup for my ride to work.

The street sweepers were spraying down Chaoyangmen South Street as I hailed a cab and drove north toward the Olympic Green. As we pulled onto the fourth ring road in north Beijing, I could see the red glow of the Bird's Nest. The Water Cube next door was fluorescent blue. Ling Long Pagoda was lit from top to bottom like a Christmas tree.

The Olympic Green was already buzzing. A small line had formed at the security check, and inside, the press center journalists were sitting at the computer stations the Beijing Organizing Committee had provided, finishing their opening ceremony stories. I ordered a second coffee from the McDonald's inside the press center and hopped on a golf cart that ferried me to my post at Ling Long.

The opening theme song the CBC used on the first day of the 2008 Olympics in Beijing was the same one the network had used since I was old enough to remember watching the Games. As I sat in the studio at six o'clock in the morning, the anthem was all it took to forget that I had already been working for two hours, that I had slept only four hours the night before, that I was already exhausted after a week of preparations, and that I still had fifteen very early mornings to go.

I watched the opening montage on a monitor and glimpsed the host on set—a legendary Canadian hockey commentator named Ron MacLean. I had grown up watching Ron MacLean on *Hockey Night in Canada*, the CBC's flagship NHL broadcast, quibbling with his costar, the loud-mouthed former coach Don Cherry. I remember seeing them when I was only a kid, watching Wayne Gretzky–era Edmonton Oilers games in my basement with my dad.

I watched MacLean on set, sitting on his $2,000 chair and preparing to go on air, and soaked up the theme song. I got a little misty-eyed. In a few hours, events would begin. This was huge.

My days as a research assistant during the Olympics went like this:

3:00 a.m.—Alarm. Push-ups. Eat yogurt and a banana, prepare coffee, hop in a cab to the Olympic Green.

3:50 a.m.—Arrive at press center. Head downstairs to McDonald's to grab a latte from McCafé. (I swear by McCafé. At Ling Long Pagoda the only coffee available tasted like bile after a few cups. McCafé lattes saved me on many mornings.)

4:00 a.m.—Arrive at Ling Long Pagoda. Monitor news-wires and international media for anything that might be useful for the show. Look for information about major events coming up that day and analysis of the previous day's events. Send anything useful to Dave or the head re-searcher, a kind, intense woman named Karen. Continue monitoring the news throughout the morning.

(One of the first things I noticed about the international media's coverage of the Beijing Olympics was just how bad some of the parachute reporting was—that is, journalists who arrive in a place they know nothing about but write about it as if they do. The *New York Times* commented on the oddities of Chinese cuisine. The *Toronto Star* lamented Beijing's ancient alleyway neighborhoods—about five years too late. Countless newspapers and magazines pointed out Beijing's butchered Chinglish signage. These stories had Beijing-based foreign reporters in hysterics. One night a writer friend pointed out that bureau reporters highlighting other journalists' clichés had become the biggest cliché of all. But I often got frustrated with some of the reporting in international media as well. A year in Beijing had made me defensive of the way the city was presented.)

5:30 a.m.—Make toast with peanut butter. Drink third cup of coffee.

6:00 a.m.—The prime-time show begins. I watch Ron from the monitor and wait for instructions from Dave and Karen. During events or commercials, the three of us scurry to find any useful information Ron might need for the upcoming segment.

7:00 a.m.—One of the tech guys comes by my station and takes my order for breakfast from McDonald's—my third breakfast of the day. (Over the course of the Olympics, I would put on about ten pounds.)

7:00 a.m.–12:00 p.m.—Do whatever Dave and Karen ask of me, which is often very little. I try to sleep at my desk, or sometimes sneak outside for fresh air, even though it is strictly forbidden while the show is on air. It had been explained to me that I might be needed at any time to find information for the hosts whenever they needed it. "If they call on us for anything, we need to have it right now—*right now*," Karen had said to me, snapping her fingers. I soon learn that this rarely happens, and every once in a while I grant myself a break. That is, until one day when Dave confronts me after I leave the studio for fifteen minutes. He tells me through quivering lips that I must never leave during a broadcast. Ever. I'm a prisoner of Ling Long Pagoda.

Noon—Lunch, my fourth meal of the day. Every day is the same: soggy sandwiches and fries.

1 p.m.–3 p.m.—Work the late show, called *Pacific Prime*. Not much is required of me for this show, so I usually read magazines and watch events from the monitor.

3 p.m. onward—Use my press pass to watch live events. Over the course of the Olympics I watch diving, swimming, track, basketball, beach volleyball, tennis, and more. Later, I meet friends for dinner and watch events at bars until my eyes start drooping, which is usually around 9 or 10 p.m. Most nights, I go to sleep around midnight.

Then I do it all over again.

It didn't take long for some of the initial Olympics euphoria to fade, for me and everybody else I talked to. A few days after the Games began, a deranged Chinese man stabbed an American couple—including the father-in-law of the U.S. men's volleyball coach, who died from his wounds—and their Chinese guide in the Drum tower in Beijing. (The assailant then jumped to his death.) Several elements of the opening ceremonies had been revealed as fraudulent: the fireworks shown on television were actually computer animated; minority performers were exposed as costumed Han Chinese; and a performance by an adorable young girl turned out to be lip-synched, the song actually performed by a child deemed insufficiently cute by the event's organizers. The weather wasn't helping, either. The city had been shrouded by smog and fog since the opening ceremony, and by Day Three it was pouring rain.

After a few days, work started to get tedious. Sometimes it all felt like an episode of *The Office*. I spent full twelve-hour days looking up information on athletes and events, printing out page after page, and filing each one alphabetically in a cabinet in case one of the hosts needed to know, say, who won gold in men's coxless pair rowing in the 2000 Sydney Olympics.

I pointed out more than once that this information would be much easier to find, and more quickly, on the Olympics' very own website that contained such data, or via Google, for example.

"You can't rely on the Internet," Karen told me. "What if the Olympic website goes down? Or Google?"

"I really don't see that happening."

"What if the computers break down?"

"All of them?"

She grew frustrated. "Look, I've been doing this longer than you. You have to prepare for the worst, even if the worst never happens."

I frowned and returned to printing out documents that I would file away and never use.

The Games went on. Michael Phelps won his first of eight gold medals. The U.S.-China basketball game drew an estimated one billion viewers. And spirits were high despite the heat and humidity and overbearing security.

As often as I could, I went to watch events. The first one I attended was beach volleyball, hosted in a temporary stadium at the east entrance of Chaoyang Park. The stadium was heaving. My friend and I sipped one-dollar cans of Tsingtao as the announcer led the curious crowd through the wave, and cheerleaders from China and elsewhere, dubbed "Beach Babies," outfitted in lime-green bikinis, danced to Chubby Checker. It wasn't exactly the Olympics in the Athenian sense, but it was definitely amusing.

A few days later, I went to the Water Cube, arriving halfway through the men's three-meter synchronized diving event. It was packed. No surprise since the Chinese were dominating. Fans waved China's red and yellow flag and chanted, "Zhong Guo jia you!"—"Add oil, China," the Chinese equivalent of "Let's go!"—and cheered politely for other competitors.

I went to the tennis courts to watch Rafael Nadal play an unknown Russian. I sat alone in the media section and wondered if, from Moscow, Julia was watching this, too. After the match I wandered to center court to watch Roger Federer, then ranked number one in the world. I bought a can of Tsingtao and took a seat in the media section. The stadium filled up slowly, and by the end of the first set there were still empty seats near the top.

The media section was only half full. I leaned back in my chair and rested my feet on the seat in front me. Work was done for the day and I felt wide awake despite a serious lack of sleep. I took a deep breath, looked up at the blue sky overhead, and held up my can of Tsingtao, offering a toast to nobody in particular.

Not a day had gone by over the previous sixteen months when I hadn't thought and talked about the Games. And whenever I did, I was thrilled. I watched the city transform. And now that they were here, and I was seeing them, living them, I felt let down, not because they weren't grandiose and spectacular— they were—but because they would soon be over, and with them would go a major justification for my life in Beijing. It was as if the pillars of my China life—*China Daily*, my friends and colleagues there, Julia, the Olympics—were all gone or going, and without them I had nothing left to lean on.

Over the course of the Olympics I grew increasingly uneasy and was affected by a lingering sadness. It seemed somehow a disappointment that years of effort came down to just a couple weeks—and then what? The stadiums empty, the banners come down, the crowds go home. Would Beijing still be on anybody's radar after the Games? Would it still be on mine?

Sleep deprivation does strange things to a man. I was sleeping an average of about three hours a night, and on some nights I caught maybe an hour or two. I felt like I was the subject of a cruel experiment. On a given day I might drink eight to ten cups of coffee and eat a half-dozen meals. I felt, at times, at the brink of sanity. I needed to drain my bladder every ten minutes, and my personal hygiene was suffering. More than once I caught a whiff of my own body odor on mornings when I slept too late to wash myself and forgot to apply deodorant. The doughnut around my belly was growing by the day.

As time went on, I grew increasingly agitated and lost sight of the fact that, in reality, where I no longer lived, CBC had actually provided me with an incredible opportunity. But more often than not I felt sorry for myself, dwelling instead on the long hours, early morning, menial tasks, and little pay. When I found out that another expat worker doing a similar job was being paid $1,000 more because he'd been hired in desperation at the last minute to fill an empty spot, I almost quit.

My outlet was a young Chinese woman named Hong, who had been hired a year earlier, when she lived in Toronto, to be a sort of cultural liaison. Hong was pretty, and I had immediate fantasies of an Olympics fling from the moment I saw her, although it never came to fruition. Even though we had broken up, Julia was still very much on my mind throughout the Olympics, especially as my mental state veered closer toward instability.

Hong's job in Canada had been to prepare background information on Beijing and China, and to coach the talent on how to pronounce Chinese words and names, a task at which she failed miserably. During the actual Olympics the CBC had little use for Hong, and although she was still required to come in at dawn, she spent most of the day sleeping in a bed she had made for herself in the studio used for the late French-language broadcast.

In between our two shows, when we had a short break, Hong and I would go outside for cigarettes and I would vent. I think she liked the drama.

"You should just quit," she said, egging me on.

"Maybe I will."

"You should. Go for it."

I nodded my head, rehearsing lines in my brain that I might say when I handed in my resignation.

But I didn't quit. Instead, I sulked under my breath and showed up a few minutes later each day to see if anybody would do anything about it. I was going crazy with fatigue. There were other times, though, when I snapped out of it and the gravity of the place and time hit me with full force.

One evening after work, for example, I went with a friend to the Bird's Nest to watch the men's hundred-meter sprint final, featuring the aptly named Jamaican extraterrestrial Usain Bolt. We drank cans of Tsingtao and watched one of the Olympics' marquee events. I fell asleep during the heats, but for the final I was wide awake as I watched Bolt obliterate the field, looking back and pulling up with ten meters left, arms raised, crushing his own record time. The crowd was euphoric. We had seen something historic and we knew it. I felt guilty for any bad thought I'd ever had toward the CBC, and I promised I would work harder and without complaint, a promise that lasted about a day.

"Are you watching this?"

It was my friend Will texting. I looked over at the TV screen nearest me and saw the women's triathlon.

"Watching what? Triathlon?" I texted back.

"Liu Xiang," Will wrote. "He's out."

Shocked, I called Will and he told me that Liu Xiang, the Chinese hurdler who had won gold in world-record time in Athens 2004, had pulled out of the Olympics because of an Achilles injury. I went on the newswires to confirm it was true. This was massive—the biggest story of the Olympics—and the CBC had missed it. Why hadn't we cut to it? I wondered. Why are we still broadcasting the triathlon?

"Liu Xiang's out!" I hollered out to everyone around me in the studio.

"Who?" Karen said.

"Liu Xiang. The hurdler. Why aren't we covering this?"

It's difficult to put into context the gravity of Liu Xiang's exit from the Olympics. In China, Liu Xiang was something like LeBron James, Roger Federer, and David Beckham—combined. People adored him. Before the Olympics, a poll asked one million Chinese their wishes for the Beijing Games. Watching Liu Xiang win his second gold medal ranked first. (Holding a successful Olympics was fourth.) In China, Liu's pockmarked face was featured on billboards and advertisements everywhere, for Nike, Lenovo computers, Coca-Cola, Cadillac, a cigarette company, and more.

Of course, I knew Liu Xiang's importance—I had been in China for the previous year—but nobody else in the studio did. I was in disbelief that CBC had not covered his story, or at the very least had not turned to the event after he pulled out. It felt almost like a personal slight—*how could they do this?* I had moved over a notch on the Foreigner/Chinese Identity Spectrum.

I was up from my chair walking up and down the studio, arms flailing like a rabid monkey.

"Why aren't we covering this? This is unbelievable."

None of my colleagues said a word. Some were avoiding looking at me entirely. After a few moments of me raving at no one in particular, one of the technical workers, a thirty-something Canadian who also lived in Beijing, pulled me to the side.

"I don't think you should say anything more."

"Why? This is bullshit. This is the biggest story of the Olympics."

"These people are professionals. They don't like to be told they're wrong."

"But they are wrong."

"Maybe. But do you hear anybody asking your opinion?"

He was right. I sat down at my post, and when my blood settled, I avoided my colleagues' eyes out of embarrassment. CBC hadn't covered Liu Xiang's heat because they didn't care. Sure, I did, but what was a huge story in China was a nonstory in Canada. From then on, I kept my opinions to myself.

I got over Liu Xiang and so did the Chinese. The country went on to win fifty-one gold medals, the most of any country at the

2008 Olympics. The weather improved and every day of the second week was sunny and clear. As the events wound down, the consensus was that the Beijing Olympics were a success. I felt proud for the city I had seen transform over the last sixteen months, and on the last day of the Olympics, as I looked over the Bird's Nest from Ling Long Pagoda one final time, I knew that despite my fatigue, I had made the right choice to work for the CBC.

Still, I was happy the Olympics were over. I was near the end of my tether as a research assistant. One more early morning, one more Egg McMuffin, one more mundane task, and I might have snapped. By the sixteenth and final day of the 2008 Olympic Games, I desperately needed to get drunk. Very, very drunk. I sent out an e-mail to anyone in Beijing who might be up for a party, and as soon as my shift ended, I said goodbye to my coworkers and cabbed to a bar in Sanlitun to watch the men's basketball finals with Will and his girlfriend.

"It begins," I said as I sipped my first Stella Artois as a free man.

My giddiness soon subsided, and I found myself drifting off as a group of us watched the closing ceremony on the patio of the same restaurant where we had watched the opening ceremony. More than once, I fell asleep, my chin resting on my chest before my friends woke me up and reminded me that this was supposed to be my big night, my one chance for a real Olympic party.

We moved to a club called China Doll, and I started passing out in a booth. A friend noticed this and surreptitiously slipped me a little plastic bag filled with white powder, under the table. But after I went to the bathroom for a line, I was hit with a strange anxiety, followed by a moment of clarity when I told myself that for my own benefit I should probably go home. Instead, I ignored my own advice and ordered more drinks.

Rob showed up. We hadn't seen each other in months. We caught up briefly and then he drifted into the crowd. That was the last I saw of him—not just that night but ever.

At one point I ran into a young woman I'd been friends with since my early days in Beijing, and we talked over a few drinks in our booth. Apparently the alcohol and drugs had cocooned my conscience because I managed to push aside any thought of Julia, and the two us soon took a cab to her place. We rolled around on her folded-out futon for a few minutes, but nothing happened. Sixteen days of exhaustion and malnutrition had taken a terrific toll.

I got dressed, apologized, and took a cab home.

I woke early. I was ravenous. It was seven o'clock and I was used to having my third breakfast of the day by then. My heart raced and my brain stung. I felt guilty and slimy about the night before—all of it. I ate whatever food I had left—oatmeal, a cup of yogurt, a banana—and drank half a liter of water before trying in vain to go back to sleep.

I felt awful, and it wasn't just the hangover. As I walked around town that day, it became clear that something was missing. There was a void in post-Olympics Beijing, and it was evident from the moment the Games ended.

I was alone and trying to come up with ways to kill the day, but in the pit of my fattened stomach was the weight of despair. The Olympics, one of the main reasons for coming to China, were done. Whenever I'd felt down in the previous year, whenever I felt lonely or frustrated or had a Bad China Day, I could always say, Oh well, the Olympics are coming. Now they were gone, and so was my girlfriend and most of my friends. Beijing didn't just *feel* like a ghost town, as it had some days that summer; it *was* a ghost town now.

I had a foot massage and went to a movie. On the way home I walked past a busy market, my head in a daze as I watched foreign visitors using their last hours in China's capital to buy cheap goods to give to their friends and family back home, where they would all be in a day or so.

But not me. I was still here. For those of us left in the city, there was a sense of gloom, and it lasted for days, weeks, even months, and throughout that time I had one terrible question always—persistently—lurking in my brain.

What now?

10

Dinosaur Bones and Brothels

In the weeks after the Olympics, my options were limited. As the financial crisis hit in North America, the journalism job market was bleak, and I wasn't enamored of the prospect of going back to the grim existence of a freelancer in Canada. I looked for work in Hong Kong, where a few friends had moved, but heard much of the same. Hiring freezes, layoffs. Apply again in a few months.

I was stuck in Beijing and anxious about what to do. The Olympics had worn me down, and I was slow to get back into the freelance groove. The previous sixteen months had gone by so fast, and I was finding that, as I expected, I was missing the comforts of *China Daily*.

I missed Julia, too. We had stayed in touch over the course of the Olympics, and now that they were over, I decided I would visit her for a week in Moscow. The Russian embassy in Beijing had other ideas, however. Only foreigners with resident permits, which I lacked, could apply for a Russian visa. My travel plans were thwarted, so Julia and I came up with Plan B: a week in Thailand.

Tanned and stunning, she met me at the Bangkok airport, and the next day we traveled to Koh Phangan, a popular island in the Gulf of Thailand and home of the Full Moon Party. We rented a bungalow on a quiet beach, and for a few days I let go of all my apprehension about life in Beijing.

We spent the week swimming, riding around the islands on motorbikes, drinking, and sleeping in. It was heavenly, but with each day the weight of knowing we would soon have to say goodbye again grew heavier. When we parted ways at the airport after seven nights together, neither of us brought up the obvious question—what were we doing? We cried and kissed and said goodbye, and she told me she would come visit me in Beijing during her winter break. We didn't say it, but we were now, unofficially at least, in a long-distance relationship.

While I was still in Thailand, a friend e-mailed asking if I wanted to work for an English-language news magazine in Beijing. The publication, called *Asia Weekly*, was owned by a journalist from England, Jasper Becker, who had lived in China for decades. It covered Asia from the Beijing office and was based on the same concept as the *Week*, a popular British news digest. The pay wasn't great, but it was a respectable publication. I figured I could work at *Asia Weekly* for a few months, continue freelancing in my spare time, wait out the financial crisis, and plot my next move.

I returned to Beijing and started the new job, and for the first time since the Olympics, I felt stable. I had friends at the office and the work was interesting. I restarted Chinese classes with Guo Li, whom I now met for private lessons at a Starbucks near my home. I bought Chinese character flash cards that I carried with me everywhere, flipping through them whenever I had a spare moment. I started thinking of freelance stories I could work on. I was rejuvenated.

Three weeks later, the magazine folded.

Asia Weekly had been in financial trouble for some time, and Jasper spent months trying to secure financing. When the last of a string of potential deals fell through, he decided the magazine couldn't continue. Perhaps down the road he might bring it back to life, but for now it was being shuttered.

The afternoon Jasper told us he had run out of money and was suspending publication, the staff went to a bar in Sanlitun and drank beer and tequila shots until we could barely walk. We would worry about work and money later, we figured.

I woke at dawn the next day with a debilitating hangover, no job, no prospects, and no Olympics on the horizon. I had no money left after Thailand and wouldn't until I got my one and only paycheck from *Asia Weekly*. My roommate, Jon, had recently left the city and I was covering the rent at Comrade Wu's place by myself. After a year of being financially comfortable at *China Daily*, and with a steady flow of funds throughout the summer, I would now need to call my parents and ask for help. I struggled to get back to sleep as questions swirled around in my foggy brain. *Why am I still here? What am I doing with my life? What should I be doing?* These questions were too big to answer—I didn't even know what I wanted to do with my morning. Beijing felt empty again after a short reprieve. A long winter awaited.

Once again, my options were few. There are three kinds of work for a foreign journalist in Beijing: state media, such as *China Daily*; international bureaus, which are sparsely staffed and tough to crack; and freelancing. With no desire to reenter the state media and no job offers in international media, I reluctantly resumed my career as a freelancer.

The staff of *Asia Weekly* continued to go into the office after the magazine folded, a way to provide us newly unemployed a semblance of routine. One of the magazine's editors was Tom Mackenzie. Tom was the same age as me, from the United Kingdom, Jude Law–handsome and with a good reporter's instinct. We had met through friends on my first weekend in Beijing, a year and a half earlier. Tom had arrived in the city in early 2006 and, like me, had put in his time in state media before joining *Asia Weekly*. Tom and I got along well and had become good friends over the summer.

Only minutes after Jasper told us he was closing the magazine, as the staff absorbed the news in silence, Tom popped his head over his computer and called my name from across the office.

"Mitch," he said. "Trip?"

I didn't know what he had in mind—or how I would pay for it—but I didn't care. I was in. We decided we would report a few stories while on the road, but which stories, and where, we had no idea. After a few brainstorming sessions, we were still without a plan.

Tom and I realized this trip would have to be more than just an adventure. We were both in our late twenties and not where we wanted to be in our careers. Tom wanted to be in broadcasting; I wanted to be writing features for international publications. We both knew that to take our careers to the next level we needed to establish names for ourselves, and we felt like we were running out of time. Whatever stories we were going to report, they needed to be good.

A week after he shuttered the magazine, Jasper took the *Asia Weekly* editors for lunch. He apologized for what had happened and said he was confident we could all make it as freelancers if we resold our stories in different markets.

"Don't look for stories that all the foreign press is doing," he told us. "Make sure to repackage the stories and sell them three, four times. And remember, sex sells."

Sex sells . . . Back at the office after lunch, Tom and I thought about sexy stories we could sell. And then it came to me: Maggie's—the nightclub frequented by lonely expat businessmen, certain *China Daily* foreign experts, and Mongolian prostitutes.

Maggie's, which had recently reopened after being shut down throughout the Olympics, had never brought me anywhere near sexual temptation. The few times I'd gone there left me feeling depressed and guilty, but ever since the night of Potter's birthday party, I had been curious about the club and the Mongolian women who frequented it. I had never spoken with any of the Maggie's girls about anything substantial, but I wanted to know their stories. Why, with so many available Chinese women, so many *poor* Chinese women, were the working girls who populated Maggie's, the Den, and other hookup bars in Beijing frequented by expats Mongolian? How did they end up in China? What brought them? Maggie's had been closed during the Olympics, and rumors had surfaced about several murdered Maggie's regulars, all Mongolian prostitutes. It was a story waiting to be written.

Tom and I did some research online. We found the U.S. State Department's Trafficking in Persons report and read that trafficking was a growing problem, with between 3,000 and 5,000 Mongolian women and girls lured or forced into prostitution in foreign countries each year. Many were recruited by deceit, often by friends and relatives, and the vast majority ended up in China. Many came to the bars and karaoke rooms of Beijing, Shanghai, and other major Chinese cities; others ended up farther south, in the saunas and casinos of Macau, the Las Vegas of Asia.

We found a story posted online by a nongovernmental organization about human trafficking in a city on the Chinese side of the Mongolian border, called Erlian. Neither of us had heard of it. We learned that Erlian was known for dinosaur bones discov-

ered in a dried salt lake in 2006, and that it was the city in which
the trans-Mongolian train—en route to Ulaanbaatar, Mongolia's
capital, and Moscow—stopped to switch gauges.

According to the story, Erlian, a thriving oil town, was also a
major human trafficking hub, the first stop before victims traveled farther inland, and the last stop for human trafficking victims, who, fearing discrimination at home, had no other place
to go after being trapped in brothels abroad. The article told of
streets in Erlian lined with brothels and of abused trafficked
women who lived and worked in tiny, filthy apartments.

Tom and I searched the Internet for any similar articles written in the mainstream press. We found nothing. This was a great
story, we thought, and we started plotting our strategy to report
it. We drew up a list of potential contacts and threw out a few
possible dates for a trip to Erlian, where we would, somehow, get
into the brothels and find trafficking victims.

Tom and I contacted several NGOs to find out more. They confirmed the problem and filled in some of the blanks. Most of the victims were uneducated and desperate for a way out of poverty. Some
were already prostitutes but had been misled about pay and con-
ditions; others were enticed by advertisements in local newspapers
promising overseas scholarships or vague offers of employment. Recruiters usually had contacts in destination countries—often women
who had once been trafficked themselves.

As soon as the women reached their destination countries,
NGO workers told us, they were routinely abused, physically and
mentally. Many were beaten, forced to take drugs, raped, and
repeatedly sold. Trafficked women often found themselves in a
system of "trapped bondage," in which employers demanded re-
payment for travel and other costs. The debts could be crippling.
Some girls ran away, but most, lacking money, travel documents,
and help of any kind, were forced to stay for several years.

Some women who found their way back to Mongolia continued to suffer. Many needed counseling for depression and treat-
ment for sexually transmitted diseases. They were shunned by
their families. With no work experience and few options, some
returned to what they knew, becoming traffickers themselves or
returning to prostitution in cities like Erlian.

Our plans continued to move forward. Tom contacted a friend
of his named Esso, a former Mongolian journalist who lived in
Beijing, where she was raising her two teenage sons. She would
come along as our translator.

We got in touch with a photographer, Jim Wasserman. Jim
was a forty-six-year-old from Philadelphia who had worked for
news outlets around the world. He'd been freelancing in Beijing
for three years. We decided to meet at a bar in the Holiday Inn
in Lido, a place known as a hangout for Mongolian prostitutes.
Over beers, we told Jim about our idea—travel to Erlian and later
south to Macau to write a story we hoped to publish in a major
American outlet. He was up for it.

In an attempt to get a head start on our reporting, we tried
talking to some of the Mongolian girls who had gathered in the
bar. They were happy to chat, but not about their stories.

"This could be tough," Tom said.

In truth, I wondered if we would be able to get the story at
all. We didn't know what we would discover in Erlian, and I was
skeptical that we would even find trafficking victims, let alone
get them to talk to us. But jobless and broke, I figured we had
nothing to lose.

"Don't worry," I lied, taking a sip of my pint. "We'll figure it
out."

The night bus from Beijing to Erlian smelled of feet and body
odor and cigarette smoke. Passengers sprayed cans of air fresh-

ener to mask the cocktail of odors, but to no avail. It was after midnight and outside it was cold and black.

There were about fifty other passengers on board, most of whom were speaking Mongolian. They carried with them large red, white, and blue plastic sacks wrapped in masking tape and packed with cheap goods bought from Beijing markets to sell back home, across the border.

Everybody was crammed into rows of bunks. I couldn't sleep. Lying at awkward angles trying to squeeze my stretched frame into the tiny bed, I tried to read a book to the glow of a pocket flashlight held between my teeth.

We arrived in Erlian at 5 a.m. in the dark and cold, still in China but barely. A cabbie took us to a hotel. When the night attendant showed us a room, cockroaches scurried under the beds. I had stayed in hostels with cockroaches and worse in my travels, but after the long and sleepless bus ride, I needed something more comfortable. We all did. The second hotel the driver showed us was passable, with clean rooms and hot showers. Beside the beds in our rooms was a sex kit with condoms and various pleasure enhancing ointments—the first sign of Erlian's sex trade.

After a few hours of sleep, we set off for the city's market. Within minutes, we were approached by two gnarled old Inner Mongolian women with black teeth who asked if we were looking for girls. It was before noon. We told them no but asked where we would find them. On the north side of town, they told us, on Golden Bridge Street.

We continued walking through the city. In Erlian's center square was a statue of a naked woman with flowing hair holding a globe extended in a palm, the paint chipped and yellowing. It's the kind of kitsch you expect to find in China's forgotten cities, but this one stood apart from the statues of Mao and other heroes of Chinese history. We asked locals what it was supposed to symbolize. The beauty of Mongolian women, they told us.

Around the corner from the square was the town market, a heaving place where dozens of Jeeps were parked, loaded with goods, drivers standing nearby, smoking, waiting to make one of the many daily trips across the Mongolian border. We hired a taxi driver to take us around town for the day, a thirty-three-year-old ethnic Mongolian named Havar. We asked him questions and he answered in Mongolian, via Esso. Yes, there are Mongolian girls here, he said, "many, many girls." Havar said the girls cost about 300 yuan—fifty-five dollars—for the night, but the price drops significantly depending on the their age and "experience."

We asked Havar to take us to the brothels. He pulled up outside a police station around the corner from the red-light district, Golden Bridge Street. A large arch marked the street's entrance. We decided that the four of us together would attract too much attention, so Esso and I would go in first to see if we could talk to anybody, and Tom and Jim would go in later.

It was a bright afternoon and Golden Bridge Street was showing signs of life. In glass-fronted rooms, women of varying ages were curled up on couches, yawning and watching television. Some swept floors and cleaned windows lined with dolls and stuffed animals; others walked over to a grocery store down the street to buy cigarettes and bottles of green tea. Every few minutes, a taxi pulled through the tall archway at the mouth of the street, next door to the police station, to drop off a girl who had worked through the night.

I was nervous walking down the street, very aware of my own presence. We had not seen any Westerners in town, and there I was, tall and obvious, walking down a street lined with brothels in the middle of the day. I felt as though everybody was watching me, but when I looked around at the women in the windows, and the groups of men in leather jackets smoking and talking, I noticed that nobody was paying attention at all.

Esso, young-looking in her late thirties with long, straight black hair, stopped in front of a room where several girls lounged on stained couches.

"Do you want to talk to them?"

I hesitated. "I don't know. Do you think they'll talk?"

"Come on." She grabbed my arm and swung open the front door.

The room was littered with ashes and cigarette butts. A puppy played with a chunk of chipped drywall on the floor and drank from a bowl of curdled milk. Sitting under a poster of a half-naked American blond, three young women smoked Esse Light cigarettes on two small couches.

The girls inside barely looked up when we walked in. It seemed as if they had just gotten out of bed, hair disheveled and wearing baggy sweaters and sweatpants. Esso told them we were journalists working on a story and that we wanted to ask them a few questions.

One of the women—chubby, with heavy makeup, green nail polish, and dyed auburn hair—shrugged. "Okay," she said.

Her name was Alimaa. She was twenty-three. She told us she worked late the night before and was exhausted today. Two years earlier, in Ulaanbaatar, she and a friend were recruited by two men to work at a karaoke bar in Beijing. When she arrived in the Chinese capital, her recruiters told her she had to work as a prostitute. They made it clear she didn't have a choice.

"They took us to different rooms in a hotel and showed us Chinese girls who had been raped," she said as Esso translated and I wrote in my notebook. "They said, 'Take a look, this is what will happen if you don't do this.'"

I took notes furiously, trying to capture all the details. This is exactly what we needed for our story, and we were getting it in the first interview. There is a certain numbness a journalist gets when reporting a story like this. You're transcribing horrors into your notebook, but not really processing it; it's like a surgeon desensitized to blood. I could hear Alimaa's story, but I couldn't feel it. Later, I would feel terrible for her and others like her, but for now I was focused on one thing: getting the story.

She went on. After Alimaa was brought into the hotel in Beijing, she slipped her passport in her boots and, later that night, escaped. For two days and nights, she hid at a construction site before a Mongolian contact in Beijing brought her to Erlian. Broke and with no place to go, Alimaa started working in a brothel. She had been in Erlian ever since.

Another woman in the room, named Gerlee, a twenty-two-year-old with a round face, rosy cheeks, and a faded tattoo of a heart on her shoulder, explained the economics of the job. She gave 30 percent of what she made to her boss, a pint-size Chinese man who came in and out of the brothel throughout the conversation, seemingly oblivious to our presence. The boss paid the rent and the girls lived in the back room. When I asked her if she felt trapped, Gerlee, who came to Erlian after a falling-out with her Inner Mongolian boyfriend, said, "I'm just looking for money. It doesn't make it good or bad."

Esso and I thanked them and walked back to the car.

"That was incredible," I said, sitting down in the backseat of Havar's car. "We got it."

I relayed Alimaa's story, and when I was done, Tom and Esso went back into Golden Bridge Street to do more interviews while Jim and I went for a walk. Jim was eager for the soft afternoon light to hit so he could go back and get photos. I pushed out the uneasy feelings from what I'd just heard; I was experiencing the rush of knowing we had a good story. During our walk, I fell partway into a sewer and thought for a minute I'd broken my leg.

We spent that afternoon making trips in and out of brothels, and Jim went back alone to take photos. The rest of us sat in Havar's car, driving slowly up and down Golden Bridge Street, watching the scenes unfold on the street and inside the windows. The women posing, trying to lure customers. Men strolling by, hands in pocket, checking out the selection. It felt like we were undercover cops, and it was both thrilling and shaming.

Later, Havar drove us to the outskirts of town. There were dozens of apartment blocks, brand-new, sprawling, and bought with oil money. A high school had just been built and looked as though it belonged in Orange County, complete with a soccer field made with artificial turf. Erlian was a strange town, wealthy and depraved, and I felt the twisted pride of a traveler who has somehow ended up in a place he doesn't belong.

The next morning, while we were walking around the town square, the same two black-toothed Inner Mongolian women approached us. They had dark, leathery faces and sucked on sugar cubes.

"You want girls?" one of the women asked us via Esso. "I can get you some for three hundred yuan each. They can go to your hotel room."

We said no and asked her if she knew how the girls ended up here. She said that trafficking was getting harder; in the previous year, border police had stopped traffickers bringing twenty-four women into China. Still, she said, the trade was thriving. "Many, many girls work here. Some girls know they will be working as prostitutes," she said. "Some don't."

The second woman brushed up beside Esso.

"Are you Mongolian?" she asked. "Can you find us girls? It's good business. If you can find us five girls, the brothel owners will pay you two thousand yuan each."

Esso politely declined.

None of us wanted to take the night bus back to Beijing. We agreed to pay Havar 1,000 yuan—about $160—to drive us back to the city, an eight-hour trip. We drove past the Statue of Mongolian Beauty downtown and continued out by the new apartment buildings and the high school. Outside of town, we passed crude statues of dinosaurs—a brontosaurus, a T. rex, a triceratops—built to commemorate the bones found in the bed of a dried salt lake.

We talked excitedly about how good a story we had, congratulating ourselves on a great job. Later, when telling friends about the trip, I would feel guilty about not feeling guiltier while I was in Erlian, speaking with women with crushed lives—guilty about the life I led compared to the lives of the women we interviewed.

Havar drove us to Beijing in his shitty little car—some Chinese brand I'd never heard of, a rust bucket that felt on the brink of collapse at all times. The seats were too small, but I was used to this after a year and a half in China. I rested my knees on the dash and watched the sun set over the grassy Inner Mongolian plains.

A few weeks later, Tom and I took the train to Guangzhou, in the Pearl River delta, twenty-four hours from Beijing. We spent the train journey reading books and talking about our story and trip and future plans. We were embracing new identities as freelance writers abroad. It felt like we were the stars of our own films.

Jim flew down and met us in Guangzhou, and the three of us took a two-hour bus to the gambling mecca of Macau, the former Portuguese colony turned Las Vegas of Asia. We came to report the second half of our trafficking story, but we had no idea how to do it. NGO workers had warned us that Macau could be a violent place, and nobody with a vested interest in the sex trade would be pleased with three foreign journalists wandering around town asking too many questions.

Macau is an odd town. For centuries it was a Portuguese colony, but it had been handed back to China in 1999. Because of the same "one country, two systems" policy that allowed Hong Kong to retain relative independence from the mainland, Macau had flourished as a gambling destination. About five times more money flowed through Macau than Las Vegas.

But Macau lacked much of the fun of its American equivalent. The major hotels—the MGM, the Wynn, the Venetian—although flashy and just as impressive as their Vegas counterparts, felt soulless. The restaurants and bars they housed were quiet; the casinos were for serious gamblers only. The bars out on the streets downtown, lit up with neon signs and housed on the ground floors of nondescript office buildings, pumped freezing air-conditioning and brutal European club music through their open windows.

The three of us checked into a fleabag hotel on narrow street in Macau's old city. We were on the main island, a few miles but a world away from the glitzy hotels on the Cotai Strip, and we spent the first day wandering our neighborhood.

The buildings were in disrepair. Air conditioners leaked onto the sidewalks below, staining the walls of buildings as the drops of water snaked their way down. There was a rustic feel to the old city, where people ran small shops at street level and gathered on benches to talk and smoke. It was a mix of Portuguese and Cantonese. The food was delicious—we ate at a Portuguese restaurant that served chicken with rice, salted fish, warm bread; and at a Cantonese hole-in-the-wall offering dumpling soup and slices of duck. The city seemed stubbornly nostalgic, proud of its past and unsure of the new reality of gambling dollars and private jets.

We walked through thick crowds on the cobblestone streets of Senado Square in the center of the old city, a UNESCO World Heritage Site, not far from churches and houses of worship from several different faiths. From certain streets in the old city, we could see the Grand Lisboa, the gold-windowed, lotus-shaped abomination that served as a line in the sand between the old, quaint, charming old city and Asia's Vegas.

We walked over to the Grand Lisboa, through its packed casino floor, and across a sky-walk to its predecessor, the Casino Lisboa, a Macau institution built by gambling magnate Stanley Ho in 1970. The Casino Lisboa was a gaudy, shiny, sparkly freak show, with garish chandeliers and men in terrible suits and women with big hair wearing too much perfume. The Lisboa felt like the set of a Coen Brothers' movie.

"This place is like a shag carpet," Jim commented as he snapped photos, "or like your aunt's house, where everything is covered in plastic."

Signs of the sex trade were everywhere in Macau, ranging from freelance prostitutes trolling the casinos in major hotels to entire floors in smaller hotels dedicated to "saunas." The young women who staffed the saunas came mostly from the Chinese mainland, as well as from Southeast Asia, Taiwan, South Korea, and Mongolia. Many of them were sold to sauna owners and were forced to work. Their passports were confiscated and they were housed in tiny dormitories. If they complained, they would be threatened with violence or rape. The year before, according to one of the NGO workers we'd interviewed, a fifteen-year-old girl's tongue had been cut out by her captors after she sent text messages pleading for help.

In Macau, we arranged to meet a Mongolian woman named Naran, an outreach worker from Ulaanbaatar doing an internship with an international NGO in Hong Kong. She was twenty-four years old, tall and slim, with long black hair and prominent cheekbones. She had spent the previous four months seeking out Mongolian sex trade workers in Macau and Hong Kong, attempting to learn their stories and, if possible, offer help.

"They don't want to speak to me," she said over Cantonese food during our first night in the city. "They worry about getting killed."

Tom asked how she was able to meet the women at all.

"I pretend to be one of them."

"A prostitute?" he asked.

"Yes. I tell them I'm on a visa run from Hong Kong, and when we talk, I ask them about their health and if they feel safe." She went on. "Traffickers control everything about the girls. They threaten to call their families and say they're working as a slut in Macau. The pimps treat the girls as moneymaking machines, and they control them by any means to keep them in debt."

After dinner, Naran walked us around to bars and saunas where she knew Mongolians worked. She stopped outside Eighteen Sauna, attached to the Golden Dragon Hotel. Lights in rainbow colors danced up and down above the entrance next to an illuminated dragon in gold and red. At street level, young men in suits tried to lure customers passing by on the street.

We talked about how we were going to report this. Clearly, it wasn't going to be as easy as Erlian, and the prospect of violence came up when we mentioned to Naran that we were going to try to interview the women. We decided that Tom and I would go into the sauna first and pretend to be customers, and Jim would enter later and try to get photos with a concealed point-and-shoot camera.

Tom and I climbed the stairs inside to Eighteen Sauna. We were greeted by an attendant—twenty years old at most, with a brush cut and a baggy suit—who handed us laminated menus with peeling corners. A "Taiwan Model Massage," the most expensive item on the menu, went for $1,914 Hong Kong dollars—about $250—followed by Korean, Chinese, and Filipino massages, at varying prices. About halfway down the list was a "Mongolian Massage," for HK$1,705.

"We want to see the girls first," Tom said.

"No problem," the young attendant replied.

He grabbed Tom by the elbow and escorted us down a short hallway to the dimly lit bathhouse. The circular room, lined with shower stalls along the wall, smelled of soap, while steam rose from a large, peanut-shaped hot tub in the center of the room, where a few dozen men—mostly Chinese, with a few foreigners—waited, wrapped in red towels.

To electronic music, a line of about seventy women wearing lingerie were paraded before the men, circling the hot tub. Each woman had a number pinned to her bra. I was surprised at how beautiful some of them were. Others seemed drained and withdrawn, and several had bruises on their legs.

The men were quick to choose, walking down the line to stand opposite their preferred girl. They touched and flirted. They had one hour.

Tom and I watched from the doorway, the attendant standing behind us.

"This is even more depressing than I thought," Tom whispered.

The attendant leaned in between us.

"Fifteen percent government tax," he said, tapping his thin index finger on the menu. "Hand jobs are cheaper."

We spent a few more days in Macau, visiting more saunas posing as customers and attending a conference on human trafficking, at which Naran spoke. We had everything we needed and decided it was time to go back to Guangzhou, where we planned to report another story.

On our last day in Macau we took a cab to the Cotai Strip, home to most of the major casino-hotels, including the Venetian, the biggest casino on the planet. We walked around the hotel's cavernous halls; I bought a magazine from a souvenir shop and ate a fifteen-dollar slice of lukewarm pizza from the food court. There was a fake canal snaking through the hotel, with depressed-looking Middle Eastern men rowing gondolas. They offered us rides to nowhere, and we politely waved them off.

For a few minutes the three of us stood on a bridge over the canal and watched it all happen. I thought about the women we'd seen over the last few days. What were they doing right now, I wondered, the girls from the saunas? Did their parents know where they were? Did they have friends here? They were young girls. Did they have plans for the future? Where would they go next—to one of the brothels of Erlian? To Maggie's in Beijing?

I took some coins—a few Macau pataca—from my pocket, made a wish, and tossed them in the water below.

"Let's get out of here," I said.

11

Chocolate City

We wandered the streets and alleys and garbage-strewn crevices of central Guangzhou, the southern Chinese metropolis once known as Canton, on the Pearl River delta, and marveled at what was for sale.

Everything.

There were oversized stuffed animals, Christmas decorations, fake plastic trees, neon signage, buttons, and bulk candy. There were paper, plastic, and reusable bags; stationery, sneakers, and scooters; Jay-Z T-shirts and LeBron James jerseys and pleather jackets. Butchers sold parts of animals I couldn't identify. One shop had the flattened, dried-out face of a dead pig dangling from its awning, like some macabre Halloween mask.

We arrived in Guangzhou from Macau in the middle of the week. We shared a room in a hostel on the south side of the Pearl River. I was on a tight budget, living off my one and only check from *Asia Weekly* and some money I had borrowed from my parents.

That morning, we set out exploring. It was a humming city, the Asia of my imagination. Beijing could be chaotic, but Guangzhou was different: the hot, humid, sweaty mayhem of a southern Chinese city. In the old part, the narrow streets were warrens of chaos lined with palm trees. Overhead, elevated freeways clogged with traffic offered views of apartment towers with barred balconies strung with drying laundry. The new areas displayed the city's growing wealth, featuring soulless apartment complexes, wealthy residents with spotless Audis and Mercedes, and high-rise buildings plucked from the Hong Kong skyline.

Tom, Jim, and I wandered the city that first day, stopping for noodle soup, drifting in and out of shops, and asking the prices of things we'd never buy. My Chinese was lower-intermediate now and I enjoyed the broken banter with shop owners: I feigned anger when they blatantly tried to rip me off, and I walked away once I'd haggled them down to a tenth of the original price.

Guangdong province was nicknamed "the World's Factory." In the fall of 2008, when we visited, it was home to 28,000 industrial firms, including 15,000 overseas-funded businesses. It made 75 percent of the world's toys and 90 percent of its Christmas decorations (in a country that doesn't celebrate Christmas). In Guangzhou, the provincial capital, it was all available directly from the source and at a discount.

Over the years, this access to cheap goods had attracted traders from around the world. When it was known as Canton, the city was China's first port opened for trade with foreign countries. The British, Americans, French, and other world powers settled on a small island called Shamian, and evidence of Guangzhou's colonial history remained in the form of ornate European-looking buildings that housed overpriced, mediocre restaurants, and a Starbucks filled with American couples waiting to adopt Chinese babies.

By 2008 the most visible foreign community in Guangzhou was African. These were the people we had come to meet. What had been a small group of a few hundred traders a decade earlier numbered as of 2008 as high as twenty thousand, according to the few articles we could find. The Africans living in Guangzhou dubbed the community "Little Africa," or "Chocolate City." Its residents came from Nigeria, Senegal, Sierra Leone, Liberia, Angola, Tunisia, and elsewhere. They came to buy jeans, shoes, fake iPods, wigs, makeup, and whatever else they might be able to sell back home.

We thought it was a great story, one of the "big" stories Tom and I were after. Tom had read about the community in a Hong Kong newspaper, but we found that the story hadn't been covered much internationally. It was interesting, counterintuitive, and timely. Trade between Africa and China had been soaring, but most stories focused on the other direction: Chinese involvement and investment in Africa. Both Tom and I were surprised to hear of the scope of Guangzhou's African community. We planned to sell the story to a top-tier publication—the *New York Times*, *Time*, the *Guardian*. Somebody, we figured, would buy it.

Little Africa was actually in two areas near the city center, both surrounding large markets. One area was predominately Muslim, the other Christian. The men (most of the traders we would meet were men) who frequented the markets bought bulk goods that they shipped back to their home countries, where a relative or a friend would distribute them. For the most part, the communities had been allowed to thrive. The markets that catered to them were fully stocked and bustling, and nearby were African bars and African restaurants, unregistered African churches, and African mosques. Many of the traders had lived in Guangzhou for years. Some had settled down with Chinese wives.

But the rising cost of goods, currency inflation, and a faltering world economy had put pressure on Little Africa. Business was suffering. More crucially, China had been granting African traders only short-term visas or denying them outright. Africans who allowed their visas to expire were often imprisoned or forced to pay hefty fines. And the community was facing increased persecution at the hands of police, a crackdown that coincided with a growing number of Africans—eight that year—being sentenced to death for smuggling drugs into China.

We were clueless about how to approach the story. We had no contacts in the city and had done little in the way of preparation. During the afternoon of our first day in the city, we took a taxi to Tian Xiu market in the mostly Muslim area of Little Africa. The market was several stories high and wig shops dominated the ground floor. Barack Obama–wear was popular. He had been elected president a few weeks before, and several shops sold T-shirts and hoodies with a picture of the president-elect, and the words in English, "The First Black Man to Sit in the White House."

We stopped for coffee nearby and debated how to make inroads with the traders. Three white guys wandering a market filled with black guys was enough to draw suspicious glances. We deployed Jim back in the market to take photos, and Tom and I went out to the quieter side streets adjacent to the market to scout out a few people to interview.

On a leafy street just around the corner, two African men were loading large boxes into the back of a van. One was tall and wearing a black T-shirt; the other short with a goatee and a navy sweater. Tom and I walked up and watched them work.

"Hey, what are you guys doing here?" I said, and as soon as I did, I winced, realizing that it was a stupid question, something a cop might say to a suspect in the movies. "I mean . . . what are you up to in Guangzhou?"

They looked at each other. The stocky man in the navy sweater said, "Who are you? Why you want to know?"

"We're journalists, living in Beijing," Tom said. "We're down here doing a story about African traders like yourselves."

They both laughed. "Why you want to do a story?" the man in blue said. "There's no story."

"Maybe. But we're just curious. So what are you guys doing this afternoon?" Tom asked.

"Working," the taller one said.

"What's in the boxes?"

"Why?"

Tom and I exchanged glances. We tried a few more questions and got nothing. This was going nowhere.

"Okay," I said, "thanks for your time."

Tom and I walked back toward the market. We stopped outside a convenience store, bought bottles of water, and sat down on the curb outside.

A tall African man walked by and asked for a lighter.

"Sorry, don't have one," I said. He started walking away and I called out. "Hey, where are you from?"

His name was David and he was from Mali. We talked for a few minutes and he invited us into his store, which was in an alley around the corner from Tian Xiu market.

We took seats on fake leather chairs inside, and he offered us bread and a sugary orange drink. David had a lanky frame and dark skin, and wore baggy jeans and a black hooded sweatshirt. I sat back in the pleather chair and took notes while Tom asked questions.

David had lived in Guangzhou for four years. He liked living there, he told us, and he liked working with Chinese. But rising prices were killing him. He bought whatever he could sell, whatever he could afford.

"G-Star is popular. Diesel. Depends. Depends if you can get the cheap price," he said.

He picked up a folded pair of dark G-Star jeans and tossed them on my lap.

Guangzhou was changing, David said. His friends were leaving. He could only get one-month visas these days, and so he had to leave town every few weeks for Macau or Hong Kong in order to renew his visa. The costs added up.

"It used to be more fun living here, yeah," he said. "This time is not easy. There are many problems, yeah. Sometimes business is good. Sometimes not good. This is business, you know."

We thanked him and exchanged numbers. Tom and I walked back down the street to the market, where Jim was still busy taking pictures. We wandered up to the second floor and browsed the stores.

In one shop, a man sitting relaxed in a chair—the chair back leaning against a wall and his foot resting on a stool—called us into the store. He was a small man with a large, round head, a trimmed goatee, and mini-Afro. He chewed a toothpick.

"You want to buy anything?" he said.

I looked around the store: it had the same hip-hop clothes and Obama shirts as every other store on the floor.

"Not really," I said, running my hand through the hair of a curly black wig.

He laughed. He told us his name was Kimba and he was from Niger. He said he also owned a leather goods store nearby that we should check out.

Tom asked him how his business was doing.

"Look, see for yourself. There are no customers. It's shit."

We asked him why things were so bad, and he blamed the visa crackdown.

"Every night police come and check passports. They go to people's homes and break down doors. They said after the Olympics they'd normalize regulations. That's bullshit." He sat upright in the chair and played with his toothpick. "When I arrived here a year ago, they were welcoming. And you know, there are a lot of Chinese in Africa. In Africa, they are welcomed and they get visas, no problem. But here, it's completely different now."

We thanked Kimba for his time and continued around the market. I thought about what he'd said. While China had been cracking down on visas for all foreigners since before the Olympics, racism did seem to be at play in Guangzhou. At the time there was a current of racism against Africans in China; several times Chinese had told me that they like foreigners "but not *hei ren*"—black people. Before the Olympics, when police were trying to clear Sanlitun of drug dealers, they did so by indiscriminately rounding up African-looking people in the bar district, including the son of Grenada's ambassador.

The next morning we went to Canaan Export Clothes Wholesale Trading Center, in the Christian African neighborhood. The market had opened six years earlier to cater to African traders. It was busy, but several of the shops were closed.

In the loading area we met Chuks, who was counting stacks of jeans with his business partner. Each month the twenty-nine-year-old bought bulk clothing that he shipped back to Nigeria, where his brother sold the goods at a markup. For two years Chuks had run a successful business and created a comfortable life for himself in Guangzhou.

He was well muscled, dressed in a formfitting navy sweater and patterned white vest. He smelled of cologne and had a Stringer Bell confidence to him. He had done well in China, but as he sorted a pile of stonewashed denim, he told us that his good run might be coming to an end. Rising costs were eating into his profits, and the visa crackdown, which traders claimed was often being violently enforced, was making it difficult to do business. He was thinking about going home.

"It's getting worse every day," he told us. "Maybe some Chinese think Africans aren't good. They don't want too many Africans in their country."

Jim took some photos of Chuks, and Tom asked him and his partner more questions. I went into a nearby store that sold coats and asked the owner, a Cantonese man, if I could take a seat and have a rest. Across from me was a young African, leaning back in a chair, his legs stretched out. He was thin and had a shaved head. He nodded as I sat.

The owner offered me a can of Sprite, and I asked the two men how they knew each other.

"Business partners," the Cantonese man said.

The African man nodded again.

"How long have you lived in Guangzhou?" I asked him.

"Few years."

"You like it?"

"I like the girls, man."

"You have a Chinese girlfriend?"

"I have Chinese *girlfriends*. It's too easy, man."

He told me his name was Chris, and he went on to explain, in great detail, how much he liked Chinese women. Eventually I steered the conversation back to his work, and he told me he was thinking about going back to Africa or somewhere else in Asia. He said a friend of his who had let his visa expire had been forced to go into hiding out of fear of the police. The friend had no options—he couldn't work, he couldn't leave. He was worried about going to jail.

"It's fucked, man," Chris said.

It was a sobering experience for me talking to men like Chris.

Having lived through the highs of the Olympics, and experienced the ease and riches of the Western-foreigner lifestyle in Beijing, it was startling to see how greatly the lives of Africans in Guangzhou contrasted with mine. These were the dark sides of the foreigner experience in China, which could be too easily ignored amid the constant circus of expat Beijing.

I exchanged numbers with Chris and thanked the owner for the Sprite. I met Tom and Jim and we continued talking with traders in the market. In interview after interview, we heard the same story, one we would hear over and over again throughout our week in Chocolate City. In markets, mosques, churches, and chicken shacks, the traders told us the same thing: they were getting screwed.

On several afternoons we found ourselves on the grounds of the large cathedral in central Guangzhou. Some days we spoke with the Africans gathered there; other times we took seats on the benches outside and relaxed in the warm air, reading our books or testing ourselves with my Chinese flashcards. By midweek I had developed a stomach bug, so I often ended up lying in the shade, rubbing my belly and running in and out of a bathroom in an annex building beside the church.

One day we met an African man named Austin Jack. He was sitting on a step inside the church gate, reading a Bible. He was tall and broad-shouldered, well dressed, and wore reading glasses. Tom approached him while he read and asked if he'd be willing to talk, and Austin opened up immediately.

He said the church was the only place in Guangzhou where he felt completely safe. "The moment you leave the church grounds, anything can happen," he said. Like so many others, Austin was growing frustrated with the way the Chinese treated Africans, while the Chinese who went to Africa for work were welcomed.

"The Chinese make money from Africa," Austin said, "but they want to stop us from doing the same here. To me, it doesn't make sense."

Austin invited us to attend church with him on Sunday and said we should interview Father Paul, who conducted Mass. He took us to Father Paul's office next door to the cathedral, and we arranged an interview the following day.

Father Paul's upstairs office was large and sparsely furnished, with afternoon light flooding the room from behind his desk. Father Paul was a small Cantonese man with thick glasses and hair parted to the side. Tom and I sat across from him as he served us biscuits and tea and went into a lengthy introduction of himself. His English was terrible, and I often lost the thread of what he was saying. I gathered that he had studied in the Philippines and worked in Guangzhou for three months. There were half a million Catholics in Guangzhou, he said, but his congregation was mostly African. They used the church as a meeting place for community groups, gathering in the crumbling annex next door to play music, sing, and hold prayer groups.

Tom and I asked him specific questions about the troubles his African congregation was having—visa woes, altercations with police, struggles with their businesses. Father Paul soon became evasive, replying to several questions with answers like "I don't know about that."

After less than half an hour Father Paul had had enough of our questions. "If you want to know about them, ask them," he said, leading us out of his office.

That Sunday we attended Mass with Austin. Father Paul delivered the sermon in unintelligible English to an audience of seven hundred African traders. They listened under the cathedral's high ceiling, chandeliers, and closed-circuit television cameras. We sat toward the back, and as I looked around at the rows of black heads, I had one of those moments that occurred every so often in China: when the reality of the situation I was in became needle-point clear—*here I am, in a church in Guangzhou, China, with seven hundred African men*—and I could barely believe it, thankful for whatever it was that led me there. It was for moments like this that I lived in China.

After Mass, the congregation spilled out to the cathedral grounds and into the annex, where they danced to the rhythm of guitar and African drums for much of the afternoon.

One evening, while strolling one of the markets, we met Hugo. Hugo was twenty-nine years old, tall and lanky and dressed in baggy clothing. He was from Aba City, Nigeria, and had a broken leg. He leaned on a cane as he told us the story of how it happened.

"The knock on the door came very early in the morning and I knew straightaway it was the police," he said. "They'd been raiding homes and taking people away since August, so I knew they'd found me. My visa was expired. I jammed the door shut and jumped out of the apartment window."

He landed hard on the concrete below, shattering his right leg. He was in agony.

"The police left me there for ten hours before taking me to the hospital." He had a twelve-inch scar on his leg and what he figured was a permanent limp. But he insisted he wanted to stay in China.

"It's still easier to make a living here than in Nigeria." He sighed. "But it's a frightening place to be."

Throughout our week in Guangzhou, everybody told us we needed to speak to Pastor James. If you were an African in Guangzhou and you had a problem, you called Pastor James. After several

phone calls and much convincing by us, Pastor James invited
Tom and me to meet him at his apartment in a prosperous suburb
a half-hour drive from the city center. No photos.

His wife greeted us when we arrived. She was short and
stocky with her hair pulled back into a ponytail, tight against
her scalp. She seemed nervous and avoided our eyes as she spoke.

"Pastor James is eating," she whispered. She nodded toward
her husband, who was sitting at a table in the kitchen, about five
feet away. He didn't look up, didn't say hello, didn't so much as
acknowledge our presence. "He'll be with you in a moment."

She sat us down on a couch in the living room next to the
kitchen, where Pastor James continued to eat. She put on a DVD
of an African minister delivering a sermon on Revelation 1:5. Tom
and I watched in an awkward silence and Pastor James's wife gave
us apples while we waited. Occasionally, Tom and I exchanged
glances—glances that said, "What the fuck is going on?"

Pastor James—dressed in a red Adidas hoodie, black cordu-
roy pants, and black leather shoes—joined us after another fifteen
minutes. He placed a chair across from us as we sat on the couch,
apple cores in our hands. He was cross-eyed, and when he began
talking, it was difficult to discern to whom he was speaking.

Pastor James was from Nigeria and had preached the Gospel
in Guangzhou since 2004. He used to have a good space he used
for a church, but the authorities closed it down in 2007. Now the
church moved around, sometimes cramming into hotel rooms.

"It's not easy. This is a communist country. Religion is still
underground." He described his role as part pastor, part social
worker. "Every day I receive calls for help from people in trouble," he told us, adding that some Africans bring it on themselves
by "engaging in dubious things," like selling drugs. He said
that most Chinese were friendly and that he had many Chinese
friends. "They just don't want us to spoil their country."

When the interview was finished, Tom and I caught a cab downtown. Pastor James was the last of the interviews we needed. We had spoken with dozens of traders during the week and listened to and recorded their stories. Jim had incredible pictures and we had all the angles covered. We had a great story. Now we just needed to sell it—easier said than done.

We took the train back to Beijing. In our sleeper cabin that night, I watched *The Sopranos* on my laptop and chatted with Tom about our stories. We were both happy to be going back to Beijing, back to our expat fantasy lives. The trips had made me more excited than ever to be living in China, and they helped take my mind off Julia, who was living several time zones away and whom I wouldn't see again for months.

Throughout the trip we marveled at how liberating our freelance lives were. As relatively well-off foreigners in China, we had so much freedom while so many others around us did not. Living in China at times felt like being a spoiled child who was allowed to run rampant. At the same time we had the freedom to escape to the comfort and safety of our lives in Beijing, or to our lives back in Canada, or America, or England.

The day we arrived back in Beijing, I went to a friend's apartment for Thanksgiving dinner, as far away from the miseries of Chocolate City and the Eighteen Sauna in Macau as could be imagined. It occurred to me that this was the nature of expat life as I knew it. Living in a bubble. I could take a peek outside of it, but before long it sucked me right back in.

As fall became winter, Tom and I met every day at Café Zarah, a small coffee shop near the Drum and Bell Towers that served as our de facto freelance office, to work on our pitches. We started at the top, e-mailing *Time*, the *New York Times*, the *Wall Street*

Journal, the *Guardian*, the *Times* of London. Every editor we contacted told us we had great stories, really moving, but just not for them. Good luck elsewhere. We worked down the list of publications, but nobody seemed to want the stories. Sex, it turned out, did not necessarily sell, and neither did the woes of Africans in China. Whatever the case, for several weeks we couldn't find a home for the stories.

These were supposed to be our *big* stories. I had been so convinced they would sell that I became increasingly disillusioned with every rejection. "I just don't know what we're doing wrong," I told my parents over the phone one night.

But, in fact, we had done everything right. We had good stories, we did the research, we believed in our subjects, and we reported them well. And we did eventually sell the stories. The trafficking piece was published in the weekend magazine of the *South China Morning Post*, an English-language newspaper in Hong Kong, and the Chocolate City feature appeared in *GlobalPost*, a start-up Web magazine. Both were solid publications, just not one of the marquee brands we'd been aiming for. I was proud of the pieces, if a bit disheartened, and the trips confirmed for me that China was filled with fascinating and heartbreaking people and places. Even though the stories weren't the monster successes we were hoping for, the trips gave us confidence that we were good reporters and that if we kept looking hard enough, we would find the stories we wanted.

A few weeks later, one of the Africans I'd interviewed in Guangzhou called me. I was riding my bike on the way to meet friends for dinner. At first I couldn't place who he was, but then it clicked. It was the man I'd met in Canaan market—Chris, the cool Nigerian who told me about his fondness for Chinese women as we drank Sprites with his Cantonese business partner.

"He's dead," he told me, his voice distant on the phone. Chris said that a friend of his, the friend he'd told me about that day in the market, the one who had been forced into hiding, had died.

"What happened?" I asked.

"The cops, they came to his home, they chased him, he jumped from the balcony. He was still alive, but nobody helped. The police wouldn't take him to the hospital for twenty-four hours. He died. He fucking died, man. You have to tell people, man. You have to write about this. Can you help? Can you?"

I couldn't. There was nothing I could do, really, except write the story we'd gone to report, a story that would likely have no real impact whatsoever. And suddenly it all felt so futile. We had gone to Erlian and Macau and Guangzhou to tell the stories of people who couldn't tell their own, to expose injustices. But the only thing we had exposed, I felt, was the vast divide between the lives they led, and the ones we did.

12

The Bachelor

"You look like a vampire," Tom said.

"Did you bring that suit? Or was it theirs?" our friend Alex chimed in with a laugh as the three of us drank pints one Saturday afternoon in the winter of 2009. "It's pretty hideous."

I rubbed my temples. A vampire in an ugly suit was not the image I wanted to project as one of *Cosmopolitan* magazine's 100 Hottest Bachelors in China. Unfortunately, Tom was correct; I looked like a character from *True Blood*. The magazine's art department had gone a little heavy with the makeup; my face looked powder-white, my eyes dark, as if I was suffering from a terrible hangover. My hair was jet black and styled to look a little like Charlie Sheen circa *Men at Work*. I wore a navy and white striped shirt under a double-breasted, tan-gray checkered suit. I looked gaunt and smug.

I flipped back to Tom's picture, a page before mine.

"Yours isn't much better, Tom," I said.

Tom's photo, like mine, took up half a glossy magazine page. He looked slightly drunk, with a wide smile and his hands out in front of him, palms down, as if he was performing some kind of mating dance or trying to regain his balance.

"At least I don't look like a corpse," he said.

"I was going for a brooding look."

It was nearing Valentine's Day and the issue—an annual supplement to the Chinese edition of *Cosmo*—had arrived on newsstands across the country. More than one million copies, the editor told us. Beside our portraits were brief bios, including hobbies (mine: watching movies, playing basketball, reading, playing guitar); what we like in a woman (funny, confident, not too tall, not too short); the words we live by ("treasure every day"—which the editors had made up on my behalf); as well as our e-mail addresses.

Before the shoot, Tom and I had made a bet about who would get the most e-mails, which we figured would be somewhere in the dozens. We agreed that the first to reach one hundred e-mails would have to buy the other dinner. We fantasized about receiving e-mails with photos attached of gorgeous, scantily clad women.

The timing was good, too. I was single again.

Earlier that month, Julia and I broke up. For real.

She had visited Beijing for a few weeks that January. It was strange, the first week, to resume a relationship after not having seen each other for four months, but by the second week we were back where we left off.

Before she arrived, I'd imagined us breaking up when she left, but toward the end of her stay, that seemed impossible. On her second-to-last night, however, after we returned from a bar drunk and slightly stoned, she broached the subject.

"Sladki, we need to talk," she said as we lay on the couch in Comrade Wu's apartment. She said that she was nearing thirty and needed to be in a relationship that was going somewhere. With her in Moscow and me in Beijing, that didn't seem likely between us.

I got angry with her for bringing it up at all, even though it was obvious we needed to address our relationship. I had been thinking the exact same thing but, for the last few days, had been trying to push the thoughts aside. "Why would you ruin our time together by saying that?" I said. We went to bed that night with no resolution, and the next day we were too drained to make any decisions other than to wait and see.

We had another teary goodbye at the airport. We hugged for longer, and this time, when I let go, I didn't say I would see her later because the truth was, I didn't believe it. I walked away, and when I got to the bottom of the escalator, I turned back and ran up to see if she was still there, but she was gone.

I took a taxi to a Café Zarah, but I couldn't get any work done. I didn't want this to be it. I didn't want to get married or have kids, but I wanted to be with her. I knew that. I didn't know if I was in love with her, but I felt something like it.

I tried to chase out the thought that we might never see each other again, and then I thought it a cruel cosmic joke that I'd found a girlfriend from Moscow—why Moscow? There were so many places I'd like to live, but not Moscow.

"Either you move to Moscow, or we have to break up," she said, a few weeks later, over Skype. It wasn't exactly an ultimatum—it was the reality of our situation. It had been an agonizing few weeks, stuck in a limbo between knowing we had to break up and not wanting to do it. I couldn't take it anymore, so I'd called her that night to see if we could get some clarity.

"Move to Moscow? I don't even know what I'd do there."

"You can live with me. Can't you freelance here?" she said. "You know I can't come back to Beijing. I need to finish my school."

She told me to take some time to think about it, and I did. For a while, for a few days even, I decided that, yes, I would move to Moscow. Moscow would be my new home. I'd move there for her.

"*Moscow?*" my mom said one morning as we talked over the phone.

"Yes, Moscow. But only for a few years, until she finishes her degree. And then we'll move to Canada."

"How are you going to get her into Canada? It's not easy to immigrate to Canada, you know."

"I don't know. Maybe we'll get married."

Married. This was the first time in my life I had ever uttered that word in reference to myself and in a nonsarcastic way. It scared me to say it out loud. I knew there was something special between Julia and me, and I wish we'd had more time to see where it went. But I wasn't ready for marriage. I wasn't ready to live in Moscow. I barely knew if I loved her.

I was miserable for the next week. I missed her terribly, but I knew we had to end it. One evening, after steeling myself all day, I called her and said I couldn't do it.

The *Cosmo* shoot, like many China adventures, happened randomly. A few months earlier, as we walked out of a coffee shop near the Drum and Bell Towers, Tom received a phone call from a former colleague of his at a local English-language newspaper who was now an editor at *Cosmo*.

"You want me to be one of your bachelors?" Tom said into his phone. "Wow, you must be getting desperate."

"We are," the woman confessed.

Tom laughed into his mobile. She asked him to bring a friend. Tom covered the phone.

"Hey, Mitch, do you want to be in *Cosmo* for their Valentine's special?"

"Really? Don't they need to see my picture first?"

"Do you need to see his picture?" Tom asked the editor.

She did not.

A few weeks later, Tom and I arrived at the *Cosmopolitan* offices in downtown Beijing. A young woman met us in a coffee shop downstairs and escorted us to a studio on the building's top floor, where we were greeted by a photographer from Hong Kong named Leon; Tom's editor friend, Liu Jia; and a makeup artist and hairstylist. We were led over to the wardrobe section of the room, where a dozen men's suits were hanging on a rack behind a curtain.

I tried on a few jackets and held up pants over my jeans. I called over the editor, Liu Jia.

"I don't think these are going to fit me," I said, holding up a pair of pants several sizes too small.

She hurriedly flipped through the rack and pulled out a checkered suit. "Try this," she said, closing the curtain as she left.

The pants were snug and the cuffs of my shirt stuck out several inches from the jacket sleeves. The suit looked like something that might be worn by the pervert cokehead cousin in a mafia movie.

I exited through the curtain.

"Looks good!" the photographer hollered from the set.

"It's not really my style."

"It will have to do," Liu Jia said. "It's the biggest we have."

In the makeup room, a young woman applied beige powder to my cheeks and forehead. The hairstylist, meanwhile, yanked at my unruly hair with a brush. She added water and pulled at it more, trying to slick it back.

"I don't think that's going to work," I said. "My hair's pretty thick."

The makeup artist offered some advice in Chinese. I didn't understand it all, but I got the idea. "Like *Mad Men*," she said.

Once finished, I strolled back into the studio, where Tom was already in the middle of his shoot. I felt queasy watching it. The photographer had Tom doing all sorts of ridiculous poses. Laugh shots. Hysterical laugh shots. Dance shots. Lunging-at-the-camera shots.

Tom seemed to be enjoying it. More than that, he was making it look natural.

I sidled up to the photographer.

"I don't know if I can do this," I muttered. "I mean, I can't do this dancing stuff."

"Don't worry," he said, still snapping shots of Tom. "We'll do what makes you feel comfortable."

We soon discovered that there was only one pose that made me comfortable: serious face, no smile, sitting down, hands resting easily on my legs or in my pockets. The photographer had snapped about forty of these—"Good, good, yes, sexy look, nice"—when Liu Jia approached and demanded more variety.

"Let's try it with a smile," Leon said.

"I look stupid when I smile on camera," I protested.

"Let's just try it. If it's no good, we won't use it."

I smiled.

Leon snapped a shot or two, and then he and Liu Jia conversed quietly in Chinese.

"Okay, let's try it without the smile again," Leon said.

After a few shots he asked me to try standing up. I stood and he laughed.

"Those pants are really tight, ha-ha."

"Yeah, I know," I said, tugging at the material around my thigh. "They were the biggest ones."

We tried a few more poses, some sitting, some standing, hands placed here or there, arms crossed, chin down, face tilted left or right.

"I think we're good," Leon said after ten minutes.

"I'm sorry I couldn't do any better."

"That's okay." He flipped through photos on his camera's screen. "Some people are just naturals. Some people . . . aren't."

I wasn't sure how to take that. "But you've got enough, right?"

"I think so." He paused. "We'll see."

"But you're definitely going to use us in the issue, right?" I asked Liu Jia. "I mean, you already took our bios. You already have our e-mail addresses."

"We'll get in touch," she said, shaking my hand. "Thank you for coming."

Tom and I changed out of our suits and bade farewell to Leon and Liu Jia at the elevators.

I sighed as the elevator doors shut. "Damn it," I said. "They're not going to use me for sure."

So it was with some surprise when I bought the Valentine's issue of *Cosmo* from a Sanlitun newsstand on a chilly afternoon to find my picture on page thirty-six of the Valentine's special. I was thrilled. I might have looked like a vampire, but I was the Don Draper of vampires. I was among the top one hundred hottest bachelors in the most populous country on earth, a country of 1.3 billion people, including about 700 million men. Forget one in a million; I was one in *seven hundred* million. Never mind that I had been asked out of desperation.

After the issue was published, we waited for our flood of e-mails. But the electronic levees held. A day passed, a few days, nearly a week. Neither Tom nor I received a message. We scaled our bet down from first to reach one hundred to first to reach fifty. And then the first to get to twenty-five. First to ten? Whoever got the first e-mail received a pint of beer, we agreed.

Tom got the first e-mail. He rejoiced. I fumed. The next day I received a message from a Yahoo account with the subject line "from cosmo":

Hi, Moxley;

I am ———, come from cosmo. could you make frined with me ?

with the best wishes.

from ----

As the days passed, more e-mails arrived in my inbox, never a flood but a steady stream. Over the next few weeks I received dozens of messages from women named Daisy, Sunny, Coral, Evan, Lucy, Cherish, Princess, and more. Some notes were short and to the point ("hi, I saw your picture"; or, "I am Chinese girl. Do you like China?"), some were complimentary ("I saw you there with mature and polite. I like that kind of guy."), some confusing ("Your name sounds like my favorite Micky, but you looks more serious than him :)~").

Several girls e-mailed both Tom and me the same message, and a couple sent group messages to the entire cohort of one hundred bachelors. Some asked if we could be friends. Some if we could be lovers. One asked me not to call the police on her:

HI

*MY NAME IS ———, I AM A CHINESE GIRL. I AM
A NURSE IN ———, FUJIAN. YOU KNOW FUJIAN.
IT IS VERY BEAUTIFUL, AND I HOPE YOU CAN
COME HERE.*

*OH YOU MAY FEEL SO STRENGE, WHY I KNOW
YOUR E-MAIL. BEAUSE I SAW A BOOK AND IN
IT THERE IS YOUR PICTURE, AND MY ENGLISH
TEACHER COMES FROM THE SAME COUNTRY
WITH YOU, AND DID THE SAME JOB BEFORE.
SO I WANT TO TELL YOU IT, JUST IT. . . . PLEASE
DON'T CALL POLICE, BECAUSE I AM NOT A BAD
GIRL, THANK YOU*

A few were from gay men. One sent photos of himself in
military fatigues. Another wrote from the e-mail address
iamhomo@———.com:

So are you gay or not?

A tiny minority included photos—including one voluptuous
woman (who might have been a man) in a sexy nurse outfit. Each
message was a tiny thrill, and my and Tom's competition intensified. Whenever we received a new note, we would announce it by
yelling to each other across Comrade Wu's place, where Tom had
recently taken a room, or by texting taunting messages.

In the end, neither Tom nor I cracked a hundred; I topped out
at eighty, edging out Tom by a few messages. (He never bought
me dinner.) But with all the online attention, I was gaining the
confidence I needed to tackle the dating scene in the analog world.

The weeks after Julia and I broke up were terrible. I felt gutted. But deep down, I knew I had made the right call. I ached—and would for months to come—but as spring arrived, I grew increasingly comfortable with my newfound independence.

Still, I reentered the dating game with some trepidation. After two years in the capital, I'd learned that dating in China was considerably different from dating in the West. Most foreigners lived in China for a finite period—a few months, a year, a few years—and for that reason the expat lifestyle often felt a lot like college. There was a lot of binge drinking and random hookups. Relationships tended to be short and sweet. Many people, like Julia and me, learned the hard way that maintaining a serious relationship between two individuals from different corners of the globe in a foreign city could be difficult, especially when both parties planned to eventually leave. Once burned, many people, like myself, were wary of making the same mistake twice. As a result, there were a lot of single expats in Beijing. And for a single man in his twenties, it could be a lot of fun.

I don't want to speak about their dating experiences on behalf of foreign women in Beijing, but I can say that many of my female friends complained about the talent pool of foreign men in the city. A few of my best women friends called their pub quiz team "The Goods Are Odd"—"the goods" being Beijing's population of foreign guys, "odd" being the best way to describe them. Beijing did indeed draw a strange assortment of expats, and there was no shortage of young Western men who wanted to use their time in China to mostly get drunk and chase girls.

Foreigner-Chinese dating was a whole other world unto itself. As a disclaimer, I should say that there are many successful, loving, long-term foreigner-Chinese relationships. But in my experience, I found that dating between foreigners and Chinese could be complex and often volatile. The very concept of "dating" is entirely different for many Chinese; in fact, very few actually *date* at all. In the West, a single person might try out different partners without commitment, dating several people at once. Sex is usually introduced into the equation long before there's any mention of "boyfriend" or "girlfriend" or "exclusive" or "relationship," and most definitely before "love."

In China, it can be the *exact* opposite. "Love" might be uttered at the very beginning of relationship, via text message, or in wild, teary declarations after the first date. In the West, couples ease into relationships; in China, they dive in headfirst. A lot of foreign men living in China take advantage of this dynamic, but the aftermath is usually nasty. I tried my best to avoid dating anyone who was interested in a serious relationship when I wasn't, but I learned the hard way, more than once, the stark differences between East and West concerning matters of the heart.

Not long after I had arrived in China, almost two years earlier, I met a nice young woman with the English name Mary who attended business school at the university across the street from *China Daily*. She was pretty and smart and spoke perfect English. We met one Saturday night at the Noodle Shop, while my friends and I were drinking at a table across from her and some of her classmates. My initial intentions were straightforward: to take her home. She withstood my initial charms but agreed to meet me for coffee later that week.

After I sobered up and we went for our coffee, I knew that we wouldn't be more than friends. She was sweet, but she was too young and a bit naïve and I didn't want to take advantage of that. We met for coffee a few more times, and one evening we went for a stroll by the polluted river near *China Daily*. She told me about her family and friends and said she was moving to Shanghai after graduation to work for a European shipping company.

She complained openly about the Chinese government, and I was surprised by her hostility toward it.

"You know, a lot of students apply for Communist Party membership. But I didn't."

"Why not?"

"Because I don't believe in it."

"Really? Do you think China would be better off with a democracy?"

"Of course it would be better. I think ninety-five percent of Chinese people believe that."

I enjoyed talking to her and regretted that she was moving. We could have been friends, I thought. But I could tell she was thinking differently. She seemed to be looking for some assurance that I found her attractive.

We walked back to the university and sat on a bench near the basketball courts. She was silent for a few moments and then turned to look at me.

"Can I ask you something?" she said.

"Okay."

"What do you think of me?"

"I think you're great."

"Do you like me?"

"Sure, I like you, but to be honest, I'm not looking for a relationship or anything."

She looked toward the empty basketball courts.

"So we're friends, right?" she said.

"Yeah, we're friends."

A few days before she left for Shanghai, we went for coffee at the university. I wished her luck, shook her hand, and we said goodbye.

Later that night, I was playing pool with Rob in Sanlitun

when my phone rang. The voice on the phone explained that she was Mary's friend.

"Where are you? Mary is very drunk," she said. "She wants to talk to you."

"Me? Why?"

"I don't know. She just says she wants to talk to you. She's very drunk."

"I think maybe you should take her home and have her call me tomorrow."

A few minutes later, Mary called me herself. She was weeping and said she had to see me right away. She said she was downstairs from the bar I was in, waiting for me.

When I found Mary in the busy alley below, she was almost hyperventilating. Her eyes were red and makeup-smeared.

"Whoa, what's wrong? Why are you crying?"

She took a few deep breaths.

"What?"

"I . . . I . . . love . . ."

I knew it was coming, but I tried to stop it anyway.

"Please don't say—"

" . . . you."

She started wailing. "I have to tell you this. I love you."

"But . . . but we've only known each other for two weeks. And we're not even dating. We're just friends. Remember? We talked about it."

"I know," she said between flustered breaths, "but I feel like . . . we're more than . . . just friends."

"Even if we *were* more than just friends—which we're not—you're moving to Shanghai in a couple of days."

"I thought . . . we could do . . . long distance."

"Long distance? No, that's not an option."

The floodgates were opening. I didn't know how to handle the situation so I stiffened up and leaned against a railing, waiting for her to stop. After a few minutes, she calmed down and dried the tears from her eyes.

"Can I ask you a question?" she said.

"Uh, I'm not su—"

"Did you ever like me?"

"Yes, I like you. But just as friends."

"Okay," she said, sniffling. "Friends."

We shook hands, as friends, and never saw each other again.

Nearly two years later, the first date I went on as a newly single man in Beijing—not to mention one of China's 100 Hottest Bachelors—was with a girl named Mei Mei (which means "Beautiful Beautiful" in Chinese). It was a disaster.

Mei Mei was a Beijing socialite and had a reputation of dating guys with money, something I decidedly did not have. We had met through friends the previous year but had barely spoken the few times we'd bumped into each other. She was the type of girl who when she walked into a bar all eyes turned to her, and not always in a good way. The kind of girl whom guys fantasized about and women loathed. She wore laughable outfits, a ton of makeup, and carried herself with an air of condescension. She was intimidating, and maybe because of that she was surprised when I asked her out for dinner out of the blue one night. (I was slightly inebriated.) She said yes and a few days later, I texted her to arrange a time.

We met outside Workers Stadium. As she stepped out of her car, my heart started pounding. She was wearing jean shorts that were the size of panties. Six inches of her tiny belly were exposed. A belly-button ring glittered. Her heels were four inches high, and she had fake eyelashes extending off her eyelids like hair combs. She looked absolutely, totally, 110 percent absurd.

I panicked for a second at the idea of one of my friends spotting us together. Thinking on my feet, I suggested we go to a Chinese-owned Italian restaurant across the street, where, after two years in Beijing and many times passing by the establishment, I had never seen more than one or two patrons dining at a time.

She agreed. I exhaled.

I ordered spaghetti; she ordered a lasagna she didn't eat and coffee she didn't drink. She spoke virtually no English, and I ran out of things to talk about in Chinese after fifteen minutes. I was still taking lessons with Guo Li almost every day, but my conversational abilities remained limited. For the next forty-five minutes Mei Mei smoked cigarettes and texted her friends on her iPhone, while I twiddled my thumbs and prayed for it to all be over.

A few weeks later, I went out with a former Miss China contestant who called herself Angel. She hosted a show on Chinese television and we met at a magazine party. The following week, we went on our one and only date, in the same bar where we'd met. I was feeling melancholic that night and didn't really want to go on a date. I was tired and wanted nothing more than a massage and a movie, but I pushed through anyway, for the story of going out with a Miss China contestant, if nothing else. I arrived early and ordered a glass of wine. She arrived an hour late; I was on my third glass. As soon as she walked in and sat down on the stool beside me, I knocked over my wineglass and it smashed on the bar, sending small pellets of red wine onto her dress. We parted company after an awkward hour. That was the last I saw of Angel.

Eventually I got the hang of being single in Beijing again, and I enjoyed it, mostly. But more often than not I just never felt on the same page with the Chinese women I went out with. That's not to say I didn't meet a lot of intelligent and charming Chinese girls. I did; I just found it difficult to bridge the cultural, not to mention linguistic, gap. And I shudder to think what many of them thought of me. When I went on dates and had to use my Chinese, I became Tall Rice, and I found Tall Rice's charms to be limited with the opposite sex. Whereas Tall Rice was quick to make people laugh with his poor Chinese and could break the ice like no other, being slow and stupid only went so far with women.

So I mostly went out with other foreigners, but I didn't find anything serious after Julia. I enjoyed the freedom of living in China, and because I was always in Beijing on a rolling basis—maybe another six months, maybe a year—it never seemed to make sense to enter into a long-term relationship. At least that's what I kept telling myself.

My extended bachelorhood was good news for my friend Ola, who was looking for single men to put in a bachelor auction that summer. Ola was from Poland and ran an event planning company that focused on things like speed dating. We had met through a mutual acquaintance the year before and became quick friends. She had invited me to her singles events on many occasions, and I always declined. I initially turned down her request to do the bachelor auction, too, but eventually capitulated.

Ola was thrilled. I was skeptical.

"Oh, come on. It'll be fun," Ola said. "Plus, it's for charity."

I tried to back out more than once, but Ola kept playing the fun/charity card. A few days before the event, I met with her and her business partner, Allison, at Café Zarah, and they peppered me with questions that would be used for my onstage Q&A. Questions like "What's the most romantic thing you've ever done?" and "What's a secret nobody knows about you?"

My answers were weak, and Ola and Allison exchanged worried glances.

"Come on, Mitch, just answer truthfully," Ola said.

"These questions are crap," I said. "If you had better questions, I'd give you better answers."

"Look, if you *really* don't want to do this, we won't force you," Allison said, her brow furrowed.

I sighed. "No, it's fine. I'll do it. It's for charity, right? Okay, a secret nobody knows about me . . . I like to watch romantic comedies on airplanes."

"That's good," Ola said, scribbling my answer.

The idea of a bachelor auction terrified me. Standing in front of a crowd of women like a circus monkey while they bid on what would surely be the most awkward date ever did not seem appealing, despite Ola's assertions that it would be "fun."

On the night of the bachelor auction, I guzzled pints of Stella as the crowd started to form. Ola instructed me to "go mingle," but, instead, I just chatted with a fellow bachelor who was as nervous as I was. I'd brought a few friends to watch: Kathleen and Michelle, two women I had met through friends in the first few months I was in Beijing. They came more or less to watch me squirm, and they seemed to relish the fact that I was so nervous. When they saw that I wasn't only nervous, I was *terrified*, they tried to comfort me. "Oh, you'll do fine, don't worry," Michelle said.

It didn't help.

The first bachelor went for 800 yuan, about $125. The next went for a disappointing 300 yuan. Only two women bid on him, and I could tell from offstage that he was embarrassed and angry, which is exactly how I would feel—and might feel in a few minutes, since I was up next.

The whole Q&A portion was a blur, and it seemed to me that nobody was paying attention. After my answer about rom-coms on airplanes, the bidding began.

There was a brief pause.

"Two hundred yuan!" someone yelled.

I couldn't make out who it was under the spotlights. Another pause.

"Three hundred!" another woman yelled.

I recognized that voice.

"Three hundred yuan? Come on, ladies, we can do better than that!" the host, Allison, said into the mic.

A long pause.

"Four hundred!"

A *looooong* pause.

"Five hundred!"

There was a bidding war between two women. Two women I knew. Two women who were at the auction entirely on my behalf.

The bidders were my two friends, who, it struck me all at once, were saving me from the humiliating fact that no one else was bidding. Thank you, Kathleen and Michelle.

Kathleen won out at seven hundred yuan. I hopped off the stage and hugged her.

"That was awful," I said. "I need a drink."

"You owe me," she said.

It turned out I wasn't one of the hottest bachelors in China, after all.

13

The Beijinger

"Hello. My name is John," I said—slowly, painfully, enunciating every . . . single . . . syllable. "I like *tig-ers*."

My voice-recording partner, Kristin, wasn't paying attention. I cleared my throat. She poked her head up and leaned toward the mic. "My name is Jane. I like pandas."

"Question," I said, reading from the text in front of me. "What animal does *John* like?"

By the spring of 2009, this is how I was making much of my money. I was writing the odd article, but without a consistent gig I needed extra income, and voice recording provided it. It was a common part-time job for native English speakers in Beijing, and it was remarkably easy. Tom recorded once in a while and had referred me to his boss, who went by either Mr. Wang or Wang Shushu (Uncle Wang), an affable fifty-something with a head of dyed-black hair.

It turned out I was quite good at voice recording—"You have strong voice," Uncle Wang told me after my tryout shift. Basically, the job entailed sitting in a studio reading English texts that would be put on CDs and used in schools and universities throughout the country. Millions of Chinese were learning English, and voice recorders were in high demand. I recorded three or four times a week, four hours at a time, and was paid about fifty dollars an hour for my efforts.

Uncle Wang was a great boss. He used to be a medic in the army but now made his living working sometimes sixteen hours a day in the recording studio. He had a wife and son, but he told me he didn't like going home. "Come to work is very interesting," he said, in broken English. "Money, money, money."

The problem was, voice recording was boring to a degree I never imagined possible. The studio was a stuffy little room built into an apartment Uncle Wang rented. Occasionally, when my partner was reading a monologue, I could take a minute break and read a page of a book, but the rest of the time we recited mind-numbing dialogues and stared at a computer screen Uncle Wang had placed in front of us so we could check our voice levels and recording time. More than once, I suggested to Kristin that physicists should study the space-time continuum in that room: four hours felt like a geological epoch.

As dull as I found voice recording, it kept me in the life-style to which I had become accustomed. Mine was an easy life that included sleeping until I felt like getting up; long, slow days reading and writing in cafés; an hour here and there at the gym; Chinese lessons; evenings having dinner and drinks with friends or going for indulgent, two-hour, ten-dollar massages (no happy endings). Weekends were a boozy haze; Fridays and Saturdays, without question, were nights out, either at bars or clubs or house parties or all three. There were birthday parties and going-away parties and coming-back parties and (insert excuse for party here) parties. Once in a while, I would head down to Shanghai or Hong Kong for out-of-town parties. Sometimes it felt like life in China was one big party, and it was thanks to voice recording that I was able to keep it all going. Just barely.

Expat life was a never-ending adventure, and for the most part, I loved it. My circle of friends was growing. My freelance assignments, although not enough to pay the bills alone, kept me motivated, and my Chinese continued to improve. One day I remarked to Tom that I was the happiest I'd ever been in Beijing. China was addictive, and as I celebrated my twenty-ninth birthday that April, I wondered if I was too hooked now to break that attachment.

But in the midst of it all I would still get sharp pangs of reality. Once, around my birthday, I woke in the middle of the night in a state of panic and realized that I had only a year left in my twenties, that I was nowhere near where I wanted to be in my career—I had published only a handful of stories so far that year—and that I was still living a life with little responsibility, with no money, no job, no girlfriend, and no semblance of what I had once perceived as a normal life, before I got to China.

My heart was racing—it felt like there was a man inside my chest beating a bass drum. I thought: What am I doing here? Where is this all going? What *should* I be doing? I lay in bed in Comrade Wu's rental apartment, with mattress springs digging into my back, and stared at the ceiling for what felt like hours. There was no clear path ahead of me. I had one year to figure it all out, I told myself. The end of the party.

The idea of turning thirty tormented me. I still felt inadequate whenever I met another journalist who had achieved more than I had. And I felt ashamed when, before voice recording came along and gave me the finances I so desperately needed, I had to ask my parents, who always remained supportive, to bail me out again, the day I looked at my bank statement and realized I was $10,000 in debt and had four dollars in my checking account.

Beijing, meanwhile, had become so familiar that it startled me when—while walking around town, or sitting in a cab, or waking up in the morning—I would think, Holy shit, I'm in Beijing. I still live in *Beijing*. The Chinese capital was my home, but it also wasn't. Canada was my home, but it also wasn't. I wanted to be in two places at once, and I still didn't know how to make that happen.

I didn't have any answers, so I made the easy choice: I stayed. If I didn't make it as a journalist, I decided, my time in China would be for naught. I needed to work harder, pitch more, write more, focus on my goals, and be more responsible with money. I became dedicated to doing those things (except, if I'm honest, the last one).

I felt an immediate weight lifted off my shoulders. I became focused on building on what I had achieved so far. I paid $1,500, borrowed from the Bank of Mom and Dad, to have a professional-looking website designed, and I got slick business cards made at Kinko's, featuring my name in both English and Chinese. I set up an office in our spare room with a desk overlooking the *hutong* below. On the desk I placed a small potted tree and a ceramic frog used for tea ceremonies that is meant to bring good luck and money, which would be a very welcome development indeed.

And then I started planning my next trip: Mongolia. Jim and I had been thinking about traveling to Mongolia since the previous fall, when we reported the human trafficking story. We wanted to look at the aftermath of trafficking and interview women who had returned home. We had a few other stories in mind, and a presidential election there was on the way, so we decided now was the time.

It was a risk. We didn't have any clients for the stories, and I would be paying for the trip on my credit card. I worried about a repeat of our previous trips: coming home with stories nobody wanted to buy.

I'd had some success as a freelance journalist in China, with stories in the *Guardian*, *Foreign Policy*, *CNN*, and half a dozen Canadian publications, but I was still waiting, and hoping, to further break into the American market, which I figured was key for me to move my career to the next level.

Mongolia, I hoped, would be the ticket. The country, bordering China to the north, was underreported and increasingly relevant, sitting on resource riches that the government seemed intent on squandering. Foreign countries were clamoring to start digging, and Mongolia, once home to the greatest conquerors the world had ever seen, was worried about twenty-first-century economic colonization, namely at the hands of the growing superpower to the south: China.

Our lineup of stories included the trafficking follow-up; a piece about the mining industry; coverage of the upcoming election; and, by far the most intriguing, a report about the emergence of a neo-Nazi movement in Mongolia. The latter story was directly linked to China, which had been conducting more and more business with Mongolia, much to the displeasure of many Mongolians, who, having suffered for decades under iron-fisted communist rule as a Soviet satellite state, feared Chinese encroachment in their country.

The neo-Nazi movement was at the fringe of a very real current of nationalism in Mongolia. The young men who made up this movement were full of venom, targeted at Chinese living and working in Ulaanbaatar, the capital. They were mostly hooligans, but the threat of violence seemed real. There had been reports of Chinese business owners being assaulted in Ulaanbaatar, and one prominent Mongolian neo-Nazi was in prison for killing his daughter's boyfriend, also a Mongolian, who had done nothing more than study in China.

We arrived in Ulaanbaatar late at night, after a fifteen-hour delay in Beijing on account of high winds. We took a cab directly to a bar with our host, an English photographer named Peter. Around 2 a.m., we headed back to Peter's apartment, where he almost got us beaten up after arguing with a taxi driver over the fare. There was some pushing and grabbing in Peter's dark stairwell, and the driver left to go get backup while we hurried into Peter's apartment and locked the door.

It was a fitting introduction to life in Mongolia, one of the toughest countries—with the toughest people—on earth.

It was May 2009, and Ulaanbaatar had four seasons each day. Morning was spring, the afternoon summer, evening fall, and night was winter—frigid, dark, and depressing. The city was dusty and run-down. It was home to just over a million people, with half the population living in outlying yurt slums, which had inadequate everything—plumbing, services, electricity. Beyond the capital was a sprawling country of grassland, desert, and forest, home to a largely nomadic population.

Jim and I woke early and walked from Peter's apartment to Peace Avenue, which cuts Ulaanbaatar in two, running the length of the city. We were an odd couple, Jim and I. He was eighteen years my senior, closer to my mother's age than mine. He was bald with a stocky build, and he wore a brown leather jacket over loose button-down shirts, with baggy Levi's and big black hiking boots. He had a calm demeanor that put people at ease, and he was one of the most genuinely kind people I'd ever met. When we worked together, I always wanted to get what we needed quickly and move on. Jim, on the other hand, was slow and methodical. He wanted to take a thousand pictures when all we needed was one. It drove me insane. But somehow we made it work, pushing each other until we got the stories done and having great adventures in the process. He became one of my closest friends in China.

In late morning we met our translator, Zaya, who had been referred to us by a Beijing photographer. We had e-mailed him before our arrival and arranged to meet in a café in central Ulaanbaatar. He wore a T-shirt and baggy jeans, and was his mid-twenties with a chubby, friendly-looking face. I asked him a few questions to gauge his English and wondered if it was good enough for the assignment, but we were anxious to get started and didn't want to waste time finding a new fixer. We told Zaya our story ideas and offered to pay him twenty-five dollars a day, plus more if he drove us around in his beat-up car. He didn't speak much during our meeting, and I was skeptical that he'd be able to get anything done at all. I mistook his easygoing demeanor for laziness.

Zaya, it turned out, would be crucial to everything we did in Ulaanbaatar. Within an hour, in fact, he had a meeting set up with the leader of Mongolia's neo-Nazis.

"How did you find him so quickly?" I asked as we drove down Peace Avenue toward the department store where we were scheduled to meet the neo-Nazi.

"Ulaanbaatar is small place." He shrugged.

We met Zagas Erdenebileg, the fifty-year-old self-proclaimed leader of Dayar Mongol (All Mongolia), one of the country's most prominent neo-Nazi groups, in a back alley behind the State Department Store. The alley was empty and shaded by the department store's back wall. When we pulled in, he was already there, leaning against a car and looking at his mobile phone. Zagas was middle-aged, short, with an average build, black hair, and a pockmarked face.

Zaya introduced us from the driver's-side window and invited Zagas to take a seat in the passenger seat of the car. The neo-Nazi leader sat in the car and started talking, and he kept talking for the better part of an hour. He refused to answer any questions directly and instead went into a long and convoluted history of Mongolia and the Nazis.

He talked. Zaya translated. I scribbled in my notebook.

"If our blood mixes with foreigners', we'll be destroyed immediately," said Zagas, who had run for parliament, unsuccessfully, four times. He loathed the Chinese, accusing them of involvement in prostitution and drug trafficking, and revered Chinggis Khaan (aka Genghis Khan), who he said influenced Adolf Hitler, another man he professed to admire. I asked him if he considered his adoption of the beliefs of a regime that singled out and executed people with "Mongol" features from among Soviet prisoners of war to be in any way ironic. "It doesn't matter." He shrugged. "We share the same policies."

His rant continued uninterrupted for forty-five minutes. I got bored and doodled in my notebook. When he was through, we exited the car to say goodbye. As Jim snapped a few shots, another car pulled up in the alley, driven by a young man with a shaved head, a swastika tattoo on his chest, and a bullet on a chain hanging from his neck. This was Shar Mungun-Erdene, the twenty-three-year-old leader of the two-hundred-member Mongolian National Union. Whereas Zagas came across as a bit of a buffoon, Shar was intimidating. Maybe it was his outfit, or his youth, but he struck me as someone who was no stranger to violence.

We asked him for an interview, and he agreed to meet us the next day.

He drove up to a fountain in a public square where we'd arranged to meet, and Jim, Zaya, and I crammed into his compact two-door. I was nervous as I got in his car. The square was empty, and it crossed my mind that Shar and his storm troopers might want to teach us a lesson about Mongolia's neo-Nazis.

I asked him about his group. The MNU, he told us, took vigilante action against lawbreaking foreigners, mainly Chinese. When I asked him what kind of action, he replied, "Whatever it takes so that they don't live here." He was trying to convey a macho vibe, but soon enough he came across as an overzealous adolescent, and it didn't take long before any intimidation I had felt about him was gone. He was, I realized, a kid—a misguided kid. At one point he opened his laptop to show us pictures of himself and his neo-Nazi buddies. Beside folders titled "Guns" and "Skinheads" were others with names like "My Car" and "Mom in Japan."

It was difficult to assess how real—or how dangerous—the neo-Nazi movement was. There had been violence, but it was sporadic. Around town, neo-Nazi graffiti was common. "Shoot the Chinese" was spray-painted on a brick wall near a movie theater. We saw a pair of swastikas and the words "Killer Boys . . . ! Danger!" on a fence in a yurt neighborhood. There was even a Nazi-themed bar, complete with SS wax figures and other Third Reich kitsch. Jim and I went there to check it out early one evening. Again, I was nervous about entering a Nazi bar, and I walked in with some hesitation. But within a few moments, I realized that it was no neo-Nazi hangout, just a grossly offensive theme bar, a twisted, Nazified Planet Hollywood. (The bar owners confirmed that the motif was just a gimmick.) We drank our beers, paid the bill, and left.

A social worker we interviewed told us the movement didn't enjoy large support, and it would likely subside as more Mongolians were exposed to the outside world. But the threat appeared to be real, at least for now. One night at a bar we met a twenty-five-year-old American who told us a story about the time he was accosted by neo-Nazis at a nightclub because he was cavorting with a Mongolian woman.

"After they showed me a swastika, my initial thought was, This isn't going to be a normal fight. They wanted to send a message," he said. As things escalated, the Mongolian girl he'd been hitting on ushered the young American from the bar and calmed his accosters, saving him from what might have been a savage beat-down.

Beat-downs, in fact, were not at all uncommon in Ulaanbaatar. At night there was the edge of menace in the air, and several people—including locals we met—warned us of Mongolians' fondness for fisticuffs. One night we went to a nightclub, and every few minutes a fight broke out, as if for sport.

Going out in Ulaanbaatar could be a surreal experience, as we learned the first weekend we spent in the city, while visiting Amrita Nightclub with Peter, the English photographer who was letting us crash at his apartment, and a few of his friends. It was one of those nights when I felt like I was out just for the sake of being out, forcing back vodkas and orange juice, and stuck somewhere in the gray haze between boozy fatigue and drunkenness. The club was loud and gaudy, filled with Mongolian girls in short skirts and potbellied Russians in bad suits. The type of place you'd expect to find in a city like, well, Ulaanbaatar.

Jim and I were about to call it a night; we were tired after a full week of reporting. I took a last sip of my drink. "Let's go," I said.

As we stood to leave, the music stopped and a team of busboys cleared the dance floor. Peter grabbed my arm and whispered in my ear.

"You'll want to stick around for this," he said.

From backstage, two young women in nurse outfits emerged. Within two minutes, they were naked, swaying lazily on the sticky dance floor to the Black Eyed Peas.

Interesting, I thought.

The nurses bowed to the audience and exited backstage. Replacing them were two child acrobats, one a teenager and the other ten or eleven, both wearing sparkling green spandex. The teenager lay down on a bench and flipped the younger one in various loops and spins. The kid was a real showman. Between stunts he ran to the front of the dance floor with a huge smile and cupped his hand over his ear, Hulk Hogan–style, soaking up the applause.

Next up was another stripper, this one in a leather dominatrix outfit. She pulled a French traveler from our group onto the dance floor, sat him down in a chair, and gave him a lap dance. Later, she led him to the stage, pressed him against a pole, and removed his pants. The crowd went wild.

The craziest part had yet to even begin, and I had come to expect nothing less from this city. After all, Ulaanbaatar was a place with a Nazi bar, where the only chain restaurant was a Kenny Rogers Roasters, a town where you risked a beating just by stepping out of your front door.

In keeping with the city's Nazi theme, a Mongolian man appeared onstage wearing a black leather vest with a swastika on the back. He blew fire, swallowed a sword (with some difficulty), and lay on a bed of nails while his female assistant smashed bricks on his chest with a sledgehammer. After each stunt, he tossed his mane of black hair over his shoulder and took a mammoth swig of vodka.

For a finale, he ate a lightbulb, holding the microphone to his cheek so the audience could hear the glass crunching between his molars.

With that, my mood had changed. I poured another vodka and orange juice and leaned toward Peter.

"That," I said, "was awesome."

We spent two weeks in Mongolia in all, and by the end of the second week our stories had come together. Jim and I were burnt-out and were ready to fly back to Beijing. With a few days left before our flight, I e-mailed an editor I knew at *Time* magazine about our Nazi story. The magazine accepted the piece. We sold the rest of our stories as well, and we actually made decent money from the trip. We proved to ourselves that this could actually be done, and the last year of toiling as a freelance journalist all of a sudden felt justified.

Once all of our interviews were wrapped up, Jim and I went out of town for a weekend, staying in a yurt and relaxing for two days in a national park—hiking, riding horses, eating long meals with the family that provided our accommodation.

The following Monday, we bade the crazy Mongolian capital farewell. Zaya drove us to Chinggis Khaan International Airport and we flew home.

Back in Beijing, Tom and I started looking for a new apartment. If the city was going to be my home, at least for the time being, I wanted certain comforts. More than anything, I needed out of Comrade Wu's claustrophobic rental apartment.

Among the creature comforts you are forced to give up as a foreigner in China—sanitary public toilets, reliably safe food, properly fitting clothes—the most basic are domestic. Unless you're on an expat package with a multinational company, most foreigners in the city live in Chinese-style apartments like any normal Beijinger. The quality of these places varies greatly.

Compared to many, Comrade Wu's place was a steal for a three-bedroom, centrally located apartment in Beijing. But it seemed to be falling apart before our eyes. Cupboard doors were coming off their hinges in the kitchen; strange smells emanated from the constantly plugged drain; the washing machine was destroying my clothes. I could feel every spring in my fifty-dollar mattress. I wanted something better. I wanted sunlight, a microwave, a dryer, a bed that didn't feel like a medieval torture instrument. I wanted something more comfortable, something . . . Western.

Tom and I decided to look for a new place together, and we enlisted the help of a small army of real estate "agents" found on various expat listings websites. Each agent seemed to ignore our every request: Two-bedroom apartment? Here's a one-bedroom. Oh, don't worry, you can use the living room as a second bedroom. Just hang a curtain! Big windows/lots of sunlight? How about tiny, barred windows/no sunlight? No more than 5,000 yuan? Here's one for 10,000 yuan.

Meanwhile, I broke the news to Comrade Wu that we were moving out. He and I met in the apartment complex's rental office. When I told him, he got out of his seat and shut the door. He wasn't pleased, so I lied and said I was moving back to Canada temporarily.

"For financial reasons," I told him, in Chinese.

When I asked about the damage deposit, he said I shouldn't expect it back because of the broken air conditioners and the kitchen cabinet doors. I explained that both problems had existed from around the time I'd moved in. Comrade Wu sighed.

"Mi Gao, we have good *guanxi*," he said—good relations. "But your roommate, Tom, I don't like him. He doesn't get up off the couch when I come in. He goes to his room. You call me comrade because we're comrades. Tom and I aren't comrades."

I apologized on Tom's behalf, even though I didn't actually believe he had committed any of Comrade Wu's perceived slights. I said I was sorry, too, about the damage to the apartment. By accepting responsibility for the damage, even though it clearly wasn't my fault, I was giving Comrade Wu, my landlord, face. After more than two years in China, I was finally learning. I had moved over another notch on the Foreigner/Chinese Identity Spectrum.

In the end, he returned half the deposit.

I waited in the office as he went to get the money. He came back in, sat down, and slid the cash across the table. I reached to pick it up and he grabbed my hand and looked me in the eyes.

"Mi Gao," he said. "We're comrades."

"Comrades," I agreed.

I stood and shook his hand. He held it for a moment, and then I turned and walked out of the office. It was the last time I saw Comrade Wu.

Eventually an agent showed Tom and me an apartment in a building called Sun City, near Dongsishitiao subway station and just outside the east second ring road. The apartment had a spacious living room and a big bay window overlooking the second ring. It had a dryer, a bathtub, a microwave, hardwood floors, antique furniture, two televisions, and soft lighting. I loved it. It was a bit more expensive than we had wanted, but nothing a few more voice-recording hours couldn't handle.

We signed a year lease.

That summer was epic. It was better even than the summer before, the Olympic summer. I had a big, diverse group of international friends: they were writers, photographers, filmmakers, NGO workers, Americans, Europeans, Chinese, all staking their claim in the world's biggest boomtown.

Something funny had happened to Beijing in the wake of the Olympics. There was no exodus of foreigners, no long-term post-Olympic depression. The city didn't all of a sudden become dull, boring, and forgotten, as so many, including myself, had predicted. In fact, it got better. People from all over the world were arriving every day to learn the language, explore the city and country, and pursue opportunities that didn't exist back home because of a stagnant economy. People were opening new bars and restaurants. They were creating art, writing books, making films. They were teaching yoga, building lives, and making money.

I was also finding my place in post-Olympics Beijing. I was more or less making the progress I wanted to in my career, and my confidence as a journalist and writer was growing.

There was a unique energy to Beijing. It was a city emerging as a world capital. It was exhausting to live in a city that frantic, but it was also intoxicating. We were out all the time because we didn't want to miss anything. We were a part of something special, something historic. Beijing felt like Paris must have in the 1920s. Anybody who would be anybody was there.

But there was a troubling element to the expat experience, as well. We were part of a floating generation. Guo Li, my teacher/friend/therapist/shoulder-to-cry-on, once told me about the term *bei piao*. It literally translates to "Beijing floaters" and describes a person adrift, or floating, in the city. It was meant to apply to young Chinese, like Guo Li, who came to the capital for school or work and ended up in a life that could sometimes feel meaningless and lonely, in which you are constantly stressed about relationships and money, far from friends and family and with an uncertain future.

Increasingly, the term could be applied to foreigners like myself: those who came for the short term but ended up staying much longer than planned, addicted to the ease of life, the adventures, the constant stimulation. But the expat existence could be deceiving. Friendships, for example, could be fleeting. Especially during summer there seemed to be an endless stream of going-away parties. The more good friends that left, the more desensitized I became. There were good people in Beijing, definitely, but it was hard to develop friendships like those I had at home, friendships built over years of shared history.

And despite all the fun we were having—I was having—a

certain sadness was always there, lingering just below the surface, and sometimes it would take over and stay for days. I felt it when I worked alone at coffee shops and when I stayed home at night to watch movies. I felt it in Uncle Wang's studio, where I suffered long, soul-destroying hours of doing nothing but reading texts and thinking. I would become so full of regret—regret at being so far from my family. Regret for letting go of Julia, for pursuing selfish goals. I often wondered if it would be worth it in the end. Living in Beijing felt at times like a self-imposed exile.

But I was addicted to China now, for better or worse, and even though I felt like the life I was leading had an expiration date—April 13, 2010, my thirtieth birthday—I still wasn't ready to give it up. One day in Chinese class with Guo Li, we studied a chapter that included a discussion about babies, and it gave me the chills. The thought of having kids, even at twenty-nine, terrified me.

There were two different worlds for me now: *this* world (Beijing, youth, adventure, recklessness) and *that* world (Canada, movies four nights a week, cooking at home, fatherhood, security). Whenever I thought about moving home, I reminded myself that I could still have all of those things, but *this* life—in Beijing, twenty-nine years old, a young writer abroad—I would never have again.

The day Tom and I moved into our new apartment in Sun City, I had no doubts. I looked out of our big window toward the second ring road below, at the traffic, at the buildings—the Poly Theater, the Swissotel—at the hustle and bustle on the streets and alleys below. It was a hot summer night and the entire city seemed to be out. The sun had just gone down; the sky was purple-navy, and at street level the pollution mixed with the streetlights to give off a surreal orange glow that I will always associate with Beijing.

I felt a surge of pride. This was *my* place. This was *my* city. I was, and forever would be, at least in part, a Beijinger.

14

Rent a White Guy

In the fall of 2009, I was offered work as a quality-control expert with an American company in China I'd never heard of. No experience necessary—which was good because I had none. I would be paid $1,000 for a week, put up in a fancy hotel, and wined and dined in Dongying, an industrial city in Shandong province I'd also never heard of. The only requirements were a fair complexion and a suit.

The job offer came via my friend Ernie, a Californian and longtime Beijinger I'd met the summer before through Julia. He told me to call his friend Kevin for details.

"I call these things 'White Guy in a Tie' events,'" Kevin told me over the phone. "Basically, you put on a suit, shake some hands, and make some money. We'll be in 'quality control,' but nobody's going to be doing any quality control. You in?"

I was.

———

The opportunity couldn't have come at a better time. I desperately wanted to cut down on my hours at Uncle Wang's, but even with consistent freelance work I was finding it nearly impossible to earn a living as a writer. Since I was then (and am still now) incapable of budgeting, without voice recording I would have been drowning in a heaping pile of debt big enough to fill the Bird's Nest.

Fueled by the success of the Mongolia trip, within a matter of months I traveled to the Philippines and Burma for stories, and I was making inroads in the U.S. market. If someone had told me when I was nineteen years old that a decade later I would be living in China working as a writer, contributing to influential newspapers and magazines and reporting from across Asia, I would have said something to the tune of, *"Fuck yes!"*

While the reporting trips made for excellent fodder on my Facebook newsfeed, my day-to-day work life in Beijing was mostly uneventful. I spent most days sitting at Café Zarah wondering why editors weren't e-mailing me back, getting excited about a new story idea only to discover it had been done twenty times before. I would often wake up late, go for a coffee, check e-mails, and drink more coffee. Once or twice a month a story of mine would go to print, but I wasn't making anywhere close to a decent living, despite Uncle Wang's generous wages. All told, I was earning about $20,000 a year.

The big 3-0 loomed heavily. In some ways, I had achieved what I'd always wanted: Adventures abroad. Writing for a living. Doing interesting things in interesting places with interesting people. And although I was aware I'd look back on this period as one of the best times of my life, the same questions kept resurfacing: What should I be doing? Where should I be? When will I become a real adult?

How long, I wondered, could I keep this up?

These were hard questions to answer. But one thing was clear: If I was to keep my life as a writer afloat, I needed a break. A big one.

The fake-businessman trip seemed like an opportunity for another random China adventure, a good story to tell friends over beers. But it was an adventure that, months later, would change my life in unexpected ways. The trip would turn out to be exactly the big break I was looking for, although I had no idea at the time.

It was one of my voice-recording partners who first told me about fake-businessman jobs, where Chinese companies hired foreigners to sit in meetings and pretend to be part of the company. It was an often lucrative gig for underworked expatriates in China like myself. She knew people who had been paid $1,000 for a day of meetings. I asked around, and it turned out this kind of work was quite common. In fact, companies sometimes posted ads online for white people to sit in business meetings. One friend of mine, an American who worked in film, was paid to represent a Canadian company and give a speech espousing a low-carbon future. Another was flown to Shanghai to act as a seasonal-gifts buyer. At one point, there was even a fake-businessman recruitment agency in Beijing. I thought it would make for a great story, and earning $1,000 for doing nothing sounded like Christmas come early.

The obvious question was why Chinese companies would want to hire foreigners to pretend to be part of a company. No one seemed to know for sure, but the best guess was that it had something to do with face. Hiring fake businessmen was one way to create the image—particularly, the image of connections— that Chinese companies craved. Guo Li, my Chinese teacher and invaluable source of insight on all things Chinese, was at first aghast about how much we were getting paid, but she then put it this way: "Having foreigners in nice suits gives the company face."

It wasn't so different from my time at *China Daily*. There the foreign experts were 50 percent copyediting drones, 50 percent window dressing. We were there, in part, for show. Same with fake businessmen. I was essentially stepping back into a job as a professional wallflower.

After dusting off my ill-fitting market suit and investing in a new pair of shoes and a haircut (image is important to the fake businessman—in fact, it's everything), I woke one Thursday morning to catch a 7:45 flight to Dongying. There were six of us in all—three Americans, two Canadians, and an Aussie.

Ernie, in his late thirties, was a high-intensity conspiracy theorist and one of the funniest people I'd ever met. We had met on the trip I took to Inner Mongolia with Julia and some of her friends, and we hit it off right away. He'd made me laugh until I cried more than once in the time I'd known him, and he had also forced me to sit through hours of documentaries about the Bilderberg Group and its plot for world domination.

Ernie showed up at the airport wearing a black suit and carrying nothing but a small shoulder bag, big enough for a laptop but not much more.

"Is that all you're bringing?" I asked.

He looked himself up and down. "What else would I need?"

Chris, a young computer nerd, was carrying with him two suitcases and a shoulder bag. I asked him why he needed so much stuff for just a week.

"Oh, I'm staying for a few months," he said.

"To do what?"

"I have no idea. Quality control?"

"Do you have any experience in quality control?"

"Ha-ha. No."

Kevin, a tall Canadian with a goatee, briefed us on the details. We were supposedly representing a California-based company that was building a high-tech facility in Dongying. Our responsibilities would include making daily trips to the construction site, attending a ribbon-cutting ceremony, and hobnobbing with people of varying degrees of importance. The rest of the time would be ours to spend as we wished. During the ceremony, one of us would have to give a speech as the company's director. That duty fell to Ernie, the oldest of our group. His business cards had already been made.

Dongying was home to Sun Tzu, the author of *The Art of War*, and that's about its only claim to fame. The landscape was dry and bleak, with factories in all directions. We were met at the airport by Kim, a young Taiwanese with a brush cut and leather jacket, whose company, we were told, had been subcontracted to manage the project. Driving into town, the excitement we felt about posing as fake businessmen for a company we knew barely anything about was almost overwhelming. We were giddy as schoolgirls.

The lobby at our hotel was dimly lit and smelled like bad seafood. "At least we have a nice view," Ernie deadpanned as he opened the drapes in our room to reveal a scrap yard. A truck had been stripped for parts, and old tires were heaped into a pile. A dog yelped.

After a quick rest, we suited up and Kim drove us to the company's temporary offices. These were small rooms with cement floors and metal walls arranged around a courtyard. The six of us had our own office space. On each desk were a hard hat with a company decal and an orange safety vest with an oversized zipper that read "D&G—DOLOE & GOB8ANA."

We took a quick tour of the factory—an army of migrant workers was about six months away from finishing—and then returned to the office and sat for hours. No instructions were given about what we should be doing, so mostly we tried to sleep at our desks. Flies buzzed around the room and boredom set in. We could hear Ernie rehearsing his speech in a room across the courtyard.

Since nobody ever told us why we were there, we spent much time speculating. Our best guess was that the company hired us to make the project look more important than it was. A ceremony was scheduled for the next morning, and we were told local dignitaries and the media would be there. When a Chinese company builds a factory, it's not news. It's another story when a big American company builds one, not to mention sends over its representatives—fictitious as we were—to check up on things.

I carried a notebook in my pocket and jotted notes throughout, increasingly aware that I had stumbled upon a great story: "Can't believe this is actually happening . . . We chat about sports, NFL mostly . . . Workers walk past, peeking through the door, we sit at our desks, suit jackets hung on chairs, hard hats in front of us. Smile and wave . . . Company has printed off an itinerary for tomorrow . . . breakfast @ 7:45, ceremony @ 9, speech by Director Ernie . . ."

Nobody, not even Kevin, was sure what we were supposed to be doing while we sat in our office. According to the itinerary, our duties were finished at the end of the next day. But we were scheduled to stay for a week. Kevin told us to sit tight and await further instructions.

"I wish I brought a magazine," Brad, a quiet American lawyer, lamented.

"What will we do this weekend?" I asked Kevin as I flipped

through the sheets of paper on my desk. "There's nothing on the itinerary."

"We'll see. There might be some important people to meet."

Ernie leaned toward me and whispered, "It's becoming clear they're just making this up as they go along."

The next morning was the ceremony—the main event, the central reason for our trip.

I'm still not clear what the ceremony was for—the factory was still just a shell—but it was obviously a big deal. On a side road next to the construction site, they'd set up a red carpet. Pretty girls in red, dragon-patterned dresses greeted visitors, and Chinese pop blasted from the loudspeakers. Down the street, police in shiny yellow vests directed traffic. The mayor was there with other local dignitaries, and so were the TV cameras and reporters.

We stood in the front row wearing our suits, orange safety vests, and hard hats. As we waited for the ceremony to begin, a foreman standing beside me barked to workers on the construction site to stop what they were doing and get out of view. They scurried behind the scaffolding, and the cranes stopped.

"Are you the boss?" I asked the foreman in Chinese.

He looked at me quizzically. "*You're* the boss," he said.

Actually, Ernie was the boss. After a brief introduction, "Director" Ernie delivered his speech in English before the hundred or so in attendance. He boasted of the company's long list of international clients and emphasized how happy we were to be working on such an important project in Dongying. When the speech was over, confetti blasted over the stage and fireworks popped on the dusty field beside us. Absorbing it all, I felt like we'd pulled off a clever ruse. Almost like a teenager who'd successfully lied to his parents about smoking.

On the walk back to the office, Kim told us what we'd all started to suspect: that for the next five days we'd have to sit in the office for eight hours a day, doing nothing. Or we could choose to go back to Beijing a few days early—for half the pay.

Ernie was livid. I think the director role had given him a sense of entitlement. "You're kidding, right? We have to sit in that box all day?"

"No," said Kim. "You can walk around the courtyard, too."

Back at the office, Ernie, still fuming, asked Kevin, "You didn't know about this, right? That we'd have to sit in this shit-box all day?"

"I knew we'd be doing nothing."

"Nothing is one thing. Sitting in a fly-infested metal shitbox is another."

Later, Kim again presented the option of going back to Beijing a couple of days early. Contemplating sitting for days in the fly-infested metal shitbox, I accepted the redundancy package.

That night Kim and a couple of the Chinese guys took us out on the town. We started in a rip-off Western-style bar, with Beatles posters on the wall and a young man onstage singing incomprehensible English lyrics.

From there, we moved to another bar across town, where we'd heard all the foreigners hung out. Opening the door to a one-room pub with a pool table in the middle revealed a pasty-faced gang of English teachers with one lone Chinese woman, presumably the owner. They eyed us suspiciously.

I asked one of the teachers what other bars were good in town.

"This is pretty much it," he said.

"You guys come here every weekend?"

"Pretty much. Thursday, Friday, Saturday." He shrugged. "It's got a pool table."

After an uncomfortable few minutes with the teachers, we moved on to the city's only nightclub, where Kim's middle-aged Chinese coworkers bought us bottles of whiskey and ice tea. The club was at once welcoming and hostile. Young girls and their gangster-looking boyfriends eyed us, but for different reasons. It wouldn't have shocked me if one of us had gotten laid, another stabbed. We were the only white people in the bar, and several club employees were dressed in over-sized animal bodysuits.

By midnight we were hammered. About an hour later, Kim, who had previously said we had the next day off, broke the bad news.

"Well, we better get going. Gotta be back at the office by seven forty-five."

We protested.

"If you're not there by seven forty-five," Kim said, "don't bother coming for the rest of the week."

It wasn't clear who we were fooling. For the next two days we sat in the office, swatting flies and dozing at our desks. Surely any passerby would realize we weren't really working. And yet there we were, high-level employees of some American company that didn't really exist. We were so important, in fact, that Chris and Sam were both asked to stay for *eight months*—eight months of waking up early, putting on a suit, and doing nothing—in exchange for a salary of $4,100 a month. (To be fair, they then received quality control training, although I'm skeptical that either of them ever performed a quality-control–related task.)

It would be easy to write this off as a quirky "only in China" anecdote, but at the heart of it was the enigma central to Chinese business and life—face. By donning a suit, touring a factory, attending a ceremony, and sitting in an office for a few days doing absolutely nothing, we were apparently giving face to the company, the project, and the city.

It would be a mistake to attribute the fake-businessman phenomenon to any type of racial inferiority complex with the Chinese. It's true that Western people and Western products—the West in general—are admired in China. But it's not a racial thing. China is an increasingly confident nation, and Chinese people are deservedly proud. They're also proud that foreigners are interested in their country. But they don't think that people with white skin are better than themselves. We're just exotic, and all we did in Dongying as Westerners in suits was add a little exotic prestige. We were just PR tools; we gave a little face to a small company in a small city in the middle of nowhere.

Still, after a few days I felt guilty. I thought about how little the workers made; I figured it would take them four months to earn what we were making in one week. Everybody treated us with such great admiration and deference that I was tempted to grab one of the workers by his shoulders, shake his bony frame, confess that we were frauds, and thrust a bunch of crumpled bills into his calloused hands. The whole episode started to feel wrong.

The trip was a perfect, albeit extreme, example of the artificial reality that is the expat universe. Did we deserve to be paid $1,000 for this? Absolutely not. One hundred percent not. We weren't even that good at being fake businessmen with our unfashionable suits, our three-day beards, our perpetual hangovers. But most of the time we acted as if we were worth every penny, whining about getting up early in our crappy hotel and having to sit in our metal office all day, dozing at our desks or reading magazines.

If you are a foreigner, China can give you fraudulent confidence, and it's when you forget that you really aren't that special that it can get dangerous. Most of us were in our late twenties through thirties, living out our very own Judd Apatow movie. Our only responsibilities were to put on cheap suits and get out of bed on time. How do you leave a life that presents you with scenarios like that?

Kim picked me up in an SUV on my last morning. The others were staying a few days longer, while I was clocking out early. We drove to the airport, and he asked questions about my life in Beijing. I was starting to like the guy. I was happy to be going home early, but something (easy money?) still prompted me to say, "Let me know if you need me to come down again."

He seemed a bit surprised. "Yeah, come any time you can. Lots happening," he said. "We need people for a week every month. It'll be better next time, too. We'll have new offices."

He paused before adding: "Bring a computer. You can watch movies all day."

The trip was a journey into the bizarre, and I knew I was on to a good story. I had no idea it would be a life-changing story. When the article I wrote about the trip to Dongying was published in the *Atlantic* eight months later, I thought the story would come and go. Instead, the reaction was shocking: I had blown the whistle on the fake-businessman scheme, and the whole world, it seemed, wanted to know more.

Within a few days I was getting phone calls from international news outlets wanting to interview me about my experience. I received dozens of e-mails from people around the world— unemployed graduates, teachers, pilots—asking if I could find them pretend businessman jobs. My career seemed to be finally taking off. Kevin was livid. And I had become something of a celebrity among Beijing's expat community.

I was the "Rent a White Guy" guy.

15

The "Rent a White Guy" Guy

I didn't see any of it coming.

After I came back from Dongying, I sat in Café Zarah with my notes and wrote the story of my experience as a fake businessman. And then I waited. For one, I didn't know where I could sell it. It was a great story, but few of the publications I knew accepted humorous, personal narrative pieces, and I didn't know if the angle was strong enough for a top-tier publication. After all, most foreigners living in China had heard of the fake-businessman gigs, and many had done it themselves. It was a funny story, but it didn't seem like anything new.

I also didn't want to get the organizers of the trip, Kevin and Kim, in trouble. Although I had openly taken notes throughout the weekend, I didn't tell them I was going to write anything. The story was supposed to be more of a quirky China anecdote, not an indictment of the company, but I still thought I would give it some time before trying to sell the story so that it would be more difficult to track down the company that had hired us.

I set the story aside and resumed my normal life. Work was going reasonably well: I accepted a part-time assignment as a stringer for an international newswire based in Rome, and I continued to freelance for international publications, sometimes traveling elsewhere in China and Asia for assignments. Traveling kept me content; it kept Beijing fresh. Making the transition back to North America was always in the back of my mind, but as long as I was content and my parents were happy and healthy, I was going to stay. I felt like I was on the right track: I had published in American magazines, had steady freelance work, and had cut down on voice recording. I perhaps hadn't accomplished as much as I'd hoped for, but I was doing all right.

In April 2010, I turned thirty. Celebrating my thirtieth birthday in the capital of China was not something I had foreseen in life, but I was thankful for the way things had turned out. Life was easy, satisfying, and constantly amusing. The anxieties I'd had about turning thirty—about career, money, the future—had started to fade. I was in the right place at the right time, and I knew it.

A few friends threw a party for me in their courtyard home, not far from Dongzhimen subway station. Their apartment was packed with people—old friends and new friends and friends of friends I didn't know. We drank a vodka punch outside in the courtyard on the cool April night, and I gave a speech for my friends that left me nearly teary-eyed.

I was presented with a birthday gift: a headless and limbless mannequin outfitted in black lingerie. I was still single, after all. We drank for hours in the courtyard and at midnight went to a large club near Workers Stadium and danced—yes, even me—until dawn. I woke up the next morning a thirty-year-old with a killer hangover and a real sense of optimism I hadn't had in years.

Around the time of my birthday, I pitched the Rent a White Guy article to the *Atlantic*. I had been looking for buyers for the previous few months, trying publications in the United States and Canada, with no luck. I had almost given up selling the story when one day I flipped through an issue of the *Atlantic* and saw a story similar in tone to what I was envisioning for the piece. I figured I had nothing to lose, and lo and behold, the magazine accepted my story.

During the fact-checking phase, the *Atlantic* contacted Kevin and the others to confirm the details of my account. Kevin was furious. He called me one morning while I was brushing my teeth.

"What the fuck have you done, man?" he asked over the phone. "Is this some kind of hatchet job?"

I assured him it wasn't: I had withheld everybody's last names, the company name, what the company did, and when we went. I told him the story was meant to be a funny anecdote about the business culture in China and not an exposé of the company. Kevin calmed down and said that as long as I didn't publish any of the crucial details, he would be okay with the article, although I suspected otherwise.

The article was published on the same day as the start of the 2010 soccer World Cup. My friends and I watched games on outdoor screens in Sanlitun, drinking beers and returning home at 5 a.m.

The next morning, I opened my inbox to find an e-mail from a producer in Los Angeles who said she worked with a major studio. She wanted to know if the rights to my article were available for a feature film. I read over the e-mail several times. The published article was short and, I thought, insignificant: a comic tale about something relatively common in China. Sure, it was a good story to tell friends over beers—"You made a thousand bucks to *pretend* to be a businessman? For real?"—but I had never, not for a minute, thought it could be a movie.

I went running that afternoon with my friend Paul Morris, a twenty-seven-year-old Brit who had worked as an assistant director on major movies in England. I told him about the producer's e-mail. He tried to temper my expectations.

"Producers have interns scouring the Internet for ideas all day," he told me as we jogged around Ritan Park. "They're contacting people all the time. I wouldn't get my hopes up."

Paul's advice would later prove prescient, but the e-mails kept coming. More than a dozen producers contacted me with inquiries about film and TV rights. Most e-mailed me; some called out of the blue.

One morning, my phone rang when I was half asleep, a long-distance number I didn't recognize.

"Hey," I said groggily, assuming it was my parents calling my cell phone over Skype.

The voice on the other end introduced himself as Dan so-and-so, from such-and-such a production company in Holly-wood.

"Oh, hi," I said, sitting up in my bed and rubbing my eyes.

He went on. "I loved the story you wrote in the *Atlantic*. Great stuff. We think it has excellent potential for a feature film." He listed a number of movies his company had done with various stars. "We'd love to talk more about this."

"Uh . . . okay," I mumbled. "Yeah, great."

Meanwhile, a major management company in Hollywood arranged an early morning conference call with its CEO and manager. They said they were interested in taking a crack at the project and asked me to take a look at their standard rights agreement. I told them I needed to seek out advice and was exploring my options.

"Of course," the CEO said. "You should. And if you find somebody who you think might be a good fit, please have them get in touch. The last movie we did, we got Brad Pitt on board."

Yeah, I thought, *let's call up Brad and see what he thinks* . . .

Meanwhile, strangers were contacting me from all over the world asking me to find them fake-businessman jobs. Some sent me full rundowns of their CVs:

> *I am a highly motivated business minded individual who desires a challenge in everything I do. As soon as I graduated I went straight into a high pressure sales job to increase my sales ability and rapport building skills. . . . I am naturally good at meeting people face to face without coming off as the dreaded "solicitor.". . .*

> *I have mastered the art of the international language with a smile and positive attitude along with the determination to jump into any situation. . . . If you can remember when you first started and through hard work and perseverance, and maybe knowing the right people at the right time, achieved your dream . . . then maybe you can help me get that start.*

Others sent me modeling shots. Some had unique experience to offer as a fake businessman:

> *I am from the US and was hired as a pilot for———airlines . . . I have always wanted to go to China and*

would love to be involved in one of these opportunities. An advantage that I have is that I can fly into several cities in China as many times as I would like for free.

Or:

I am a Caucasian male with excellent etiquette, style, and verbal skills.

Or:

[I'm] an old white guy with a bespoke suit or two.

At first I found it entertaining that anybody would contact me looking for a fake job, as if I was the world's liaison to employers of pretend businessmen everywhere. Then I found it sad, because the people who contacted me were mostly unemployed and had run out of options. As several of the people who contacted me said, they had nothing to lose.

One day during the "Rent a White Guy" craze, my mom called me in Beijing.

"Are you having an affair with a married woman?" she asked.

"Excuse me?"

"Look in the *Atlantic*'s comments section. Someone wrote that you're having an ongoing affair with a married woman."

I opened up the article and scrolled down through a couple hundred comments until I found it. "International Journalist Mitch Moxley . . . has recently been forced from Beijing after his affair with the wife of ———— was recently discovered," the message said. It went on to claim that I had been carrying on the affair for four months and offered as evidence an "intimate" photo of my alleged lover and me in an expat listings magazine. The woman's husband was apparently "full of murderous rage and vows to hunt Moxley to the edge of the earth. Moxley has since left Beijing but has been quoted several times saying how he targeted married women for sex as they required less care and maintenance."

I fought through my bewilderment and contacted the woman with whom I was allegedly having an affair. (We were not; the magazine photo in question was simply me, her, and another friend standing beside one another at a concert.) I gave her a heads-up in case her husband saw the comment.

"Wow," she messaged me back. "Somebody really doesn't like you."

The whole thing had taken on a life of its own. Over the course of a few weeks I was interviewed by the BBC, CNN, National Public Radio, and news outlets from Canada to New Zealand to the Netherlands. Journalists from around the world contacted me to help do their own fake-businessman stories. CNN did a story that generated more than fifty-three thousand "likes" on Facebook. *The Colbert Report* did a skit on the Rent a White Guy phenomenon.

The requests for movie rights continued to pile up. At its peak, there were some twenty production companies considering buying the rights. I needed advice. A friend in Beijing put me in touch with an agent in the city who contacted his colleague in Los Angeles on my behalf. That night, at 3 a.m., I received a call as I stumbled home slightly wobbly from a club opening in Sanlitun. The agent made his pitch. I was on board.

In July, while my agent worked with producers in Los Angeles to pitch "Rent a White Guy" to studios, I moved apartments again. Tom was going back to England, and I wouldn't be able to afford my place in Sun City alone. Paul and I and his cousin Kit Gillet, another freelance journalist, spent a month looking for the perfect apartment. We had almost given up when we finally found it: a two-thousand-square-foot space on the top floor of an old building near Lama Temple. It was the city's best neighborhood, in the *hutong*s, with cool bars, cafés, and restaurants nearby, but with a Chinese feel. On the wall of our building were characters that read: "This building has old people. Please keep quiet."

Beijing's bylaws stated that apartment buildings of more than six stories must have an elevator, and our apartment was on the seventh floor of a building with no elevator. Nobody had ever lived in the space before, but for whatever reason the building's management company had decided to rent it out anyway. It had cement floors splattered with white paint, big windows, two massive balconies, each the size of squash courts, and ten rooms in all. It felt like an art gallery. We furnished it ourselves, framed photos and hung them on the walls, built bookshelves, and bought a movie projector. It was an incredible apartment, and it cost only $1,400 for the three of us.

One day shortly after we'd moved, I sat in a nearby coffee shop and read over my journals from before I came to China. I was reminded of the dark place I was in that year in Toronto. Thinking about those days, I could hardly believe how much had changed. Over the course of three years, I'd gone from spending my days wandering around alone, bullying myself for being such a failure and writing business fluff pieces—to having Hollywood producers call me.

I shook my head. Unbelievable, I thought. What an unbelievable, incredible, mind-boggling . . .

Fluke.

The article was a mere eight hundred words, a story about a slice of expat life that is ridiculously common. One story in one magazine. But it had obviously struck a chord with a readership suffering from 10 percent unemployment, with an economy in the toilet and news of China booming in their faces every day. And my career was taking off because of it.

Still, I knew in my heart that, really, I didn't deserve much credit. I couldn't help but feel like a bit of a fraud—which, coincidentally, was also the main job requirement of a fake businessman.

Perhaps I'd found my calling.

16

Chasing the Iron Rooster

The old lady was asleep on the berth beside me, snoring. It was a guttural snore, a snore that came from the soul. It rose up from the gut, through the lungs and throat, with a brief layover in the nasal cavity and was then released with a thunder. It was an epic snore, one that might provoke thoughts of violence. Thoughts of violence within me. Toward her.

I lay in my bunk, consumed by the noise. Not just the snoring; sounds were everywhere. It was seven in the morning and the train was alive. Old men climbed down from their berths, stretching and yawning. Young women shuffled to the steel sinks at the end of each car to brush their teeth and hair. The televisions mounted to the walls of each cabin were soon turned on—at full volume—playing a low-budget Chinese historical epic. Before long, the grumpy attendants were out, pushing carts down the aisle, selling fruit, toothbrushes, and fried chicken in vacuum-sealed packages.

Sleep was futile. Outside my window was southern China's Guangxi province. As staccato images of rocky outcroppings, rice paddies, and half-built brick homes flashed by, I rolled out of bed and mixed myself a cup of instant coffee I'd brought with me.

Rule number one of Chinese train travel: bring coffee.

I had been commissioned by the *Globe and Mail* to write a travel story about riding the rails in China. The paper gave me a budget for more than a week's worth of travel. From Beijing, I'd take the twenty-eight-hour train to Guilin, in Guangxi, and spend a few days exploring the karst peaks of Yangshuo Valley. From there I would travel to Guangzhou and Shenzhen, the southern Chinese boomtown. After Shenzhen, I would take the night train to Shanghai for a day before returning to the capital.

It was a much-needed break from Beijing. For months, I had been consumed with just one thought. One word, really.

Movie.

My agent in Los Angeles had been pitching my *Atlantic* article to producers who were in turn pitching it to studios. They had been close more than once, and now there was a possible offer: a major producer was on board and a private financier was considering funding a script, which would be presented to studios once completed. I didn't have the details yet but was told to expect them in a matter of days.

Throughout the process, I hadn't been able to work on much else. I had images floating in my head of relocating to Hollywood; of sipping martinis on a private jet flying to the New York premiere; of a steamy affair with the female lead. It was all so close, yet so far, far away. It was delusional, of course, but this is what happens when you're plucked from obscurity to land a Hollywood agent. You get ahead of yourself.

Despite Beijing traffic's best effort to stop me, I made the train to Guilin minutes before its 8:58 a.m. departure. I claimed my spot on the middle berth of a second-class compartment, called a "hard sleeper." The beds were almost as comfortable as first class—"soft sleeper"—but had six berths to a cabin instead of four. The train was sold out, and my car was a hive of activity.

For reading material I'd brought Paul Theroux's 1988 book about train travel in China, *Riding the Iron Rooster*. Much had changed in China in the last twenty-two years. Much hadn't. "A train isn't a vehicle," Theroux writes. "A train is part of the country. It's a place."

I couldn't have agreed more. Chinese, in particular, don't just ride a train—they live in it. The minute a train pulls from the station, sunflower seeds are chewed, card games played, and tea endlessly gulped. Cigarettes are smoked; bodily gases passed. Passengers sleep away the hours as if on vacation, chat with strangers, or gaze out at the passing world. Riding the rails wasn't just a way to travel China, neither during Theroux's journey nor mine; it was a way to experience it.

There are two types of people on Chinese trains: sleeping people and restless people. The old lady beside me had already fallen asleep and begun her monumental snoring, which would continue unabated, except for a few meal breaks she took in bed, for the next day. I never saw her go to the bathroom, and I wondered if her bladder was the size of a wineskin. Meanwhile, a middle-aged man on the bunk below me was up and down, up and down, all morning, rustling through his belongings, chatting with his buddy, or smoking cigarettes in between cars. Technically, smoking was not allowed on the train, a rule ignored in totality.

As we traveled through Beijing's outlying regions, I lay in my bunk and read Theroux. I was the only foreigner in the car, and periodically a Chinese passenger stopped by to say hello.

"Ni hao," they'd say.

"Ni hao," I'd reply.

"Ah! Your Chinese is very good!"

Chinese have very low expectations of foreigners.

A gritty city in Hebei province rolled by. I picked over a supply of ham, cheese, crackers, and fruit that I had brought with me in order to put off consuming the gruel served in the dining cars of Chinese trains.

Rule number two: bring snacks.

Until the late 1980s, China relied on steam-powered relics to transport citizens and goods around its vast territory. Iron Roosters. By 2010, it was home to the largest high-speed rail network in the world, with 4,300 miles of track. The year before, China spent more than $80 billion on rail construction, and it had plans of adding 10,000 miles of capacity by 2020. The country already had more than 1,200 miles of routes that could run at top speeds of 220 miles per hour, with much more to come. China had grand ambitions of connecting coastal cities to the remote west, and it envisioned lines beginning in China and stretching across Asia, the Middle East, and Europe.

There were a few things about train travel the Chinese hadn't yet perfected, however. Food, namely. For dinner, having exhausted my ham, cheese, and crackers, I went to the dining car. I ordered a meal of stewed cabbage and rice with a bowl of chicken soup, and washed it down with a watery can of Snow Beer. It didn't work. Not even alcohol could make the food palatable.

I was back in my berth for lights out at 10 p.m. Some passengers had been asleep for hours. The old lady across from me was still snoring. She hadn't moved in more than twelve hours. I would have thought she was dead were it not for the snoring.

The men below me smoked in their beds, thick clouds of smoke wafting up to my bunk and into my nostrils.

I read to the light of my cell phone. It was fascinating to read of Theroux's train journey and then look around to my own. In 1988, the Cultural Revolution was still fresh in the collective memory and people were still dealing with its repercussions. In 2010, the Cultural Revolution existed in theme restaurants in Beijing. The China I knew had nothing to do with communism. Back then, Deng Xiaoping's reforms were just taking hold. Now China was a fast, materialistic, frantic juggernaut. Construction, money, epic change. The world Theroux described in *Iron Rooster* seemed so familiar (travelers in pajamas drinking tea, spitting sunflower seeds on the floor), yet so different. When he traveled China by train, the changes were just beginning. As I sat in my berth en route to Guilin, they had come to fruition. The future was here, and the Chinese seemed as comfortable in it as they were riding the train.

After midnight I prepared for sleep by removing from my bag earplugs, an eye mask, and sleeping pills (rules three, four, and five). The snoring and smoking continued throughout the night. The pills were useless.

On long train rides there's a lot of time for thinking, and that's what I did that mostly sleepless night. It was the first real thinking I'd done since the summer, when the "Rent a White Guy" article was taking off and dominating my every waking minute.

In early August, I'd gone back to North America for a few weeks. I went with fifteen friends from high school and university to San Diego for a long weekend to celebrate our collective thirtieth birthdays. We rented a house near the beach and spent four days catching up and partying like maniacs.

One afternoon we were walking from our house to the beach and I was telling my friends about my life in China. "It's weird," I said. "It's like it's not reality over there. I mean, I have no responsibilities, no mortgage or anything, no job to go to. It's like living this, sort of, fantasy life."

"Yeah, yeah, we get it. It's awesome in China," one of my friends said.

I could tell he was annoyed, but I wasn't trying to brag. The opposite, in fact. I tried to explain that living in China felt like fiction. It was a choice to opt out of being an adult, to escape the realities and responsibilities of adulthood, and I was starting to wonder if that was really such a good thing. In some ways, I was beginning to envy my friends at home—who had girlfriends, well-paying jobs, comfort, and security. They had a place to call home.

Seeing my parents in Canada also hit me hard, as it did every time. My dad had just turned sixty-eight and my mom sixty. I saw them about every six months, and every time they looked just a little bit older. I could see it in their faces, and living away from them amplified that awareness.

When I flew back to China, I lacked the same energy I normally had whenever I returned from North America. I was exhausted and unmotivated. It took me weeks to get around to unpacking my things in the new apartment, and a month before I scheduled a Chinese lesson with Guo Li. Work seemed excruciating. I had no fresh ideas and no will to dig any up.

Part of it was the anticlimax after the "Rent a White Guy" craze. Although there was still a chance of selling the article rights for a movie, I had to confront the hard truth that the movie might not happen. In July, when the hysteria was at its climax, it seemed all but certain. But I should have been heeding my friend Paul's advice—"I wouldn't get my hopes up." My hopes were *way* up. So many people seemed interested and momentum was building. But over the summer, the number of producers willing to create a package—a fleshed-out story idea with possible stars, etc.—had dwindled. Calls and e-mails from my agent were growing less frequent, and even with this new potential offer, of which I knew very little, my gut was telling me it wasn't going to happen, and that even if it did, I didn't really deserve it.

The train pulled into Guilin station in the early afternoon. I immediately rushed to the ticket office to buy a ticket for my next destination, Guangzhou, two days later. This was a massive flaw in China's ticket purchasing system: train tickets could only be bought from the departure city, an annoyance that often resulted in a mad scramble to buy return tickets as soon as a train pulled into the station.

After buying a soft sleeper ticket for Guangzhou, I took a bus to Yangshuo, just over an hour out of town, with a twenty-five-year-old Swede named Olaf, whom I'd met on the train.

"There is a Chinese conundrum," Theroux writes in *Iron Rooster*. "If a place has a reputation for being beautiful, the Chinese flock to it, and its beauty is disfigured by the crowd."

Prime example: Yangshuo Valley. The area is known for its rocky, mist-blanketed peaks, depicted for centuries in Chinese landscape paintings. But it's not the chill backpacker hangout it once was. Mid-Autumn Festival was just kicking off, and the once-quaint town was wall-to-wall with tourists, dressed in baggy plastic ponchos to keep out the rain.

On the advice of friends, I'd booked a room at a small guesthouse in a village a few miles outside of town. It was raining, but I went for a stroll around the village anyway, taking photographs of the rocky hills and the Yulong River. At night, I met Olaf in Yangshuo town and had a dinner of spicy boiled fish and fried vegetables at an outdoor restaurant. We drank beers at an expat hangout called Reggae Bar, chatting with a chain-smoking Irish musician and a group of girls from Guilin who wanted to practice their English.

The next morning, despite the rain, Olaf and I rented bicycles and rode up and down the valley, perusing the villages and stopping to take photos. The hills were shrouded in mist, and the sky was a dark gray. Rice paddies surrounded us. As we continued up the river, locals offered us rides across on bamboo rafts, which, apart from harvesting rice, seemed to be the only business going.

We stopped for a swim at a part of the river where a couple of old ladies were defeathering chickens, preparing for a Mid-Autumn Festival feast. They tossed the feathers into the water. Up close, the river was polluted. Plastic bags. A Coke bottle. A dead fish. The water felt like a tepid bath. We got out soon after getting in, and I felt itchy for the rest of the day.

Despite the itch, it felt good cycling around that afternoon, in the outdoors, in the rain. It was a beautiful place and my head was clear. This was my job, and for a few hours I appreciated how lucky I was.

Not that lucky, evidently. I woke up sick the next morning and couldn't even get out of bed. My train for Guangzhou would be leaving in the early evening, and I spent the day sleeping, sweating, and running in and out of the bathroom.

In late afternoon, I hauled myself out of bed and took the bus into Guilin. I was miserable. My stomach was in ruins, and I was sweaty with fever. On the bus, it took all the will I had to keep from throwing up on the floor beneath my feet. I put headphones on, but my seat partner kept tapping me on the shoulder to ask me questions in Chinese: "Where are you from? What do you do? Do you like China?" My head felt like it was going to explode.

My ticket was soft sleeper, on the bottom berth of a cabin I shared with a thirty-something businessman from Guangzhou. He was a car salesman and offered me glossy pamphlets of the models he sold. He was single and had a sad quality to him. "I travel all the time," he told me. "Very tired. Too tired."

A fat young man in a pink golf shirt with a dimpled bald head that resembled a honeydew melon opened the door and asked if I would move to another cabin and sleep on the top berth. I told him I wouldn't. He grunted and scurried away. Later, another man peeked his head through our door, looked at me, and said, "Be careful of your things. There are thieves on board."

I forced down a dining car meal of mushy fish, vegetables, and rice, and went back to my cabin to read. I was exhausted and weak, but when it came time for bed, I couldn't sleep. My body and head ached. The fat man in the pink shirt kept opening and closing our door, and I was convinced he was the thief in question. I had a camera and computer with me and wrapped the straps of my bags around my legs while I tried to get some rest.

I skipped Guangzhou and continued on to the nearby metropolis of Shenzhen. Thirty years ago, Shenzhen was a fishing village. In 2010, thanks to its status as a Special Economic Zone, it was one of the fastest-growing cities in the world, home to almost nine million people. The average age in Shenzhen was less than thirty years old. The city was dazzling in its newness.

I decided to make the most of my only full day in Shenzhen by doing absolutely nothing. I went to a lavish spa for an indulgent five hours of saunas, hot tubs, and massages, preparing for another long day on the train.

At the spa, I experienced my first Chinese body scrub. For this, I lay naked on a massage bed while a scrubber, a man, vigorously scrubbed my entire body with an exfoliating cream and a wet towel. When I say my entire body, I mean everywhere.

The eighteen-hour train from Shenzhen to Shanghai was newer and cleaner than the other trains I'd taken, featuring sit-down toilets (a rarity) and crisp, white sheets. I met a traveler named Nathan, from England but living in Amsterdam, who was in the cabin next to mine. We smoked between cars and drank tea in the dining car, glancing out at the green hills and crumbling villages outside.

Nathan asked about my life in China. I initially gave my standard answers. "It's awesome. I love it. There's so much going on. So much opportunity."

But Nathan also lived abroad, and he asked good questions. So I eventually answered him honestly. I told him that living in China was always up and down, that I always had mixed emotions about it.

I told him about Julia. The previous month, in Vancouver, we had seen each other for the first time in a year and a half. She was traveling across Canada with her parents, who were thinking about immigrating there.

Seeing her was harder than I'd expected. Not because I still missed her and regretted breaking up with her, but because it was clear there was nothing left. We still got along well, but we had changed too much in the time we'd been apart. Our conversation lacked the fluidity it once had; our interaction felt awkward. I went back to China with a void in my gut. I had always thought that maybe, somehow, we might end up together. Not anymore. It was a hard realization, but I had come to terms with it in the past few weeks. This was a lonely path I'd chosen in life, and I knew it probably would be for some time.

"It's hard to date people here," I told Nathan. "Everybody's always coming and going. I don't know, sometimes it just doesn't feel like real life in China. It's great, don't get me wrong. But sometimes it just feels like a cop-out."

"How long do you think you'll stay?" he asked.

"I'm always here on a rolling basis," I said. "I'll stay for maybe another year . . . or so."

After a few more cigarettes, I returned to my cabin and flipped through magazines. I shared the soft sleeper with a young family who lived in Shenzhen and was heading home for the National Day Holiday. Their incredibly adorable little boy played with a brand-new iPad until ten o'clock, when they flipped off the lights and went to sleep.

I woke from a dream. The cabin was black. The train had slowed to a crawl.

The dream started off the same as all the other going-home dreams I'd had over the years, when I would find myself at the airport about to board a flight to Canada and be struck with sadness about leaving China. I would sometimes wake up, realize I was still in Beijing, and be washed over with relief. But in this one, I was at the airport and couldn't find my ticket home. Someone was telling me I had to stay in China, that I couldn't fly. In the dream I was nearly in tears. I saw flashes of family, of friends. They were moving on with their lives, getting married, getting older. But me, I was still in China.

I opened my eyes to the darkness of the cabin. I could feel the rhythm of the metal wheels rolling on the tracks below me.

I'd been running from real life for almost four years. But someday soon this would all end—the adventures. China, for me, would end someday. Not tomorrow. Maybe not this year or next, but someday. It had to.

Real life would beckon.

We pulled into Shanghai at 7 a.m. I rushed to the ticket counter, where a long line had already formed. After a half-hour wait, I reached the booth.

"Do you have any tickets for Beijing tomorrow morning?"

"Probably not," the young man said. He scrolled through a list on his computer screen. "Actually, there's a ticket for tomorrow morning at seven a.m."

It wasn't ideal, but I was sick of trains. I wanted to sleep in a bed that didn't stop and start all night long. "I'll take it."

The next morning at 6:45, after a night of drinking pints and smoking cigarettes with Nathan, I arrived at the Shanghai train station exhausted and hungover.

I handed my ticket to the attendant on the platform. She handed it back.

"Where's my seat?" I said.

She took the ticket out of my hands, examined it again, and handed it over.

"Mei you."

I looked at my ticket and noticed there was no seat number. My mind flashed back to buying it the previous morning. Had I asked for a seat? I couldn't remember.

"No seat," the attendant said. "Standing room only."

Rule number six of Chinese train travel: double-check your ticket.

I steadied myself for a long journey, twelve hours of standing on a Chinese train. I stood outside on the platform, massaged my temples, and took a deep breath of cool morning air before boarding.

For the first few hours, before we reached Nanjing, I claimed an open seat. But then a businessman politely kicked me out. I walked down to the snack car. There were no seats, only standing tables. I made an instant coffee and studied Chinese characters for the next few hours. A middle-aged man from Shanghai interrupted my studying to practice English. His English was atrocious, and I felt a pang of sympathy for any Chinese person on whom I'd ever tried to rehearse my Chinese over the years, and for my trusty tutor Guo Li and her infinite patience.

I not-so-subtly hinted to the man that I didn't want to talk, holding up my flash cards to indicate that I was deep in study. He didn't buy it.

"You like better Shanghai or Beijing?" the man said.

"Um, they're both good. Very different."

He continued to ask me questions while I flipped through the flash cards, until finally I'd had enough and told him I was going back to my nonexistent seat to sleep.

"Very tired," I said, mock rubbing my eyes.

I returned to my car and claimed a spot on the floor in between cars. A woman, traveling with her daughter, handed me a newspaper to put on the ground. I thanked her.

"What's your name?" the daughter asked.

"Mi Gao."

"Ha-ha. That's a funny name."

The mother nodded. "Very funny name."

They were from Anhui province, traveling to Beijing to visit relatives. I helped the daughter study for an English exam, while the mother tried to doze with her head on her knees.

New passengers boarded at every stop, and soon there were about twenty people crammed between the cars, towering over the mother and daughter and me. A solidarity developed among the seatless passengers, and as the only foreigner without a seat—the only foreigner dumb enough not to have asked for a seat—I was soon a minor celebrity on the train.

There was much talk of my name.

"You know, *Mi* isn't a Chinese surname," a young man in a boxy suit said.

"Yes, I know," I said.

"Gao is a surname, but not Mi," he added.

"Mi Gao is something you eat," an older woman said. "It's a cake."

"Your name is very delicious!" someone wisecracked to much laughter.

Everyone agreed I had a very funny name.

We pulled into Beijing in the early evening. The sun was low in the horizon, and the air felt warm as the doors opened. I gathered my things and took a photo with the mom and daughter on the platform. My back was in knots and I was exhausted. I had in mind the great Chinese cure-all: a cheap massage.

During the cab ride home I thought about the trip, and then I thought about my next reporting trip, to Sichuan, just a few days later, then another after that, to write a story about surfing in the south of China. It was exciting—the life I always wanted—but I also felt drained.

I wondered: How many more twisted paths were there left to explore in China?

Plenty, it turned out.

17

Dancing Idiot

On a warm day in Beijing shortly thereafter, a young man approached me on a street in Sanlitun with a request. He was in his early twenties, short, with bushy black hair, a shiny face, and a tribal tattoo on his left arm. He introduced himself as Eric.

"Are you busy next week?" he said in nervous, slightly American-accented English.

"Why?"

"My company's filming this, sort of, music video. Can you be in it?"

I looked over to my friend, Annie, with whom I had just finished eating pitas. She shrugged.

"Do I have to pretend to sing or anything?" I asked.

"No singing."

"What about dancing? I hate dancing."

"He does hate dancing," Annie confirmed.

"No dancing," Eric said. "You just have to pretend to be, like, in love with some girl."

"Will you pay me?"

"No," he said, raising his eyebrows, "but this video will be seen *everywhere*."

Everywhere. The word lingered for a moment as I pondered the opportunity. On the one hand, I was terrified. Terrified of having to dance. Despite Eric's no-dancing pledge, I was sure he was lying, and, as already established, I have no greater fear than sober dancing. On the other hand, it might make for a good story to write, another strange *laowai*-in-China anecdote, like "Rent a White Guy."

Annie told me to go for it.

"Why not?" I said.

If living in China was like a drug, Eric was offering the chemical substance that provided the high. But as with every drug, there are ups and there are downs. For me, the highs were the moments of bewildering hilarity and adventure; the point of boozy weekend nights when things got interesting; the travels; the randomness and the unusual.

The lows, by the fall of 2010, were pretty much everything in between.

In a lot of ways, I was growing weary of my China experience. In Beijing, life sometimes felt routine: sit in cafés, go to the gym, Chinese class with Guo Li. DVDs, basketball, pub quiz. It was a good life, but not as exciting as it once was. Days flew by. Here's a thing about most foreigner experiences: despite living in one of the most chaotic, baffling, and fascinating countries on earth, eventually you settle into a routine and realize that it all seems so normal. You stop noticing the unusual things around you—in fact, the unusual things are simply not unusual anymore. And then you're left wondering: Why am I still here?

After almost four years in China, I was growing numb to it all, and in the wake of the excitement sparked by the "Rent a White Guy" article and the possible movie deal, which, in the end, never happened, I felt drained. Whenever I wasn't traveling or living out some strange story I could later tell friends over drinks, I didn't know what to make of myself.

These thoughts intensified after I traveled to Sichuan with Jim, a few days after the train trip, and experienced one of the great scares of my life. We were in the mountainous western region of the province reporting a story. On our last day, the two of us climbed to the top of a mountain ridge, looked out at the beautiful landscape around us, filmed one of those giddy "Look where we are, Mom!" videos they find after people have been eaten by grizzly bears, and then promptly got lost in a dense mountain forest with no food, no water, and no protection. We wandered for hours as the temperature steadily dropped. After much struggle and a few shed tears (on my part), we made it out minutes before sunset with only bruised egos and a nice collection of thorn lashes, but it was the first time in my thirty years that I had ever genuinely feared for my life.

The old internal debate between staying or leaving resurfaced with a vengeance in the weeks that followed, and I came close to calling it quits in China.

Then a young man with bushy hair and a tribal tattoo came along and offered yet another hit of the China drug, which reminded me exactly why I was still living in Beijing. Don't get me wrong—it's not as if starring in a music video was in and of itself enough to keep me in China. I didn't even really want to do it. But it represented everything that made life in China so addictive: experiences so beguiling and bizarre that they stay with you forever; rare moments when you are fully aware, fully present. Those moments—raw, challenging, uncomfortable, and often humiliating—make you feel alive.

It later occurred to me that Eric's offer presented an opportunity for an aspect of the foreigner experience in China that had intrigued and eluded me since I first arrived in Beijing: random stardom. Every so often I would meet a foreigner in Beijing who was marginally famous for this or that reason, generally because they had become a television personality on account of speaking good Chinese.

By far the most prominent of this group, the man every foreigner in China loved to hate, was Mark Rowswell, better know as Da Shan, or "Big Mountain." Da Shan was a middle-aged Canadian who had been a presence in China for more than twenty years. He was usually the first thing mentioned whenever I told a Chinese person I was from Canada. Chinese were fond of comparing a foreigner's level of Mandarin to Da Shan's, as in, "Your Chinese is okay. But not as good as Da Shan's."

Da Shan's Chinese was indeed very good, and he had become enormously successful because of it. Before he became Da Shan, Rowswell was a young exchange student in Beijing, learning Mandarin at Peking University in 1988. That year, he made his first appearance on Chinese television, hosting an international singing competition. Later he was invited to perform a comedy skit on CCTV's New Year's gala, which was broadcast to an audience of 550 million viewers—approximately 520 million more people than *exist* in Rowswell's native Canada. For more than two decades, Da Shan had been a ubiquitous presence in the Chinese entertainment industry and a thorn in the side of every foreigner who had ever set foot in the country.

I met Da Shan during the Olympics. He was Canada's "Commissioner General" for the Games and had come to the CBC studio at Ling Long Pagoda for an interview. Our meeting was brief; we shook hands and said hello. He waited in the studio before going on air, chatting with a couple of ladies who worked with the network. They wanted directions to a market in the center of the city. Rowswell jotted down the Chinese characters for the address, as well as the thorough directions to get there from the Bird's Nest.

"You can't just say the address in Chinese. The taxi drivers probably won't know it," he explained. "You have to be very specific—go down this alley, turn down this street, it's across from this building."

He seemed genuinely interested in helping these women, exhibiting the kind of joy I still got whenever friends came to town and I could show off my local know-how. Even after twenty years, countless TV and movie appearances, a fan base that numbered in the hundreds of millions, and I assume plenty of money, Mark Rowswell, aka Big Mountain, seemed like a completely normal dude. He wore Canadian Olympic team gear and unfashionable eyeglasses. His thin blond hair was parted to the side and he had a gap between his two front teeth. He looked like an accountant.

The second-most-famous foreigner in China was an American named Jonathan Kos-Read, also known as Cao Cao. I met him for the first time at a writers' workshop in a Beijing café called the Bookworm. He was handsome, in his mid-thirties, with what I remember as being very nice hair: brown and thick and wavy. The writing group took turns reading our stories and discussing ideas, and during his turn we brainstormed a movie idea he had involving the sexual chi of an ancient Chinese emperor.

A few years later, I interviewed Kos-Read for a story. We met at a Starbucks in Beijing's Central Business District, where he was waiting with his Chinese wife. He wore Thai fisherman pants and a loose-necked shirt. His hair was still great.

I pulled out my tape recorder and placed it on the table.

"So. What do you want to know?" he said.

Kos-Read had arrived in China a decade earlier, after graduating from college in New York, where he studied acting and took Chinese classes to fulfill a language requirement and "impress chicks." In Beijing, he worked odd jobs until he stumbled across an ad on a local listings magazine's website looking for foreign extras. The rest, he explained, was history. Since then, he had made a very healthy living appearing in more than sixty Chinese movies and television series, often playing the white villain. He displayed no vanity whatsoever about his fame and still seemed to marvel at his luck. (Once, he told a friend of mine in an interview that he "should probably be waiting tables somewhere," and his Twitter bio read, "professional token white guy.")

"What are the perks of being famous in China?" I asked.

"I suspect the perks of being famous in China are the same as perks of being famous anywhere. People are nice to me. I get hired for stuff because I'm famous. I get into places free. But nobody runs around and doesn't let me live my normal life. I'm like the Goldilocks of famous—just right."

"Any drawbacks?"

"Nope. None. It's just awesome."

A few days after our initial meeting, Eric sent me a string of text messages, all of which addressed me as "Dude." I was told to meet on Tuesday at 7:45 a.m., and to "produce a business suit, two shirts, and jeans. Can you produce it?"

I told Eric I had a suit, but it didn't fit. He told me to bring it anyway. I reminded him again that I wasn't an actor and that under no circumstances would I dance. "I don't think it's a problem," he said. "You just have to pretend to be in love with some girl."

We met with the cast and crew at an outdoor mall called Solana. At a fountain outside a Starbucks, one of my costars, a good-looking Chinese model/actor with big hair, pursed lips, and a thin nose, was busy staring into a personal mirror and trimming his goatee. He complimented me on my beard and immediately applied makeup to darken his. I was the only foreigner there. The girl I was supposed to be in love with was a pop star from Shandong province who went by the English name Marry. We waited while she was made up in a rented van parked nearby.

The director arrived, a chain-smoking twenty-five-year-old waif from Guangzhou who called himself Viko. He called me "Mitch-ee." He seemed nice, although he was visibly displeased with the wardrobe I'd brought. I was wearing skinny blue jeans, a slim black short-sleeve shirt, and brown leather boots. I had dropped and stepped on my second shirt while exiting a cab earlier, marking it with two boot prints. The suit was boxy and terrible, the one I'd had made for my trip to Dalian years earlier. Viko winced when I showed it to him.

Marry came bouncing out of the van half an hour later. She wore a flowing white dress, her hair in carefully manipulated twirls and her eyes in heavy black makeup. She was tall, with a nice smile and wide face. She looked like Winnie from *The Wonder Years* and she was clearly excited about the shoot.

We drove around to the back of the mall. Permits to film at Solana were expensive, so this was a guerrilla operation. Under umbrellas at an outdoor seating area, a team of makeup artists applied makeup and hair products on me and the other model, whom I'll call Derek (as in *Zoolander*). One woman kept trying to poof up my hair like Derek's, and I kept trying to pat it down whenever she looked away.

Meanwhile, the crew was shooting Marry up on a veranda overlooking the park behind the mall. She smiled, she spun, she swooned. It all looked very much like a Chinese music video, and I was getting nervous.

The premise of the video, as it was hastily explained to me, was this: Marry and Derek were lovers on a trip to Europe, where they meet me, a random European. Some sort of love triangle ensues. Marry is confused, Derek oblivious, and I'm eventually heartbroken when she chooses him over me.

About half an hour later, Eric handed me several sheets of paper stapled together, one of which featured movie stills, mostly of Ethan Hawke and Julie Delpy in *Before Sunrise*.

"Okay," he said, "the first shot is of you and the girl and the other guy running. Like this." He tapped on a small image of three actors running hand in hand in a European city.

"That seems weird," I said.

"Yes."

"Holding hands?"

"Yeah. It should be no problem."

It was a problem. During the first take, Derek darted out quickly, while I went for a light jog, leaving Marry awkwardly in the middle being tugged in both directions. When the director yelled "cut," everybody watching started laughing. Eric was literally keeled over.

"Mitch. Mitch!" he said, trying to contain his laughter. "You have to go faster! And don't stare at her the whole time. It looks funny."

I watched the video playback. My arms and legs were so stiff it looked as if I was wearing clothing made of metal. "Jesus," I said. My mouth was parched. "Eric, can you get me some water?"

The director put his arm on my shoulder. "You have to be more natural. And move your arms when you run."

We did three more uncomfortable takes before the director yelled, "Good take!" To put a time frame on the shoot, I had told them I had to leave for work at 11:30 a.m.—a lie. The director checked his watch. We'd just started filming but only had a little over an hour left before my deadline.

The next shot was a short scene of Derek and me sitting on a bench pretending to talk. Before cameras started rolling, Marry yelled to me, "Mitch, like Tom Hanks!" Somebody mentioned Tom Cruise. "Like Tom Cruise!" Marry said.

After we wrapped that scene, a crew member brought over two cups of melting ice cream. For the next shot I had to walk through the mall holding the ice cream and trying to look "happy and excited," and then, upon seeing the two young lovers enjoying themselves on a bench already eating ice cream, I was instructed to "look blue."

"With your eyes," Eric translated. "Look blue with your eyes."

The directions were specific: hold the ice cream like so; walk like this; keep your head down; don't use your hands or shake your head. We did four takes, and each time I thought I'd nailed it. The director thought otherwise. With each take, he looked increasingly worried until finally he glanced at his watch and said, "Good enough."

I was a star once. I was twelve years old, in seventh grade, and I had been cast as the lead of my elementary school's Christmas musical, called *Small One*. The play was based on a children's book about a young boy and his beloved donkey. I played the boy. I sang songs (*Small one, small one, small one for sale . . . one piece of silver, small one for sale . . .*) and acted my heart out. We did an afternoon and an evening performance, and both earned standing ovations as robust as strong coffee. I remember spotting my grandpa in the audience as he sprang up from his seat before anyone else, slapping his big hands together with a great force. It was the proudest moment of my young life.

The next year I was cast as Tiny Tim in our school's rendition of *A Christmas Carol*. But something had changed that year: the onset of puberty. As the boy in *Small One*, my voice was high and angelic. Not so as an adolescent. My voice cracked and couldn't decide between high and low. My performance was a disaster, and as I stood onstage struggling through my numbers, within me was growing a lifelong fear of performing.

A fear that would only be exacerbated by what was about to happen.

Marry changed into a white wedding dress, and for the last of my scheduled scenes, the three of us were positioned atop a set of stairs in the middle of the mall. Eric explained that we were to simply walk behind her while she pretended to sing her song, which blasted from a pair of speakers. There was then a long conversation in Chinese between the director, his assistant, and Marry. I couldn't understand all of it, but I did catch one fateful phrase:

Tiaowu. Dancing.

My ears perked up, and so did Eric's. He hurried over, cigarette in hand, and told the director, "No—Mitch can't dance." The director spoke in Chinese, and Eric translated. "You don't have to dance, just walk to the music. Like this." He made dancing movements.

"That's dancing!" I protested.

Eric laughed. "I know, I know. Just, you know, move to the music. Not dancing. Just moving."

My heart was racing now and sweat circles were forming in my armpits. During the first take, which seemed to span the length of a Chinese dynasty but was probably no more than thirty seconds, I was back in my metal clothes. I moved like RoboCop.

When the director yelled cut, Eric said, "Mitch, you're very nervous. You're doing like this." He imitated my RoboCop dance. "Try to act like you're flirting with her. Like you're having fun. More natural."

"But I'm not having fun and it's not natural."

The second take was as bad as the first. The assistant director pointed out the obvious—that I was awful. The director asked for one more take.

"Look," I said, "it's not going to get any better than this. This is really awkward for me. I said I didn't want to dance; you want me to dance. That last take was as good as it's going to get."

Marry told me that I needed to be "more manly—like cool man." She grabbed my arms and said: "Do you like me?"

"Sure, why not," I said.

"Well, then you have to act like you like me."

"If you wanted an actor, you should have paid for an actor. I'm not an actor."

She threw up her arms in exasperation. Viko begged for one more take. I looked over at Marry sitting on the pavement nearby in her white wedding dress, looking near tears. I was clearly ruining her big video. I just wanted to leave, to go home and wash off the humiliation. The jury was in with its verdict: I was the worst unpaid costar in the history of low-budget Chinese pop music videos.

Through clenched teeth, I agreed to one more take.

About a month later I was riding my bike through the city when I received a text message from Viko. "Hi Mith!" he wrote, misspelling my name. "The video you did with Marry is finished! I will send it to your e-mail. You are very handsome ;)"

My heart skipped a beat. When I got home, I opened my laptop and followed the link Viko had sent. My roommates, Paul and Kit, gathered around to watch. As we waited for the video to download, I wondered if I should even watch it. I swallowed.

The video, called "Le Seine," opens with bright, overexposed shots of Marry on the veranda followed by images of what I assume Viko and the others thought was Europe. (Curiously, the video's version of Europe is home to Yankee Stadium.) Then, there I am, doing an awkward little jig on the stairs beside Marry and Derek. My scenes are brief. The three of us appear running through the mall, and then I'm "looking happy" walking down the hall with ice cream in hand. If I do say so myself, the shot where I was to "look blue" is a real tour de force. My dancing part was almost entirely cut from the final edit, except for the odd glimpse of my arm or chin at the corner of the frame.

"This is amazing," Paul said, looking over my shoulder.

"Fine work," Kit chimed in.

I don't appear in the video's last three minutes. Total screen time was about thirty seconds, and I'm amazed they managed to salvage that much. In the credits I was listed as "MITH (CANADA)."

"I think we have a new nickname for you," Kit said, struggling not to laugh.

"What's that?"

"The man . . . the Mith . . . the legend."

18

Chollywood Dreaming

Some people toil for years to crack the movie business. In China, it took me five hours.

One wintry Sunday evening a few months later, in early 2011, I opened an online classifieds page looking for acting jobs and found a want ad for foreign extras needed to play journalists, police officers, FBI agents, and military personnel in a Chinese movie. I sent out an e-mail with a photo and bio at 7:30 p.m. I listed under experience acting in a Chinese music video and modeling for *Cosmo*.

At 12:30 a.m., sitting in the front seat of a taxi headed home with Paul and Kit, I received a phone call from a woman named Cathy who had an air of desperation in her voice. She said she was a casting agent and was urgently looking for foreigners for a shoot the next morning.

"Do you consider yourself fat?" she said, totally deadpan.

"Hmm. No."

"So you're not very big?"

"No. I'm tall, athletic . . . I'm not small. But I'm not fat, either."

"Okay." She paused. "Do you think you could play a police officer?"

I thought about it for a second. "Sure."

"Can you come at six a.m. tomorrow?"

"Wow. That's pretty early."

"I know it's not much notice," Cathy sighed, "but we have scientists. They're seventeen years old—"

"You have seventeen-year-olds playing scientists?"

"No—*seventy*! Not seventeen. And they get up very early. It's no problem."

I paused. "Okay," I said, "I'll do it."

"Do you consider yourself a good actor?" Cathy asked through the phone. "Could you say some lines?"

"I don't know if I'm a good actor. We'll have to see."

"Could you say some lines?"

"Sure." I winked at my roommates, who were listening to the conversation and holding back laughter in the backseat of a taxi. "I could probably say some lines."

And so began my brief career in Chinese cinema.

The music video had left me shell-shocked. In the weeks after filming, I periodically glanced at want ads online and found plenty of small-time acting and modeling gigs, but I was reluctant to seek them out. I would compose an e-mail and attach a few photos, but as I was about to hit SEND, I would picture myself standing beside Marry, atop the stairs at the outdoor mall and dancing like a moron as the director and crew looked on in horror. I would think to myself, You're a journalist, for chrissakes, and then I would delete the e-mail.

But I was on to something. It occurred to me in the months after the "Rent a White Guy" article that people in the West might want to see the lighter side of China. They wanted a break from news of growing economic might, postapocalyptic skies, excesses of the rich, and hardships of the poor. I figured that as a writer, by slipping into the character of Tall Rice and chasing the rabbit down the rabbit hole—seeking out the most offbeat, unusual, only-in-China adventures I could find—I could offer a glimpse into the *other* China, the surreal place where my friends and I lived. This, I decided, would be my new beat: Chinese Neverland.

I put concerns about my dignity aside and began looking for roles in Chinese movies.

The movie business was booming in China. Box office returns in 2010 topped $1.5 billion, a 64 percent increase from the year before, making China's movie market on target to be the world's second largest by 2015. The industry, sometimes dubbed "Chollywood," pumped out 526 films in 2010 (compared to 754 in the United States), and the government announced plans to more than double the size of the entertainment industries, including movies and television, over the next five years.

Hollywood had taken notice. Chinese-U.S. coproductions were on the rise, and Christian Bale, Kevin Spacey, and Keanu Reeves were among the stars who had sought projects in China. So eager were American studios to crack the Chinese market that MGM edited out the Chinese villains from its *Red Dawn* remake, replacing them with North Koreans. Studios couldn't afford to offend the officials who decided which twenty-odd foreign films were allowed to play each year on Chinese screens, whose numbers were growing at a rate of four per day.

The nightmare of my first foray into the Chinese entertainment industry prevented me from sleeping that night. I tossed and turned until my alarm rang at 5:30 a.m. I showered, drank a cup of coffee, and took a cab to our allotted meeting place.

There were more than a dozen foreign extras waiting in the lobby of the Kunlun Hotel in downtown Beijing. Cathy, a short woman with a round face and a knit wool cap sitting crookedly atop her head, spotted me immediately as I entered through the lobby's revolving doors.

"Mi Gao!" she shouted, reaching out her hand. She spoke to me in English. "Nice to meet you. Oh, you're not very fat. You can't play the police officer. He'll play the police officer." She pointed to a husky middle-aged man sleeping on a couch in the lobby. "You can play a military officer. But we'll have to cut your hair. . . . Not too short . . . just a little on the sides. . . . . One week, back to normal!"

I tried to protest, but she brushed me off and told me to go make friends with the other extras. I took a seat on the couch beside the dozing man, whom Cathy woke and instructed to see the casting director to see if he was fat enough to play the cop.

After a brief delay on account of a crew member's diarrhea, we piled into a minibus and drove to a studio on the outskirts of town. We were a grab bag of expat males: white-haired Americans with southern accents (the "scientists," I was told); some well-groomed Italians; and a couple of burly Eastern Europeans. The soon-to-be police officer was Bulgarian. I sat beside Cathy with the hope of ingratiating myself to her and landing more movie gigs. I learned that her biggest achievement as a casting agent was finding the body double for Brendan Fraser in *The Mummy: Tomb of the Dragon Emperor*, which had been filmed in Shanghai a few years earlier.

Cathy briefed me on the movie we were filming. Called *Qian Xue Sen*, the film was based on the true story of the Chinese rocket scientist of the same name, who, in the 1950s, after making significant contributions to the American missile and space programs, was accused of being a communist spy and forced to escape back to China, where he started up the country's own rocket program. On this day, we were filming scenes from Qian's time in the United States, which is why so many foreigners were needed. The movie was funded by the behemoth China Film Group, to the tune of $9.5 million—no small sum for a Chinese project. Several crew members and an actor were brought in from the States; they had apparently worked on the series *Lost*, a fact of which Cathy was quite proud.

Before arriving at the studio, we stopped at a decrepit hotel on the outskirts of the city, where the crew was staying. Cathy ushered us upstairs to a makeshift makeup room, where a group of foreigners were getting haircuts.

I watched the military cuts being bestowed on the heads of my fellow extras, and I suffered a mild panic attack. Haircuts in China are always a risky proposition, and I'd had a number of devastating experiences over the years. Once I walked out of the salon looking like a marine, although I repeatedly told the bored-looking stylist "not too short." My hair became a running joke among my friends for the next two weeks.

I pleaded with Cathy to spare my hair, but she insisted it would just be a trim. It wasn't. The stylist removed his clippers and took the sides down to the width of a nickel, leaving the top intact. He doused my head with hair spray and pulled big wads of hair over to one side. (The next day a friend said of my hair: "It looks a little Hitler Youth.")

Beside me, a young man who had arrived in the morning with a head of wild red hair was being sheared like a sheep.

"Did you know they were cutting your hair when you signed up for this?" I asked.

"Nope," he said, looking terrified as his ginger locks tumbled to the floor.

After some toast and instant coffee, Cathy corralled us back into the bus and we drove to the studio. I sat beside a blond Canadian from Winnipeg, named Daniel, who was the same age as me. He ran his own business in Beijing and did acting as a side gig. He had recently starred as the foreign villain in a Chinese movie and was negotiating for a recurring speaking role on a TV show.

"You don't need to be talented," he told me as we drove. "You just need to be available when they call you. It's a very low bar."

We pulled up to a large brick building. Inside, in the dressing room, a number of young aides started handing out outfits. They quickly ran out of military officers' uniforms, so my role was changed to FBI agent.

"It's a better role," Cathy insisted. "Very cool."

She flashed a thumbs-up and I changed into a baggy gray suit.

We were brought into a massive soundstage built into a former factory next door. The set was made to look like a 1950s-era FBI office, complete with old newspapers, ashtrays, and file folders marked CONFIDENTIAL. The studio was not insulated, and it was freezing; the crew wore bulky winter coats and warmed their hands with their breath. The director and art director scurried about, placing the small army of FBI agents and military officers behind desks, in semi-hidden offices, and around a big table, in the middle of the set, covered with stacks of documents.

Cathy, for some reason, was in a state of near panic, insisting that we all be quiet and still as the scene was set up. She seemed keen on making a good impression on the American crew members.

"Shut up!" she hissed, grabbing my arm as I chatted quietly with one of my costars. "They're from *Hollywood*."

My role was simple: stand at a desk pretending to talk to a young

French guy who totally did not look the part, and then I would be called to another desk where a thirty-something European military officer would instruct me to grab "that document." I then walked over to the big table at the center of the set, where a group of older scientists were examining the papers looking for evidence of Qian's Communist sympathies. I had to bring the document back to the officer.

After a few takes the director told me to "say something" to the scientist when I picked up the folder. One precious, unscripted, mumbled line. He inserted a small mic in my shirt. It was official: I had a speaking role.

I just need to take this book for a minute.

The night before, my roommate Paul had offered some advice based on my last acting role: try to relax. I noticed how nervous the French guy was and thought to myself, Don't worry, kid, follow my lead. After all, I was practically already a music video star. And this time, I didn't have to dance.

I tried to get into character, repeating in my head: *I'm a thirty-year-old FBI agent. I'm on my way to the top. I just need to take this book for a minute.*

We did the take about a dozen times and I varied my line with every take: "I need to borrow this book for a second . . ." "I need to take this off your hands for a minute . . ." "Just let me grab this folder for a few minutes."

I nailed it.

After the scene wrapped, we drank instant coffee in the parking lot outside the studio. I chatted with fellow extras about the usual expat male topic—women—and had a prison lunch of soggy eggplant, cabbage, chicken parts, some sort of rice gruel, and donkey meat flatbread.

"Acting is waiting," one of the extras said at some point in the afternoon, stating the obvious.

Several hours had passed since my one glorious line. It was getting late in the afternoon, and I was starting to doubt I'd be called upon again. It was freezing outside, so I went to the wardrobe room, where several extras had already gathered, and had a nap.

I woke half an hour later. Everybody around me was still asleep. I leaned back in my chair and put my feet up on a radiator, looking out the window at the pale winter sky. What a day, I thought. This place could be incredible.

Cathy roused us at 5 p.m. and said it was time to go home. She tried to dodge paying me the money she'd promised, saying she would meet me at a café downtown in the next few days, but I refused to leave before she handed it over, which she eventually did.

My line didn't bump me up a pay grade. Cathy paid me the standard 500 yuan (seventy-seven dollars), and a few minutes later I crammed into the minibus heading back downtown, fantasies of Chollywood stardom floating in my head.

As with the "Rent a White Guy" story, I sat in Café Zarah one afternoon and wrote out the tale of my day as a film star. It was another unique take on the expat experience in China. Again, I pitched the article to the *Atlantic*, and the magazine took it.

These were the stories the world wanted to read. I'd found my niche. My career was going great.

Everything else, unfortunately, was turning to shit.

19

"Burst into Bloom"

My meteoric rise to stardom fell somewhat short of meteoric.

Not long after the *Qian Xue Sen* movie gig, I received two calls for acting jobs—one from Cathy and another from an agent named Jackie, who had surreptitiously slipped me his business card on the bus home from the set. Cathy called about a movie, Jackie a TV show. Neither of them gave much in the way of notice—about twelve hours—and for both jobs I had previous commitments.

For several weeks afterward, I was traveling or otherwise occupied. As Daniel had warned me on the set of *Qian Xue Sen*, Chinese agents cared less about talent than about reliability. It's a one-strike-you're-out system, he told me, and I was out. My dreams of Chollywood stardom were flitting away.

But that summer, with plenty of time on my hands, I redoubled my efforts to get marginally famous, to become the poor man's Da Shan. I had a photographer friend of mine take head shots, called back the agents I knew, and started looking for more acting jobs on online classifieds.

My next potential gig came via Daniel. My phone buzzed one Wednesday night during a pub quiz. "A TV show really needs an actor for a few days starting tomorrow," he wrote. "You available?"

I told him I was and waited for instructions. He said to call a woman named Sylvia first thing next morning, which I did, about half a dozen times. Her phone was off.

At 11 a.m., I was at the gym when my phone rang. It was Sylvia.

"I've been waiting so long for your call!" she yelled into the phone in English.

"I tried calling you like six times this morning," I said.

"We need to meet you. Right now. Can you come now?"

"Right now? I'm at the gym now. I haven't even showered."

"Please, hurry. Go shower now and we will be there with the van in twenty minutes!" she pleaded. "Please, it's an *urgency*!"

I rushed to the shower and hurried to the street out in front of my gym. There I waited for one hour and forty minutes before Sylvia pulled up in a van. She was accompanied by two other Chinese men—a driver and another agent—and two other foreigners: a middle-aged American named Kurt, who was from Hawaii and wore a Tommy Bahama shirt, and a Ukrainian male model. We picked up a third foreigner, a Syrian, and headed toward the outskirts of town.

"Where are we going?" I asked Sylvia.

"To the studio. It's about an hour out of town."

"What is this show anyway?"

"A historical show. They need a foreigner to play a doctor."

We continued driving while the four foreigners tried to figure out what we were auditioning for, piecing together potential scenarios based on the tidbits of information Sylvia had provided.

When we arrived, Sylvia escorted us into a hotel lobby near the studio, where we met a producer who offered us all cigarettes. I asked Sylvia one more time for information about the program.

"It's historical, about, I don't know how you say in English . . . *Gong Chan Dang.*"

I didn't know the word so I checked my phone dictionary. *Gong Chan Dang* = Communist Party of China. The foreign doctor, I guessed, was Norman Bethune, one of the best-known foreigners in Chinese history, a Canadian who helped Mao's Communists until his death of blood poisoning in 1939. In China, Bethune is considered a martyr, and I wondered if my citizenship would give me a leg up on the role.

Sylvia led us upstairs to meet the producer. On the way, she told us, "Don't say you don't have much experience. Say you've done movies, TV shows, commercials, okay? That will be better."

A young producer waited for us in the hotel room. He was working on his laptop as we walked through the door; a cigarette was dangling from his lips. Beside him was an ashtray with a couple of dozen butts. Smoke filled the room. As we walked in, he looked at the Ukrainian and Kurt, the Hawaiian.

"Oh, *tai gao le!*" the producer said. Too tall.

My heart sank. Kurt and I were the exact same height, and the Ukrainian was a couple of inches shorter.

Next the producer looked at the Syrian, who was tanned, with dark stubble on his face.

"Oh, *tai hei le!*" he said. Too dark.

I sat down before he noticed my height. The producer stopped on me for a moment and turned to the agent.

"He's the best. Take him to the other room."

Sylvia walked me to a nearby room. She was thrilled. "This is great. He likes you. Make sure to tell him you've acted."

"Actually, I was in a movie. And a music video."

"Great! We'll put that on your résumé."

"My résumé?"

In the hotel room Sylvia asked me to upload my head shots onto a memory stick while she crafted a fake résumé for me in Chinese. A few minutes later, the producer entered and asked me to stand.

"How tall are you?"

"I'm 190 centimeters"—six foot three.

"Hmm. That's okay, we'll tell the director you're 180."

"But won't he notice—"

The producer darted out of the room, a cloud of cigarette smoke trailing behind him. Sylvia grabbed my shoulders and pulled my face close like she was going to kiss me. "It's looking good," she said. "*Really* good."

Sylvia treated us to lunch as we waited for the director's word. I was feeling optimistic. "This could be good for you," Kurt said, slightly forlorn, as we ate at a Korean restaurant next to the hotel. "Apparently, it's a recurring role."

Half an hour later, back in the hotel lobby, the first producer came down to deliver the news.

He spoke in Chinese. "Did you eat enough? Good. So here's the thing. You guys didn't fit." He looked at me. "The director said you're not quite right. You're too tall. Sorry, really sorry."

We were all slightly annoyed with Sylvia on the ride home. A simple question—how tall are you?—could have saved us all four hours of our time. I asked Sylvia once more what, exactly, the producers were looking for in the role of doctor, other than someone shorter than me.

"They want a forty-five-year-old man," she replied.

I had just turned thirty-one.

———————

An agent called me one Saturday night as I sipped champagne at a friend's wedding. A movie was being shot, he said, and the producers wanted to meet me the next afternoon. I asked if I needed to wear anything special or if I would be auditioning.

"No, nothing special," the agent said. "They just want to meet you."

The next afternoon, hungover from a long night of drinking champagne, I showed up at a studio near Beijing's Central Business District to find that it was, in fact, an audition, but not for a movie. The job was for a promotional advertisement for a Chinese television company called Blue Ocean Network. BON broadcasted English-language programing to the United States. My old roommate Tom had worked at BON before moving back to the United Kingdom the previous year, and I still had several friends at the station. I really didn't want any of them to see whatever end result would come of this, and I considered backing out and going home to nurse my hangover.

I told one of the Chinese producers that I had expected to be meeting about a movie and he waved his hand. "No, no movie. No movie." The director asked me to stand in front of a green screen and walk from left to right, front to back, pretending to look at things off in the distance. Then he asked me to walk in place, facing the camera, and act as if I was looking at the Forbidden City just beyond. There was some grumbling about the fact that I'd worn shorts and a T-shirt, and about my beard, and after a couple of minutes of walking in place, the director thanked me and said he would get in touch.

I got the part on the condition that I shave my beard. After much complaining, I relented. The shoot took up a Sunday, and I was paid $200 for my troubles. All I had to do was walk around in front of a green screen pretending to look at things that weren't really there.

It was my first and only starring role.

My friend David Fu, a Chinese-American who worked in the film industry, hooked me up with a spot on Beijing Television. They wanted a foreigner to more or less humiliate himself by performing Chinese opera in front of a television audience of millions.

I was instructed to meet at 4:30 p.m. at the Beijing TV studios downtown. Paul, Kit, and Annie came along with me, interested as they were in watching me embarrass myself. We met Ms. Li, a producer on the special National Day holiday show on which I was to appear. She escorted us into the building and brought us onto the set. The show was called *Guang Rong Zhang Pang*, which translated roughly into "Glorious Burst into Bloom." The studio was dark, with a black and purple backdrop, and purple, pink, and white star-shaped strobe lights illuminated the stage.

A few dozen people had gathered in the audience, but more than half the seats were left empty. They were old ladies mostly, and several of them were growing impatient. "When does filming start?" one belted out. "It's almost rush hour!"

We sat. We waited. My palms were sweaty. Ms. Li told me I would be called onstage and instructed to do various poses and movements common in Peking Opera.

"Will I have to sing?" I asked.

"Maybe. Maybe not. I'm not too sure."

"You don't know?"

"No. It's up to the host." She scurried off.

Eventually the host arrived. And then the three guests: female Peking opera performers. As filming began and they started the interview, I still didn't know what I would be encountering upon being called onstage. After twenty minutes, the host asked the audience if anybody wanted to come up and learn some Peking opera. This was my cue. Ms. Li nodded and I stood to go onstage.

There I introduced myself to the audience, and one of the performers handed me a baton and tried to teach me how to twirl it. Easy enough. A few minutes later I went back onstage and learned a little dance, which went considerably better than my music video routine. In the end, I was not required to sing.

I sat down, satisfied with my performance. An old lady tapped me on the shoulder and whispered in my ear.

"Hen lihai!" she said. Very formidable.

She presented me with a little notebook and asked for my autograph. I signed it, in Chinese characters: Mi Gao.

During the National Day holiday week, in October 2011, I gave a speech at my former assistant's wedding. Her name was Wei Xiao Ming, and she and her new husband, who went by the Anglicized name Mex, were married in a village of two hundred families not far from the North Korean border. ("Most of the villagers have never seen a foreigner before," the groom told me when I arrived.)

I read the speech, in Chinese, in front of a curious audience of locals in Mex's family's backyard as sappy music played in the background. Despite my growing show business CV, I was so nervous my hands were shaking and I lost my place a few times. The host, a man in his thirties wearing a sparkling jacket that looked like fish scales, helped me find my spot each time.

"Wei Xiao Ming and I started as colleagues," I said, "but now we've become very good friends. I'm happy she's found such an amazing husband. He's very handsome, isn't he?" The crowd cheered. "The bride's very beautiful, isn't she?" They cried even louder. "I wish them one hundred years of good luck and a long life together. Thank you."

When the speech was over, I looked at Xiao Ming in her white wedding dress, standing on a stage in a tiny corner of northeast China, and she was crying. It was by far the most satisfying moment I would have in front of an audience in China.

Throughout those months I felt like I was living two separate lives. One was my Facebook life; the other my real life. Facebook life consisted of all the random adventures I was having in the name of writing—chasing acting gigs, starring in music videos, mumbling a line in a Chinese movie. People left comments congratulating me on living such an interesting life and wishing me luck in my next pursuit. But Facebook life wasn't really *my* life. It was Tall Rice's.

Real life was something different. During the summer and fall of 2011, I was growing increasingly anxious about my future, about when and how I would leave China, and what I would do once I was gone. As Tall Rice, I was experiencing more adventures than I had ever thought possible. But in my real life, I kept asking myself, was I still happy in China? I struggled to find an answer.

Things were changing in Beijing. I had been in the city for four and a half years, and many of the core friends I'd made over the previous few years had left or were thinking about leaving. We had lived a life of prolonged adolescence, and now people were growing up. Social engagements were growing fewer and farther between, and people were pairing up and settling down. Some of my best friends were seeking jobs back home or applying for graduate school. On bad days it seemed like my Beijing life, which I had loved so much, which had given me an identity, was crumbling before my eyes.

My dating life was practically nonexistent except for the odd drunken one-night stand, sometimes spaced months apart. Why date when you know that someday you won't be here anymore? Partying, so key to life in China, was losing its shine. The wasted journalist abroad was getting boring and cliché.

When I first arrived in Beijing, I would walk into a bar and not know a soul. It was exhilarating. *Who are these people*, I wanted to know, *and why are they here?* A few years later, I did know. I'd walk into a bar and recognize dozens of people. Now that was starting to change. The wave of foreigners who had come to witness the buildup and aftermath of the Olympics—my wave—was being replaced by a new one of people coming from all over the world for the opportunities China afforded. They were excited to be here and they were young. Sometimes in bars and nightclubs I was starting to feel like Matthew McConaughey in *Dazed and Confused*—"I get older, they stay the same age." I would look around and notice that I was the oldest person in my group—by about five years. And I wasn't even that old.

I had lived in Beijing longer than in any other city since high school, and the fast-approaching five-year milestone weighed heavily on me. I felt increasingly guilty about living abroad, about being so far from my family, about avoiding responsibility. I was jealous of friends who were leaving and of those who had a plan for the future. But it's hard to leave the city that's the closest thing you have to a home, even if you'll never really belong there.

My head was a clouded mess. Days were spent killing time, filling it up in chunks—reading a magazine, cycling to the gym, Chinese class, followed by sitting in Café Zarah surfing the Internet and looking for things to tweet, and then getting a tiny burst of energy to write. At night: dinner, basketball, drinks, a movie.

It was all a blur. I wasn't really there. Not totally. In a lot of ways, I was starting to feel like I had when I left Toronto.

It was time to enlist my therapist: Guo Li.

Guo Li and I had been having classes together for more than three years. I use the word *classes* loosely. Mostly, I would pay her fifty yuan an hour just to sit and talk. She knew everything about me—more, in fact, than most of my Western friends in Beijing—and I knew everything about her. She was more than just my best Chinese friend; she was one of my best friends, period.

One afternoon in the fall of 2011, at a coffee shop in a mall near Dongzhimen subway station, Guo Li noticed that I wasn't my usual self.

"Mi Gao," she said, "what's wrong? You're not normal today."

I sighed and explained that I was feeling nervous about the future. I told her that many of my friends were leaving and that, although I still loved Beijing, I also felt stuck. I didn't know if I wanted to stay or go.

She nodded. "That's because you're *bei piao*."

Bei piao. I was one of Beijing's floating generation.

"I'm *bei piao*, too," she said.

We sat in silence for a few moments, both of us lost and confused in the booming capital of China.

Guo Li tried to put me at ease. "You live a good life here, Mi Gao. You travel all the time, you have so many friends, and you're not poor. You should enjoy it. You can go back to Canada whenever you want."

She was right, of course, but still I fretted. I saw two possible futures for myself. Scenario A: I stay in China, nine more years pass, and the clock strikes forty. Broke and alone, I reapply for a job copyediting at *China Daily*, spending my days trying to block out the hum of my ancient computer and the blinding fluorescent lights above my head, and my evenings in the Den, wallowing in middle-aged sorrow, following in the footsteps of Potter and his friends, drinking flat Carlsberg and smoking cigarettes bummed off young female interns I'm trying to sleep with. Scenario B: I return to North America, accept a job at a newspaper, and bore people to death with endless tales about the good life I used to live over in China.

Neither option appealed.

Not a day went by that I didn't weigh leaving, weigh the choice between two vastly different worlds, between two vastly different lives. I worried that if I stayed, I'd miss out on having a family and building a life for myself in a place I could call home. I worried that I'd miss out on spending time with my parents as they grew older, and with my friends as they settled into families.

On the other hand, I worried that if I left, I would never really find my way back in North America, that I would miss China so much it would consume me.

But I began wanting a more normal life—I wanted a stable job, enough money to be comfortable, a nice apartment, old friends, and a neighborhood pub. A weekly softball game with colleagues. Maybe a wife and a daughter. All those things that once terrified me and prompted me to run—the things that, when you boiled it right down, had driven me to China—all seemed strangely appealing.

What was happening to me? I wondered. Could it be that I was, finally, growing up?

Despite all the friends I had made over the years, and all the time I had spent in the city, the expat life in Beijing could still be a lonely one. And it became clear how much it was affecting me after I met my Future Wife.

One summer night a few months earlier, at a *hutong* restaurant not far from my apartment, I spotted a girl who was, in my mind, perfect. She was uniquely gorgeous with a cool style, somehow both sexy and modest. But it wasn't just the way she looked. I felt immediately as if I already knew her, as if I'd *always* known her, even though I'd never seen her before in my life.

I was infatuated. Nothing like this had ever happened to me before. She was sitting at another table across the restaurant, with some people I knew, and I stared at her the entire night. At one point I approached her table with the sole purpose of getting an introduction. I didn't, but I did overhear her name—Maria.

The next day I flew to Canada for a few weeks, and when I arrived, I did some Facebook stalking to see if I could find her, but to no avail. Who was this girl? What was she doing in Beijing? Was she single?

Although I had no answers to these questions, I told my mom I'd found my "future wife"—I actually used those words.

"Mom, I met my future wife the other day."

"Oh really? Tell me about her," my mom said.

"She's only the most beautiful woman I've ever seen."

"What's her name?"

"Maria."

"What does she do?"

"Well, I haven't actually met her per se."

A few weeks later, I was back in Beijing, and after a month of wandering the city with my eyes open, thinking of the lines I would use on her if I ever found her, I gave up hope of finding my Future Wife again.

Then one night I saw her in a bar. As soon as I noticed her from the door, my heart started pounding. My mouth was dry. I explained to my friend Gil, who just happened to be the world's best wingman, that I absolutely *must* talk to this girl. Gil agreed to approach her table with a concocted story about how we had all met on some previous occasion. After an awkward few minutes of listening to Gil's fabricated story, she snuck outside, and I followed. I introduced myself and we chatted for a few minutes. She was British and worked at an NGO in Beijing. She was about to go home for the night, and I blurted out something about getting a drink sometime. She said sure. I was euphoric.

We arranged a time. She canceled. We arranged another time. She canceled again. We ended up having lunch, and during the lunch she casually mentioned that she had a boyfriend. I was, even though I'd known this girl for all of twenty minutes, devastated.

A few months later, we would end up dating, Maria and I, and I was crazy about her. It didn't last long, though. Apparently I had seen too many romantic comedies on airplanes because I got very far ahead of myself. I was convinced she was going to be my ticket out of China. We rushed into things after she broke up with her boyfriend, and then she pulled away, drew in again, and a few months later, pulled away for the last time. I ignored all kinds of warning signs—she's too young, just twenty-four years old, too soon out of a relationship—and I paid for it in the end. She hadn't really been single since she was fifteen years old, she told me. Her last few relationships had been "really intense." She needed to do "the whole single-Beijing thing."

I was as heartbroken as I'd ever been in my life. As always, China had found a way to derail best-laid plans.

"Do you want to be on a dating show?"

It was David Fu again, calling me one afternoon that fall. He had an uncle who worked as a producer, and he needed a foreigner to appear on his Shanghai-based program, called "One Out of 100."

I might have been Bursting into Bloom as a Chinese stage presence, but in the mood I was in I most certainty did not want to be on a dating show.

David was persuasive. "They'll fly you down to Shanghai, all expenses paid," he said. "Maybe you'll meet your future wife."

20

Singing Elvis for the People

I took a deep breath. And another.

Don't fight this, I thought. Embrace it.

I was backstage waiting at the bottom of a set of stairs that led to the set of a famous Chinese dating show, called *Bai Li Tiao Yi*—"One Out of 100." My armpits were soaked. My bladder was ready to explode.

Deep breath.

Thirteen young women waited for me onstage. Beyond them was a live studio audience, as well as a hundred-odd viewers being broadcast via webcam on a huge screen at the front of the stage, collectively producing live rankings of the male contestants from their home computers.

Beyond that, an audience of millions.

Deep breath. *Don't fight it.*

I had guzzled about eight bottles of water but still felt cotton-mouthed. I desperately had to pee. Too late. I rehearsed my introduction in my head and mouthed the words to the song I had chosen to sing: Elvis's "Can't Help Falling in Love"—a song I figured appropriately cheesy for a dating show; one I could easily ham up.

Kevin, the director, a thirty-something Shanghainese hipster in yellow jeans and a purple hoodie—some kind of urban Joker outfit—joined me on the stairs.

"Mi Gao," he said, patting me on the back, "when they call your name, walk up the stairs and onto the stage. Remember to pause under the arch and do a pose, like this . . . " He danced a little jig. "Mi Gao, *jia you.*"

Kevin gave me a thumbs-up and walked away. I was alone.

Jia you. Add oil.

I heard the female host speaking into the microphone from the stage.

"Let's welcome our esteemed guest from Canada, Mi Gao!"

The audience applauded. I took one last deep breath and slowly climbed the stairs to my fate.

Don't fight it.

The lights were blinding. Deep breath.

Jia you.

My heart wasn't into the dating show in the weeks leading up to it, but I was committed. I had almost no clue what to expect. In the days before the show, I enlisted Guo Li to watch a few episodes and brief me. I was too terrified to watch myself.

We met in a coffee shop a few days before filming. As she sat down, she reached into her purse and slipped a notebook on the table. She had come prepared.

"Mi Gao, you know that the show is very embarrassing for the men," she told me with raised eyebrows. "You have to perform a talent—sing or dance, mostly. Then the girls say what they think of you. Most of the men get rejected. It's very humiliating."

"Fuck. Me."

Guo Li laughed. She gave me a rundown of the show. After I introduced myself, declared my "love manifesto," which each male guest was required to prepare, and performed my talent, each of the women would, one by one, tell me their first impressions. I would have to list my requirements for a girlfriend, which Guo Li helped me prepare: must be independent and confident; mustn't care too much about money; must have gone to college and have a job.

I would then choose which woman I liked most, and each of them would reveal to the audience if she was interested or not. Interested parties would give their pitch about why we should be together, and I could do the same with whomever I picked. If we were both in agreement, we could "validate" our love by walking offstage hand in hand. If we weren't feeling it, our love would remain "invalidated," and we would shake hands as friends.

"Remember," Guo Li said, "if you don't like them, say, 'Let's just be friends.'"

Dating shows were all the rage in China. The most popular, called "If You Are the One," had broken ratings records the previous year. Chinese TV was increasingly provocative, and nowhere was that more evident than in the booming dating show category. Satellite outlets, in particular, were free of the constraints placed on China Central Television, and it showed in the product. Dating shows had developed a reputation for rampant materialism and intentional humiliation, particularly of male participants, who were forced to run a gauntlet of ego destruction in the hope of finding true love, with bank statements often presented on air. In one notorious incident during an April 2010 episode of "If You Are the One," a male contestant asked a young woman if she would be willing to ride on the back of his bicycle. Her reply: "I would rather cry in back of a BMW."

I flew to Shanghai, jittery with anxiety. I had been told we were filming the next day, which I hoped would give me enough time to calm my nerves. Two of the show's employees greeted me at the airport and drove me to the studio, where I was taken into a private room for a briefing with two producers.

One was a short, chain-smoking man with brown teeth, the other a pretty woman of about forty. They explained the show in rapid-fire Chinese, and I caught about half of what they told me. They said they had already prepared a guitar for me. (During my initial interview with the episode's director I had made the mistake of saying I could play guitar.) They asked me if I had prepared a song, and I told them I hadn't.

"You can practice one," the woman said. "We don't shoot for two hours."

Two hours!? I'd been told they were filming the following day. I started to panic.

"I don't feel comfortable playing guitar, or singing, or dancing in front of an audience. I'm not prepared."

"Well, what's your talent then?" the man said, puffing his third cigarette.

"I don't have any special talents."

He was getting annoyed. "Well, you have to do something, Tell a joke, read a poem, do push-ups. Something!"

I sighed. "Okay, I'll think of something. I'll try guitar. I'm just nervous."

"Ah! Don't be nervous! It's for fun. It's to show your personality!" the woman said.

"It's a party!" the smoking man chimed in.

"If it's a party, let's get drunk," I said, only half joking.

Down in the makeup room, I pulled out the guitar. It was

cheap and out of tune, and had no outlet. One of the stagehands tried to tune it. "Good enough," he said, handing it back to me. He'd made it worse. I rested the guitar against a wall and told him I'd think of something else.

Plan B was to indulge a lifelong appreciation for *Top Gun* and belt out the Righteous Brothers' "You've Lost That Loving Feeling," but I figured that since I was ostensibly trying to *win* hearts, that probably wouldn't work. So I settled on "Can't Help Falling in Love" and looked up the lyrics on my phone.

After an hour of fretting, I was ushered onstage with the other male contestants—all of whom were Chinese—for the rehearsal. We were instructed to wait behind the stage at the bottom of the set of stairs. A producer told us to stop under an arch covered with flowers and do a pose, and then slowly walk down onto the stage, where a microphone waited. There we were to say our names, ages, jobs, and where we were from. We then would declare our "love manifesto"; an assistant had written mine on the back of a placard I carried with me.

When my turn came, I walked up the stairs, paused under the arch for a bow, and descended onstage to say my lines into my mic. I stumbled over my love manifesto several times. Then I took the mic and belted out a tenor version of "Can't Help Falling in Love."

"Mi Gao, sing to the girls!" a producer interrupted.

"But there are no girls."

"Pretend!"

I turned around and sang to a row of empty seats.

Wise men say, only fools rush in. . .

I could hear a few chuckles backstage. My voice was cracking.

. . . But I can't help (crack) falling in love with you.

"Mi Gao, Mi Gao," the producer said after I finished. "Do you have a shorter song? Something with more energy?"

"No, this is the only song I have."

"Can you sing it faster?"

"It's not really a fast song."

"Okay, okay." He mumbled something in Chinese to another producer.

I went backstage and waited nervously. Kit texted me to see how things were proceeding. I texted back: "It's just as horrible as I imagined. Did the rehearsal. About to go on. Singing Can't Help Falling in Love. Feel like vomiting."

The director, Kevin, arrived and asked me how I was doing. I told him I was nervous about the song.

"Don't worry, Mi Gao, *jia you*."

Add oil, indeed.

I chatted with the other contestants as I waited. They were all in their twenties and had come to Shanghai from across China for the show. Several stood out as being confident and good-looking. Others were so awkward and shy that I was sure they were picked simply to be humiliated. (I wondered where I fell in that spectrum.) All of the contestants were single, and they were dead serious about landing a woman.

One of the men, named Guo, a handsome twenty-eight-year-old from Shanghai dressed in a sharp suit, and whom one of the producers had nicknamed "the boss," asked me if I was looking for a girlfriend, too.

"Not really," I said. "I just thought this would be a good story to tell my friends back home."

He nodded.

"What about you? Are you looking for a girlfriend?" I asked.

He looked at me like I was an idiot. "We're looking for *wives*."

The filming began. I was scheduled to appear second to last, but I was too nervous to watch the early contestants. From the dressing room I could hear applause and laughter onstage. A young man singing. Girls giggling.

I chain-smoked an assistant's cigarettes and, after an hour of waiting, gathered up the courage to watch some of the proceedings from the side of the stage. I consumed many bottles of water. I smoked more cigarettes.

"Mi Gao," Kevin said after another half hour. "You're on."

Music blared. I squinted under the lights. Walking up and then down the stairs, I stopped under the arch, paused, and bowed toward the audience.

I walked down the stairs and through the line of single women toward center stage. I smiled at the girls as I walked past, winking at the prettiest—she was in the middle of the row, with a tiny white dress and flowing black ponytail.

I approached the mic and introduced myself to the audience.

I'm Mi Gao.

I'm from Canada.

I live in Beijing.

I'm a travel writer.

I'm thirty-one.

I believe that. . .

I read the back of my card, where a producer had scribbled my "love manifesto."

I believe that on the road of li—

I stumbled over the words and started again.

I believe that on the road of life, fate brings people together.

The hosts chuckled.

"Mi Gao, did you write that yourself?" the female host asked, smiling knowingly.

"Ha. No, they wrote it for me." I pointed over my shoulder

toward backstage. The audience laughed. The girls laughed. I shrugged my shoulders.

So far, so good.

The host asked me a few questions. I answered as best I could.

"What's your talent, Mi Gao?" the woman said.

"Well, I'm going to sing a song. But I didn't prepare, and I'm *very* nervous." I tapped my chest in front of the mic for a mock heartbeat. "So before I sing, I'm going to do some exercises. Okay?"

"Of course," she said.

I stepped away from the mic and took a deep breath. Something was happening. Something strange. I noticed, for the first time, that I wasn't nervous at all. I was totally calm. I was almost—*almost*—having fun.

I looked back to the girls and said, "Just a second."

Then I dropped to the floor, in front of the contestants, the hosts, the audience, and millions of TV viewers, and did push-ups. Ten of them.

The audience howled. They were mine.

"Jia you!" I said, taking the mic from the stand.

I burst into song.

Wise men saaaaay. . .

I walked down the line of girls, making eye contact with each of them until I got to the last line of the first verse.

. . . falling in looooove wiiiith—

I stopped and paused. I looked up and down the row, and then back to the audience.

"I can't decide. They're all so beautiful!"

The audience roared.

I broke into the second verse, the last I'd bothered to memorize, finished it with a flourish, and joined the hosts at the front of the stage, satisfied that, at the very least, I hadn't totally bombed.

The female contestants went down the line and told me their

first impressions. A lot of it I didn't understand. One asked if I would teach her English, another if I could show her around Canada. One liked my beard.

When all of them were done, the female host asked me to pick which one I liked. I wasn't to say it aloud, only to press a digit on a mobile phone she held in her hand. I looked up and down the line of thirteen contestants. Since I knew nothing about these women, not even their names, I picked the best-looking. She was tall with a wide smile and big eyes, wearing a dress so small it could have been a nightie.

The prettiest it was. Number seven. My hand was shaking as I touched the screen.

Much of the next half hour was a blur. There was a question-and-answer portion. I listed off my requirements, and, I would learn later, when the episode aired on November 11, 2011—11/11/11, which happened to be Chinese Singles Day—all but one of the contestants revealed to the audience they were no longer interested in me after I said I didn't want a girl who liked money.

It all felt so surreal and I smiled to myself at the story I would later tell friends. I was proud of myself for pulling it off and thrilled that my Chinese was good enough to do it. Five years of lessons had paid off.

Then, under the lights and with adrenaline coursing through my body, I had an experience not unlike the music video, where I felt like I wasn't really there, that instead I was watching it all happen. The anxieties and worries and doubts about my life in China, my life in general, were momentarily gone, and all of a sudden I was struck with disbelief at the moment in which I'd found myself—thirty-one years old on a dating show, a *Chinese* dating show, still there in that wild nation after all these years.

Later, in the weeks and months that followed, whenever I

thought about the strange episode, whenever I told the story, I would be reminded of all the other unbelievable places and situations I'd somehow fallen ass-backwards into over the years, and I would ask: What if it all just didn't happen? What if, instead of opening *China Daily*'s online job posting while sitting in a Toronto coffee shop on a horrible winter afternoon, I had simply folded up my laptop and gone home? What if, after *China Daily* offered me the job, I'd simply said, "Nope, that's just too fucking crazy," and stayed put? What if the financial crisis, which pinned me in Beijing, hadn't happened? What if I had followed through on one of the innumerable times when I got so sick of China I swore I was going to go home?

So many moments were now seared into my memory and forever would be: walking home from the *China Daily* offices on a warm summer night, puffing a smoke bummed from a colleague after working the late shift; looking out my window at Comrade Wu's place, watching a hazy sunset, counting down the days until the Olympics and waiting for Julia to come over; the trips—Xinjiang, Harbin, Erlian, Macao, Guangzhou, and everywhere in between; standing on the stairs of an outdoor mall, filming a music video and trying my best to lower my heartbeat; lying in bed wide awake after nearly dying on a Sichuan mountain, trying to make sense of it all. This moment, too, standing onstage being vetted by thirteen Chinese women, would be permanent. I would have it with me forever.

China was an incredible place at an incredible time, and I had lived through it. I had lived it. I *was* living it. For almost five years, I had been searching high and low for stories about China I could write and bring to the world. But the story was there the whole time: it was the life I was leading. And in the days after filming a Shanghai dating show—when I became a minor celebrity in my *hutong* neighborhood, when my neighbors started calling me Comrade Mi Gao—I realized that it was a life to be grateful for.

I realized something else that fall, in weeks after appearing on "One Out of 100," which would turn out be one of the last random China adventures in a long line of random China adventures that once seemed to stretch on forever.

I realized I was ready. I was ready to go home.

Wherever that turned out to be.

Epilogue

FALL 2012

Almost a year after singing Elvis on a dating show, after more than half a decade in China, I did what I should have done on my first day: I enrolled in an intensive Chinese language program. And the first thing I learned at school was that despite all the time I'd spent in China, despite the few thousand dollars I'd invested in private schools and countless hours in cafés with Guo Li, my Chinese language ability was still, as Comrade Wu once joyfully pointed out, terrible.

This was a humbling realization. It wasn't as if I hadn't tried. True, I didn't do much homework—ever, really—and I used most of my class time with Guo Li and other teachers to relay my problems to them and solicit advice. The Chinese language, ancient and profound, seems to have an idiom to address every dilemma, and over the years I probably heard (and promptly forgot) all of them. But the fact that I could even have those conversations, I figured, was evidence I could speak Chinese. Maybe not fluently, but good enough to chat with friends. Good enough to appear on a Chinese dating show (although to be fair, the show's editors did a brilliant job of hiding my many lapses during the program).

On my first day of intensive class, I woke at 6 a.m., made coffee, slipped on a backpack, and hopped in a cab to Tsinghua University, one of China's most prestigious institutions of higher learning. Orientation was in a building near the center of campus. There were some seventy students in the course, many of them fresh out of American colleges, and I felt like a grizzled China veteran when I heard some of them discuss their first days in Beijing. During the program director's introduction, she described life in the city. "In Beijing you should know nobody pays attention to rules of the road. So make sure you look in all directions when crossing the street," she said. A young man beside me, an American wearing New Balance sneakers, wrote in his notebook: "Look in ALL directions." He penciled a dark line under the word *all*.

The program required the equivalent of second-year university Chinese, and I was lucky that when the administrators interviewed applicants for admission, they didn't consider our knowledge of Chinese characters. My reading and writing ability was abysmal, and these shortcomings became abundantly clear when, on orientation day, we took a written test that would determine our classes for the semester. I was at a total loss; the questions might as well have been written in . . . well, Chinese.

As soon as the director finished her speech, we signed a language pledge. From then on, we were forbidden to speak English at the school or at any school activity. After signing the pledge, we stood around the classroom chatting awkwardly in Chinese, unaccustomed to the charade of speaking a second language to someone who speaks your native tongue. I exchanged short bios with several students. When I told one young woman with strong Chinese how long I'd lived in China, she looked confused. "You've been here *how* long?" she asked.

"Why are you studying Chinese after five years in China when you're planning to leave?" more than one friend asked me after I enrolled at Tsinghua. It was an excellent question, and I offered two reasons. First, I simply couldn't bear the loss of face of leaving China after so many years with poor Chinese. I had moved over one last notch on the Foreigner/Chinese Identity Spectrum. The second reason was, in the months after appearing on *Bai Li Tiao Yi*, I needed to make a change in my life. But I still hadn't figured out what that change would be.

Through the winter and into the spring of 2012, my life continued as it had the previous fall. I knew I wanted to leave China, I knew I wanted to set down roots somewhere other than Beijing, but I still didn't know where or how. Meanwhile, more friends were leaving, and I felt more trapped in China than ever. I couldn't concentrate on work and I was sleeping so poorly that I was eventually prescribed sleeping pills. Sitting in a movie theater one afternoon, avoiding work and hoping to take my mind off things, my heart started pounding, my palms were sweating, and I thought: I *have* to leave.

Then, something happened: I calmed down. I realized there was no way I wanted to leave Beijing without some form of closure: the city meant too much to me and I felt I owed it something. So I made a concerted effort to reconnect with Beijing. I started going out more, I reached out to old friends and made new ones, and I agreed to do things I would normally turn down without thinking. Finally, I enrolled at Tsinghua.

Over the months, I fell in love with the city again. Beijing is a city that grows on you. It's not like Shanghai or Hong Kong in my experience, places that grab you immediately and command your attention. During the Olympics, a foreign woman who had been working in the Chinese capital for a month told me why she hated the city: "It's dirty. It smells. The air is terrible. I think the people are rude. Do you want me to go on?" Her outburst was crass but not entirely unfounded. Beijing is sprawling and inconvenient, with horrible traffic. There are very few pedestrian-friendly areas, the air is toxic, and it's too hot in the summer, too cold in the winter.

Despite its flaws, I adore the place. It's gritty, idiosyncratic, and overflowing with character. I cherish interactions with the residents of my *hutong* neighborhood: the old folks in my building, the couple who own the laundry shop, the fruit stand ladies, the granny sitting on a stool wearing a red "Security Volunteer" armband. These are the moments I cherish and will miss most when I finally leave Tall Rice behind.

Often, late in the afternoon after hours of reading and writing Chinese characters, my brain begins to hurt, so I take my bike and cycle around the city. Sometimes I go around the Drum and Bell Tower and Houhai Lake and then wind my way south through the *hutong*s until I hit the Forbidden City. I'll stop on Chang'An Dajie at the Gate of Heavenly Peace and watch the crowds, just as intense and curious as they were when I first ventured there my first week in Beijing. Chairman Mao's portrait hangs above the gate beside the words "Long Live the People's Republic of China." The only difference is that now I can read them.

Other times I'll head north, up to the third ring road and past the McDonald's where Rob and I ate Big Macs after a long night in Sanlitun my first weekend in Beijing. I'll ride along the *China Daily* buildings, which have new white tiles on the exterior and seem to belong to an entirely different newspaper from a new era. Across the street, the noodle shop, where two *China Daily* foreign experts once came to blows, has been turned into a 7-Eleven. I'll bike north to the Olympic Green, past the Bird's Nest, where I watched Usain Bold break the world record, and Ling Long Pagoda, which is still lit up at night like a Christmas tree.

Then I'll cycle back to my sprawling apartment in the *hutong*s, which I'll only call home for a few more months.

I'm leaving Beijing in mid-April, exactly six years after I arrived in China. Sometime between now and then, I'll open my laptop and buy a plane ticket. One way. To New York.

In the meantime, I'm happily riding out my last days in China. It turns out that neither I nor Tall Rice was made for minor Chinese stardom. My line from *Qian Xue Sen* was left on the editing room floor; I appear in the film for a few seconds as a blurry figure with a bad haircut hidden in the background. My potential future wife rejected me on national Chinese television, and I still have nightmares about sober dancing in a low-budget music video, although they're slowly abating.

"Can't do it, I'm afraid," I told a friend who called with an acting gig not long ago. As I talked to him, it seemed as if for the first time since I came to China, I had no doubts whatsoever. A plan was in motion. I was ready to leave my China identity behind and start looking for a new one. "I'm retired."

Acknowledgments

To everybody below, drinks on me. I owe you that and much, much more.

To Stephanie Sun, my agent emeritus, thank you for seeing potential in an eight-hundred-word article and believing I could do this even when I wasn't so sure. This book simply wouldn't exist without you. To Maya Ziv, my editor at Harper Perennial, thank you for your hard work and thoughtful comments throughout, and for seeing the bigger story that made sense of all the little ones. Thanks as well to Katie Salisbury for taking a chance on an unknown writer hiding out in Beijing, and to James Gibney and the people at the *Atlantic* for publishing the story that started all this.

To my brother, Sean Moxley, my first reader at every step of the way, I'm grateful for your ideas and advice from proposal to final draft.

Thank you to the following people for your insight and opinions at various stages of this project: David Herbert, David Fu, Clarissa Sebag-Montefiore, Kit Gillet, Allan Pulga, Kathleen Boyce, Kevin Keane, Richard Wiltshire, Julian Wilson, Claire Pennington, and Nestor Santana. Thanks to Jim Wasserman, Tom Mackenzie, Annie Ly, Paul Morris, Julia K., Nick Houshower, and Jeff Lulewicz for being such a big part of my Beijing life and the stories included in this book. Thank you to Wei Xiao Ming for all your help over the years; you are a much better journalist than I'll ever be. And I'm forever indebted to the wonderful Guo Li—my teacher, life coach, therapist, and, above all, friend.

Thank you to the folks at Café Zarah for letting me occupy their lovely coffee shop for the better part of six years, and many thanks—and apologies—to the good people at *China Daily* for giving me the chance to come to Beijing in the first place.

Lastly, I owe everything to my parents, Joan Skingle and Ross Moxley, whose unwavering support and belief in me over the years has helped me through the many highs and lows of living abroad. Thank you for a lifetime of love and encouragement.

Mitch Moxley
January 2013